Fritz Machlup • Kenneth Leeson
and Associates

INFORMATION THROUGH THE PRINTED WORD

The Dissemination of Scholarly, Scientific, and Intellectual Knowledge

Volume 4: Books, Journals, and Bibliographic Services

PRAEGER

PRAEGER SPECIAL STUDIES • PRAEGER SCIENTIFIC

The data used in the preparation of this material were obtained and processed with the support of the National Science Foundation Grants No. DSI 74-12756 and IST-78-13383, and the National Endowment for the Humanities, Grants No. AS-24510-76-155 and AS-29912-77-1107. However, any opinions, findings, conclusions, and/or recommendations expressed herein are those of the author(s) and do not necessarily reflect the views of the supporting agencies.

Published in 1980 by Praeger Publishers
CBS Educational and Professional Publishing
A Division of CBS, Inc.
521 Fifth Avenue, New York, New York 10017 U.S.A.

Library of Congress Catalog Card Number: 78-19460

0123456789 038 987654321

Printed in the United States of America

PREFACE TO VOLUME FOUR

The first three volumes of this work were published in December 1978. This fourth volume brings the project to its conclusion. Volumes 1 to 3 were divided into six parts; Volume 4 now adds three more parts: Part 7, on "Book Publishing," presents data and findings supplementary to those of Part 2; Part 8, on "Journal Publishing," is supplementary to Part 3; Part 9, on "Bibliographic Services: Abstracting and Indexing," presents new material. Our hope to have additional information on libraries, supplementing what we published in Part 6, has not materialized, but we trust that what we are offering in this fourth volume will be received as a worth-while outcome of the gleaning of the field after we reaped the product of several years' work.

The team that did the research, analysis, writing, typing, and preparing copy for this volume consisted of ten persons, five of whom had been among the 29 who worked on the first three volumes. Their names will be listed below among the acknowledgments. The grants that enabled us to do this concluding volume will also be listed there.

It may be helpful to the reader if this preface could give him an idea of what he may expect to learn from this book. We shall be bold enough to give him three nutshells full of previews: In Part 7 he will be confronted with a first application of "cohort analysis" to the economics of book publishing. Costs, sales, prices, gross revenues, and gross margins of eight different "vintage years" of books published in a variety of fields will be examined and compared. One by-product of this analysis will be some new light on the differences in the publishing experience of university presses and commercial publishers. In Part 8, the reader will be shown new findings regarding the effects on the gross margins obtained for journals deriving different proportions of their gross revenues from subscriptions, sales of advertising space, and page charges. In Part 9, the reader may be interested in the description of the techniques employed by abstracting and indexing services in collecting, processing, and publishing the bibliographic information so urgently needed by the research community confronted with the ever-increasing flood or primary publications.

We wish to express our gratitude to those who supplied the information on which our inquiry depended, to the team that did the research work and prepared this report, and to the sponsors who financed and supported the project.

The Sources of Data

The primary data for Parts 7 and 8 came from the 50 book-publishing divisions and 38 journal-publishing divisions of commercial publishers, university presses, and learned societies. Their names were listed in Chapter 1.1 of Volume 1, pp. 4-5.

For Part 9 we acknowledge the cooperation of several persons managing some of the most ambitious abstracting and indexing services. The most generous donors of their time and expertise were:

Mr. John E. Creps, Jr., Executive Director, Engineering Index, Inc.

Ms. Eileen Machesy, Managing Editor, *MLA International Bibliography of Books and Articles on the Modern Languages and Literatures*

Dr. Robert Marchisotto, Director, Office of Scientific Affairs, Bioscience Information Service

Dr. Kenneth Metzner, Director, Division of Publications, American Institute of Physics

Dr. Mark Perlman and Dr. Naomi Perlman, Managing and Associate Editors, *Journal of Economic Literature* and *Index of Economic Articles*

Ms. Jan Strasel, Assistant to the Executive Editor, American Psychological Association

The Work Force

A list of the 29 persons who made up the work force for the project until the completion of Volumes 1 to 3 was included in Volume 1, pp. 8-9. In the following we name the members of the team who participated in the work on Volume 4:

Principal Investigator: Fritz Machlup
Senior Research Associate: Kenneth Leeson
Research Associate: Trude Kronwinkler
Adjunct Research Associate: Arthur Rosenzweig
Research Assistants: Trish Gallagher
Anthony Irace
Sharon Spellman-Olasov
Computer Analyst: O. Young Kwon
Secretaries: Robin Primoff
Sheila Trindal
Preparation of Camera-Ready Copy by Sheila Trindal

The Funds and Facilities

The research grants for the entire project were listed in the Preface included in the first three volumes. We repeat here the two grants which enabled us to complete Volume 4:

National Endowment for the Humanities
AS-29910-77-1107
Division: Office of Planning and Analysis
Title: Mining a Rich Deposit of Confidential Data on the Communication of Scholarly Knowledge
Period: 9/1/77-8/31/78 (with a no-cost extension through 12/31/78)

National Science Foundation
IST-78-13383
Division: Science Information
Title: An In-Depth Analysis of a Comprehensive Data Base on the Communication of Scientific/Scholarly Knowledge
Period: 7/1/78-6/30/79 (with a no-cost extension through 12/31/79)

New York University provided office space and equipment in the Department of Economics and contributed the cost-sharing usually borne by grantee institutions. In addition we wish to acknowledge the cooperation of the Courant Mathematics and Computing Laboratory, with its computer facilities supported by the Department of Energy under Contract EY-76-C-02-3077.

The Association of American University Presses in the role of subcontractor assumed some of the administrative burdens and thereby relieved the Principal Investigator and Senior Research Associate of many bureaucratic frustrations.

PREFACE TO THE PREVIOUS THREE VOLUMES

This is a report on the findings of several years of research by a team of varying size, up to 16 persons at the peak of activities and, because of turnover in personnel and the use of occasional consultants, altogether 29 persons over the entire period. The project was financed chiefly by the National Science Foundation and the National Endowment for the Humanities through a series of grants to New York University, with considerable cost-sharing by New York University, funds from two other sources, and supplemental contributions of money and unpaid services by Professor Fritz Machlup, Principal Investigator, and Kenneth Leeson, Senior Research Associate.

The title of the project has changed over the years, partly in order to accommodate an expansion of its scope, and ultimately for the sake of euphony. In the first application for an NSF grant the project was called "The Production and Distribution of Scientific and Technological Information." When the scope of the research was extended to include scholarly knowledge in all disciplines, including the humanities, the title underwent a commensurate expansion: "The Dissemination of Scholarly Knowledge: A Study of the Economic Viability of the Publication of Books and Journals and of the Maintenance of Library Services and Associated Activities." This was more than a mouthful and badly in need of cosmetic surgery to meet higher standards of English composition. Hence the new title: *Information through the Printed Word: The Dissemination of Scholarly, Scientific and Intellectual Knowledge*. If any reader, addicted to the "S & T" label, misses the adjective "technical" (or more correctly "technological") as an additional modifier of the noun knowledge, or information, let him be assured that the three adjectives exhibited in the title fully cover all information generated by engineering sciences; indeed, any one of the adjectives would do.

This report will probably be read — partly or fully, cursorily or attentively — by persons in a variety of fields and with very different backgrounds. This makes it difficult to write in a manner that will not be regarded as too technical by some and too simplistic by others. Publishers may scoff at our "pedantic" explanations of practices, institutions, problems and word meanings customary in their industry, while economists may find these explanations too sketchy for an outsider. Librarians may be bored with details in the descriptions of library operations, while scholars and scientists in various fields may complain that we took too many things for granted and were inconsiderate of readers not familiar with the language and activities of librarians. There is no way to meet the needs of all readers; it is impossible to have the right pitch in an exposition addressed to readers in different fields and at different levels of sophistication. We appeal to our readers to bear this in mind if they find some terms or relations overexplained or underexplained from their own point of view.

The report is organized into the following six parts: One, General; Two, Book Publishing; Three, Journal Publishing; Four, Use of Journals; Five, General Appendix on the Economics of Statistical Sampling; Six, Libraries. The first volume contains Parts One and Two. The second volume contains Parts Three, Four, and Five. The third volume contains Part Six. Additional research is still under way and may yield findings to be reported eventually in a fourth volume.

For the record we are listing here the grants from the two sponsoring agencies:

National Science Foundation

GN42274 (Changed to SIS 74-12756-A01)
Division: Science Information
Title: The Production and Distribution of Scientific and Technological Information
Period: 7/1/74-12/31/75

DSI-74-12756-A02
Division: Science Information
Title: The Production and Distribution of Scientific and Technological Information
Period: 9/1/75-8/31/76

DSI-74-12756-A03
Division: Science Information
Title: The Production and Distribution of Scientific and Technological Information
Period: 9/1/76-8/31/77

IST-78-13383
Division: Science Information
Title: An In-Depth Analysis of a Comprehensive Data Base on the Communication of Scientific/Scholarly Knowledge
Period: 7/1/78-6/30/79 (for additional research not yet embodied in the three volumes)

National Endowment for the Humanities

AS-24510-76-155
Division: Office of Planning and Analysis
Title: The Dissemination of Scholarly Knowledge: A Study of the Economic Viability of the Publication of Books and Journals
Period: 12/1/75-5/31/77

AS-29910-77-1107
Division: Office of Planning and Analysis
Title: Mining a Rich Deposit of Confidential Data on the Communication of Scholarly Knowledge
Period: 9/1/77-8/31/78

Earlier Grants for a Related Project

The material contained in these three volumes on *Information Through the Printed Word* should not be confused with a related though separate undertaking by Fritz Machlup: the updating of his book *The Production and Distribution of Knowledge in the United States* (Princeton University Press: 1962). It contained 85 statistical tables, most of which terminated in 1958. During the years 1971-1974 the National Science Foundation and the National Endowment for the Humanities had made various grants to Machlup to enable him to expand the material and bring the tables forward to 1970. When this research was completed, the project on book publishing, journal publishing, and library operations emerged as an undertaking more urgent than the writing of the second edition of the 1962 book. Moreover, it was hoped that the research on books, journals, and libraries would enrich the material for the new edition of the more comprehensive work. It is scheduled to appear, with all data brought forward to 1975, in a set of several volumes at various intervals between 1979 and 1982.

A preface usually includes a list of acknowledgements. Since the authors are indebted to so many persons and organizations that their listing extends over a good many pages, it was decided to relegate the acknowledgements to a separate chapter in Volume 1.

INFORMATION THROUGH THE PRINTED WORD

The Dissemination of Scholarly,
Scientific, and Intellectual Knowledge

Overview of the Four Volumes

CONTENTS

Chapter *Page*

Chapter		Page

Chapter *Page*

List of Tables

Table Number *Page*

Table Number *Page*

Table Number *Page*

Table Number *Page*

Table Number | *Page*

Table Number *Page*

Corrigenda for Volumes 1, 2, and 3

Volume 1: Book Publishing

1. Page 8 — The following name was omitted from *The Roster* under Research Assistants:

   Jeffrey Silver   June 1975 to August 1978

2. Page 199 — Reference in the third paragraph to (p. 2.7.6) should be to (p. 192) and reference to (p. 2.7.7) should be to (p. 193).

Volume 2: Journals

1. Page xii — "Part 9" should read "Part 5."

2. Page 39 — In line 6, "by type of publisher" should read "by type of subscriber."

3. Page 154 — The left column of the continuation page of Table 3.5.4, headed "1974," should read "1973."

4. Page 160 — The heading of Table 3.5.6 states the sample size as ". . .32 Journals (21 Published by Learned Societies, 5 by University Presses, and 6 by Commercial Publishers. . ." It should read ". . .32 Journals (18 Published by Learned Societies, 8 by University Presses, and 6 by Commercial Publishers). . ."

5. Page 162 — The final two years of data, 1974 and 1975, for Table 3.5.6 are supposed to appear on page 162, but were omitted. Instead, that page duplicates *Questionnaire on the Use and Evaluation of Economic Journals* from page 291.

6. Page 164-165 — The continuation pages of Table 3.5.7 are in reverse order.

PART 7

BOOK PUBLISHING: A COHORT ANALYSIS

CHAPTER 7.1

INTRODUCTION

This is a study of the economics of book publishing. Original data on samples of individual book titles, bunched according to year of publication to form "cohorts," are used to observe and compare the costs, prices, sales, and gross profit margins of books of various kinds. Among these are books of university presses and commercial publishers, books in the natural sciences, social sciences, and humanities, and books classified as scholarly monographs, professional-reference works, college texts, and of general interest.

The study was originally motivated by repeated claims that certain sectors of the publishing industry, particularly the type of scholarly publishing that rests in the domain of university presses, had suffered a gradual decline in profitability during the early 1970's and are even today caught in an economic pinch that has impaired, or will impair, the dissemination of knowledge among scholars, scientists, researchers, and students.[1]

OBJECTIVES OF THE RESEARCH

As originally planned, this research had four major objectives: (1) to try to determine if profits in book publishing had in fact declined over the period 1968-1975; (2) to investigate the extent to which and some of the reasons why the profitability of book publishing differs among certain of the industry's major sectors and subject areas; (3) to investigate whether annual statements of income and expense or profit and loss could serve as adequate bases for conducting comparative analyses of profitability and for uncovering trends in profits; and (4) to develop an alternative method of analyzing profits

[1] A recent expression of concern over the plight of scholarly publishing was made by the director of the University of Minnesota Press in a letter to *The New York Times*, February 3, 1979.

in which costs and revenues of different "cohorts" of books, grouped according to vintage, or year of publication, are observed over a considerable number of years of their lives.

The second, third, and fourth objectives have essentially been accomplished; the first has not. It has not been possible to draw any definitive conclusions regarding trends in profits; the samples of cohort data at our disposal were too small to allow generalizations. The analyses do, however, uncover several strategic differences in costs, prices, sales, and profits of books of university presses and commercial publishers, of books in major subject areas, and of books of various functional or publishing categories.

METHOD OF ANALYSIS

A distinguishing feature of the analyses presented in this study is their reliance on cohort data rather than on the more conventional annual data.

Conventional Analysis

Descriptions of costs, sales, prices, and profits of the book-publishing industry as a whole, of its major sectors, and its individual member firms, that are customarily prepared by trade associations, statistical branches of government agencies, independent observers, or by publishers themselves, are based, by and large, on series of annual data. Such series reflect economic conditions prevailing in successive twelve-month periods for a mixed bag of books, some newly published, others one, two, three, or more years old; they are useful, indeed indispensable, for providing information on industry-wide trends. However, annual data, particularly annual *financial* data that are used to derive measures of profits in book publishing, embody certain conceptual and practical weaknesses that call into question their suitability for analyzing profitability.

Cohort Analysis

The term "cohort" is commonly found in demographic and other statistical studies that typically focus on the behavior and influence over time of individuals who were born during a specified period. The "baby-boom" cohort is a case in point. Analogously, cohort analysis in book publishing focuses on the economic performance, in terms of costs, prices, sales, and profits, of samples of individual book titles grouped according to their year of publication and observed over several years of their lives. Titles may be grouped further to form a variety of cohorts — according to different subject areas or scholarly disciplines, according to level of readership, according to major sales outlets, and so on — which will enable the researcher or individual publisher to conduct comparative studies of the economic performances of books of these several categories.

Original Data

The data used in this cohort analysis were collected first hand from the confidential files and internal reports of 20 publishing firms — 11 university presses and 9 commercial publishers.

Each of the publishers who agreed to allow small teams of researchers to visit their premises (usually for several days) to gather the sought-after data has agreed to allow us to cite their names in exchange for a pledge that none of the findings or results presented in the study can be identified as having come from their firm. Since the data of the several publishers have all been "pooled," or otherwise disguised, the pledge is faithfully kept.

The cooperating publishers are listed here:

University Presses	*Commercial Publishers*
Columbia University Press	Academic Press
Cornell University Press	Harper & Row
Chicago University Press	Little-Brown & Company
Harvard University Press	Plenum Publishing Corporation
University of Minnesota Press	Prentice-Hall
New York University Press	Random House
Northwestern University Press	Charles Scribner's Sons
Princeton University Press	The Shoe String Press
Wesleyan University Press	John Wiley & Sons
Yale University Press	

Fixed and Variable Costs:
Of the Individual Book and of the Firm

That the emphasis of the analysis is on books, or more accurately, cohorts of books, rather than on the publishing firms as a whole raises a few issues regarding the classification of costs into fixed and variable components that may require clarification.

If one were to measure the output of a single book title by the number of copies printed, then an expansion of output would entail printing additional *copies*. If, on the other hand, one were to measure the output of the publishing company as a whole by the number of titles it produces annually, then an expansion of output would entail publishing additional *titles*. In the first instance, plant costs[2] incurred to produce the plates from which copies of the book are printed are fixed by nature — they need to be incurred only once and do not increase with the number of copies printed. The costs of paper, printing, and binding, or run-off costs, on the other hand, are variable by nature, meaning that they increase with the number of copies printed. In the second instance, where the output of the firm is expanded, both plant and run-off costs are "variable" since both increase with the production of additional titles. In this analysis, only the first of these two interpretations is relevant and, hence, plant costs constitute the fixed costs whereas paper, printing, and binding costs constitute the variable costs.

Direct and Indirect Costs

All costs incurred in the production of books whether they be fixed or variable can be classified in one of two categories — direct and indirect. Direct costs are those that are clearly attributable to particular titles and include such items as plant costs, the costs of paper, printing, and binding, royalties paid to authors, and some editorial costs. In contrast, indirect costs are more in the nature of joint costs in that they cannot be unequivocally attributed to particular titles, except by arbitrary rules of allocation that have no sound economic rationale. They include such items as the salaries of managers and staff personnel of the various departments (editorial, advertising, marketing, fulfillment) office supplies and equipment, building maintenance, warehouse storage space, and so on.

Only for direct costs will averages for groups of books be calculated in this cohort analysis. It would make little sense to calculate an average cost that included indirect components since there is no identifiable or systematic correspondence between the number of titles published and the magnitude of such costs.

---

[2]When book publishers speak of plant costs they do not mean the cost of operating a printing plant as the term would seem to imply; they mean nonrecurring costs, that is, costs incurred only in connection with the *first* printing of the book. The chief items are the costs of composition (i.e., typesetting), plates, dies and art work for illustrations and jackets

FOCUS OF THE STUDY

Though the material presented in this study deals in considerable depth with a number of topics on the economics of book publishing, there are several areas that had to be ignored altogether, largely because of the time and expense that would have been involved in expanding the research any further.

The Book, Not the Firm

The cohort analyses presented throughout this study pertain exclusively to books. It is widely known that book-publishing firms engage in a variety of activities other than publishing books. These may include publishing journals, acting as the domestic sales representative for foreign publishers, selling publishing rights to paperback houses or movie rights to the motion picture industry, to name just a few. While such activities may incur costs and generate revenues, they are beyond the scope of our research. We are not concerned here with the profitability of the whole of the activities with which book publishers may involve themselves, but only with publishing scholarly books.

Direct Manufacturing Costs

The analyses of costs shall begin with composition costs, that is, costs incurred after the author's manuscript has been accepted for publication and has been prepared for the compositor (typesetter) by the editorial staff of the publishing house. It would have been quite beyond the scope of the research to attempt as well to identify the so-called "pre-publication" costs, measured in both time and money, incurred by the authors during the period that begins with the author's original idea, includes the research and writing, and ends with the manuscript being submitted for publication. Furthermore, while some publishers actually provided estimates of the cost of editing manuscripts of individual titles, most of these estimates were based on rather arbitrary rules-of-thumb and were therefore not suitable for making comparisons among titles of different publishing houses. Hence, the study focuses exclusively on direct manufacturing costs, that is, plant costs, paper, printing, and binding costs — costs that are clearly incurred for the production of a particular title.

Scholarly Books

The research is not concerned with all types of books, but focuses solely on so-called "serious" works, those intended for use by scholars, scientists, engineers, and students in their professional or academic activities, and by general readers with intellectual interests in the arts and sciences. The types of books of interest here, whether published by university presses or commercial firms, include scholarly monographs, professional-reference books, college textbooks, and some books of general interest. Categories receiving little or no attention in the research include elhi textbooks (books used in elementary schools and high schools), encyclopaedias, juvenile trade books, and mass-market paperbacks.

CONTENTS OF THE CHAPTERS

Chapter 7.2 provides a synopsis of the major observations and findings that appear in greater detail throughout Part 7.

In Chapter 7.3 it is argued that net-income figures derived from annual income-and-expense statements customarily prepared by publishers cannot provide an adequate basis for an analysis of the profitability of book publishing.

Chapter 7.4 elucidates the concept of cohort analysis and describes some of its advantages and disadvantages compared with conventional analysis. It also describes the cohort data used in the study, how they were collected, to which aspects of book publishing they pertain, and the composition of the samples obtained with respect to type of publisher, subject area, and type of covers.

Chapter 7.5 provides both the theoretical foundations for calculating gross (profit) margins for cohorts of books as well as a number of empirical results on gross margins derived from the cohort data.

Chapter 7.6 provides discussions and numerical findings on many of the factors that lie behind gross margins, including direct manufacturing costs, list prices, margins between manufacturing costs and list prices, and discounts below list prices offered to wholesalers and bookstores. Comparisons are made between books of university presses and commercial firms; among books in the natural sciences, social sciences, and humanities; and among scholarly monographs, professional-reference books, college textbooks, and books of general interest. The chapter also contains, by way of a summary, a separate section on the plight of university presses.

Chapter 7.7 provides a glimpse of patterns of physical sales of books. Profiles of unit sales (number of copies sold) over the first six years of life are presented for books of the two types of publishers, the three major subject areas, and four functional categories. Average number of copies sold per title are given for each year of life and for all six years combined.

CHAPTER 7.2

SUMMARY OF THE FINDINGS

Chapters 7.3 through 7.7 contain, in some 175 pages, discussions of a variety of topics concerning the economics of book publishing. Some of them deal with conceptual issues, and require a good deal of delineation, or explanation to convey adequately the ideas involved; others are straightforward, involving only simple descriptions of numerical data contained in one of the numerous statistical tables. The main arguments, however, and the principal findings (or observations in those cases where "findings" may be too strong a word) are spread throughout the pages and some of them may be difficult to see clearly in a first reading of the material. Thus, as a guide to the reader who would wish to have in advance a summary of what is to be found in greater detail in the body of the study, and as a convenient enumeration of the major findings, we shall, in this chapter, provide a list of questions, either posed explicitly or implied by the analyses, along with the answers, be they tentative, partial, or complete. Elaboration on any of these points can be found in the text in the chapters indicated next to each question.

ON CHOOSING A METHOD TO ASSESS PROFITABILITY

Chapter 7.3 — *Can the net-income figures derived from annual income-and-expense statements customarily prepared by publishers be used to assess reliably the profitability of book publishing?*

It is first argued and then demonstrated with the use of simulated data that annual income-and-expense statements may provide a misleading picture of the profitability of book publishing, because of the effect on reported net income of (1) the practice of expensing in the year of publication a good portion of the costs of producing a product to be sold in future years — a practice that breaks the link between the realization of income and the incurrence of costs and (2) the effects of different methods of valuation and write down of inventory.

A number of tests using simulated data on costs and sales have shown that the application of different accounting practices regarding inventory, of which there are a large variety in use by various publishers, produced substantial variations in calculated gross margins and, by extension, net income, particularly when the proportion of sales coming from the backlist of books varies from year to year. In Chapter 7.5, real data collected from a single university press are applied to the same set of techniques for inventory valuation and write down. The substantial variations in calculated gross margins that resulted reinforce the claim that annual financial data may be misleading.

Chapters 7.4 and 7.5 — *Is there an alternative method of calculating gross margins that would be free of the deficiencies inherent in gross margins derived from annual income-and-expense reports?*

It is shown how gross margins can be calculated more nearly in conformance with the concepts employed in traditional economic theory. By using cohort data rather than annual data, one can calculate the arithmetic difference between the capitalized value of the stream of sales revenues received over the life of a cohort of titles and the capitalized value of the stream of direct costs incurred in their production, with both streams adjusted for changes in the level of prices. This difference is the gross margin as seen by cohort analysis. Unlike conventional analysis, cohort analysis can provide measures of the returns to books published in various vintage years, by different types of publishers, and in different subject areas and functional categories, all expressed in comparable dollar values.

ON CALCULATING GROSS MARGINS IN COHORT ANALYSIS

Chapter 7.5 — *What would gross margins calculated with real data collected from a sample of publishing houses indicate about the relative performances of books of various vintage years, types of publishers, and major subject categories?*

Because the number of titles belonging to each vintage year in the cohort samples available for this study is small, valid comparisons of gross margins could not be made among vintage years. The calculated values fluctuate widely from one vintage year to the next and seem to exhibit no discernable trends over the periods observed. For 15 years, 1961-1975, we procured cohort data from a university press on all of the titles it published in the period; and for 8 years, 1968-1975, we obtained cohort data from eleven university presses and nine commercial publishers on samples of the titles they published in that period.

With regard to differences between the two types of publishers and among the three broad subject areas, however, a number of observations can be stated:

While most of the cohorts of titles published by the single university press over the period 1961-1970 covered their own direct costs after six years of life, none came even close to contributing revenue sufficient to cover the indirect costs associated with their publication.

A comparison of the overall performance of the sample of titles of the eleven university presses with the overall performance of the sample of titles of the nine commercial publishers reveals that gross margins after four years of life of books published over the period 1968-1972 were far higher for the commercial publishers than for the university presses. The average of the absolute (dollar value) gross margins expressed in deflated and discounted values for 190 commercially published titles, including a few with extraordinarily large values of dollar sales, was $41,615; for 180 commercially published titles, excluding those with the extremely large values of dollar sales, $31,440; but, for 219 university-press titles the average of the absolute gross margins was only $5,850. The relative gross margins (absolute gross margins as a percentage of direct costs) were 184.4 per cent, 154.3 per cent for the two samples of commercially published titles, and only 53.1 per cent for the university-press titles.

Although the gross margins in the three major subject areas do not differ very much for the commercially published titles and do not even begin to diverge until after four years of their lives, it seems that books in the social sciences have the highest gross margins, those in the humanities the second highest, and those in the natural sciences the lowest. For books of university presses, the ranking of the three major subject areas is different from that observed for the books published by commercial firms. Average gross margins after four years of life are highest for titles in the natural sciences, less for titles in the social sciences, and lowest for titles in the humanities.

ON FACTORS THAT LIE BEHIND GROSS MARGINS

Chapters 7.6 and 7.7 — *How do books of the university presses and commercial publishers, in the major subject areas and in various functional categories differ from one another in a number of factors pertaining to levels of outputs, manufacturing costs, prices, and physical sales?*

The Sizes of Print-Runs

For the eight vintage years 1968-1975 combined, 239 titles of university presses averaged 2,860 copies printed per title in the first year of life, less than half the 6,190 copies printed of the average of 158 commercially published titles.

Number of Pages and Number of Words

For the same eight vintage years combined, the books of commercial publishers had an average of 379 pages each, or 23 per cent more than the average of 309 pages for the books published by university presses; the former titles had an average of 181,600 words, a full 40 per cent more than the university-press titles with an average of only 129,300 words.

Direct Manufacturing Costs

Average plant costs (the fixed costs of manufacturing a book) per page and per 1,000 words of text are seen to be slightly lower for university-press titles than for commercially published titles. However, the cost of paper, printing, and binding, (the variable costs of manufacturing a book) are higher for the books produced by university presses: the average cost of paper per signature (32 pages) is 30 per cent higher, the average cost of printing per signature is 67 per cent higher, the average cost of binding a hardbound book is 23 per cent higher, and the average cost of binding a paperbound book is 67 per cent higher than for the books produced by commercial publishers. Likewise, for the average book published, total direct costs (the combination of fixed and variable components of manufacturing costs) are higher on all counts for university presses than for the commercial publishers: direct costs per copy are 23 per cent higher ($4.35 compared with $3.55), direct costs per page are 50 per cent higher ($.015 compared with $.010), and direct costs per 1,000 words are 90 per cent higher ($.040 compared with $.021).

Margins Between Manufacturing Cost and List Price: Mark-Up Factors

For titles of all vintage years combined, 1968-1975, the mark-up factors of the university presses were lower than the mark-up factors of the commercial publishers. Per copy, per page, and per 1,000 words, the not-for-profit publishers established a list price for their average title that was, respectively, 3.6, 3.7, and 3.5 times direct manufacturing cost; the for-profit publishers established a list price that was, respectively, 4.8, 4.9, and 5.3 times direct manufacturing cost. For the university-press titles, mark-up factors in the natural sciences, social sciences, and humanities are 3.8, 3.8, and 3.4, respectively, and for the commercial publishers 5.1, 4.5, and 4.3, respectively.

Discounts Below List Price on Sales to Wholesalers and Bookstores

A sample of 340 titles of university presses for all eight vintage years combined had, in percentage terms, a slightly higher effective discount than did 299 titles of commercial publishers. That is, net sales revenues actually received per copy sold were 32.4 per cent below average list price for the university presses against 29.3 per cent for the commercial firms. Among university-press titles, those in the humanities had the highest percentage discounts of the three subject areas: 35.5 per cent below average list price. Among commercially published titles, those in the natural sciences had the highest percentage discounts: 32.6 per cent below list price. Discounts for the various functional categories were as follows: scholarly monographs, 35.2 per cent for 259 university-press titles and 28.7 per cent for 112 commercially published titles; professional-reference books, 29.8 per cent for six university-press titles and 31.5 per cent for 21 commercially published titles; college textbooks, 30.0 per cent for 28 university-press titles and 30.7 per cent for 113 commercially published titles; and general-interest books, 36.3 per cent for 35 university-press titles and 22.9 per cent for 30 commercially published titles. These results do not necessarily mean that university presses, in general, *offer* larger discounts than do commercial publishers. It may merely be that the university presses in the sample sold a larger proportion of their books to customers to whom higher discounts are customarily offered, such as wholesalers. This would account for the effective discounts observed.

List Prices

Average list prices of books of commercial publishers were found for all cohorts, 1968-1975, to be higher than the prices of books of university presses. Moreover, the commercial firms were apt to raise the prices of the same titles over the years of their lives at a faster rate than the university presses in the sample. Relative prices of titles in the three major subject areas for both the cohort sample and a larger sample of titles obtained from a published source exhibit an extremely interesting regularity. Of the university-press titles and the commercially published titles in the cohort sample and the titles in the Bowker series, books in the natural sciences have the highest prices, followed by books in the social sciences, with books in the humanities showing the lowest prices of the three categories. The largest differences in average list prices among the three subject areas are observed for books of commercial publishers in the cohort sample; the average title in the natural sciences was priced, in constant 1977 dollars, at $25.78, compared with $13.91 in the social sciences and $11.15 in the humanities. The smallest difference observed is for books of university presses; the average title in the natural sciences was priced at $15.46 compared with $14.39 in the social sciences and $13.89 in the humanities. Changes in the list prices of commercially published titles over the period 1968-1975 seem to have just kept pace with the general price inflation reported for the output of the printing and publishing industries, while list prices of the university presses actually declined in the earlier years of this period — reflecting the fact that nominal list prices were not increased fast enough by the university press to keep up with price inflation.

Lifetime Patterns of Physical Sales

Over the first six years of life, physical sales of 132 hardbound books of university presses published in the three-year period 1968-1970 averaged 2,052 copies per title. Physical sales of 20 paperbound titles in the same age group averaged 3,560 copies per title, some 73 per cent above the average for the hardbound titles. Some 71.8 per cent of total six-year sales occurred in the first two years of life for hardbound titles, against only 59.6 per cent for paperbacks.

Physical sales of 92 hardbound books of commercial publishers belonging to the same age group as the university-press books, averaged 5,637 copies per title in the first six years of life. Physical sales of 26 paperbound titles averaged 9,358 copies per title, some 66 per cent above the average for the hardbound titles. Unlike the books of the university presses, the sales of paperbound books of the commercial publishers are skewed more toward the earlier years of life than are sales of hardbound books, though the difference between the two distributions is far less pronounced.

Among university-press books, those in the natural sciences registered sales of 3,083 copies over the six-year period, the highest number of copies sold per average title; social sciences were next with 2,332, and humanities last with only 1,874 copies.

Among commercially published titles, those in the natural sciences registered the *lowest* number of copies sold per the average title — 2,715 copies — lower even than the university-press books in the natural sciences. Because of the much higher prices charged by the commercial firms, however, actual sales revenue were far higher than for the university presses in this subject area.

The sample of commercially published books in the social sciences contains by far the best sellers of any of the three subject areas: 11,143 copies sold per average title over six years of life. This compares with 4,621 copies in the humanities and the previously cited 2,715 copies in the natural sciences.

For university-press books there do not appear to be large variations in physical sales among functional categories — scholarly monographs, professional-reference books, college texts, and books of general interest. The highest average is for college texts, with 2,992 copies sold per title over the first six years of life; the lowest is for books of general interest, with average sales of 2,100 copies.

In the sample of commercially published titles, books of general interest had the largest number of copies sold per title: 13,620 copies of the average title sold over the full six-year period. The worst sellers were the scholarly monographs, with 4,702 copies sold per title over the first six years of life.

ON THE PLIGHT OF UNIVERSITY PRESSES

Chapter 7.6 — In summary, what are some of the strategic differences observed in the analysis of costs and prices of university presses and commercial publishers?

In terms of the standard-cost measures used, per copy, per page, and per 1,000 words of text, direct manufacturing costs were seen to be higher for books published by university presses than for those of commercial publishers, due chiefly to the fact that they publish more short-run books than commercial publishers.

Mark-ups — the multiplicative factor by which direct costs are multiplied to determine an appropriate list price — were consistently lower for university presses than for the commercial publishers.

There is some indication that effective discounts below list price on sales to the distributors of books (wholesalers and bookstores) were slightly higher for books of university presses than for those of commercial firms.

List prices per copy of university-press books were consistently lower, on average, than the list prices charged by commercial publishers. In addition, university presses tended to raise the prices of the same books over the years of their lives less than the commercial publishers. From the point of view of those who purchase and/or read the books, the lower prices charged by university presses are no doubt welcomed. However, since the titles of the commercial firms have, on average, more pages and more words per page, the buyer is actually paying more per page and per 1,000 word for the average university-press book.

With regard to the relative prices charged for books in the three subject areas, commercial publishers evidently took advantage of differences in demand conditions, charging comparatively higher prices for books in the natural sciences and lower prices for books in the humanities. In contrast, university presses charged similar prices in all three areas.

Thus, for several reasons the university presses are likely to end up with less satisfactory bottom lines on their income-and-expense statements than commercial publishing houses.

CHAPTER 7.3

ANNUAL FINANCIAL DATA OF BOOK PUBLISHERS

One of the purposes of this chapter is to try to determine whether, or under what circumstances, the net-income figures derived from annual profit-and-loss or income-and-expense statements can be used to assess reliably the profitability of book publishing.[1]

A discussion of the appropriateness of financial statements as a tool in an analysis of profitability, however, presupposes a familiarity with the accounting practices and conventions upon which they are based. A brief review of the terms and prevalent accounting procedures used by publishing firms in the formulation of annual financial statements will aid in the subsequent analysis.[2]

ACCEPTED ACCOUNTING PRACTICES AND CONVENTIONS

The type of financial statement of interest in this study is called an "income-and-expense account," "profit-and-loss account," or "operating statement." These three labels mean essentially the same thing, but to simplify the exposition only the first shall be used here. The adjectival phrase "income-and-expense" is more descriptive of the purpose of the accounts than is the adjective "operating," and the phrase "profit-and-loss" does not seem to fit comfortably in a discussion that includes not-for-profit publishers such as university presses.

---

[1]Some of the material presented in this chapter is an elaboration of material found in Chapter 2.4 of Volume 1 of *Information Through the Printed Word.*

[2]For a more detailed discussion of the accounting practices of publishers see John P. Dessauer, *Book Publishing, What It Is, What It Does* (New York: R.R. Bowker Co., 1974).

Annual Income-and-Expense Accounts

In general, it can be said that book publishers follow similar accounting procedures in preparing annual statements of incomes and expenses. Costs incurred in the process of editing, typesetting, printing, binding, advertising, marketing and distributing books are subtracted from the revenue obtained from selling books to derive a measure of annual "net income" or "net profit before taxes."

Table 7.3.1 displays a typical (though somewhat simplified) version of an income-and-expense account and, for purposes of illustration, contains authentic financial data for the years 1976 and 1977 obtained from a medium-size commercial publishing firm.

The account begins with *Gross Sales* of books, which are actual billings to customers in dollars, with all discounts deducted. Excluded are a number of other potential sources of revenue including income from subsidiary rights or from non-publishing activities such as printing plants, sales representation or fulfillment-service operations for other firms. For purposes of this illustration all such revenues have been lumped together and are shown under item 6, *Other Income*.

The second major item on the account is *Net Sales*, obtained by subtracting from *Gross Sales* credits for returned books and allowances. The sum of *Net Sales* and *Other Income* represents the entire "income" side of the income-and-expense account from which all costs are deducted to determine *Net Income from Operations* (item 7 in Table 7.3.1).

There are two major categories of cost. The first is usually called *Costs of Books Sold* (item 3 in the table), which includes plant costs (nonrecurring costs such as composition, reproduction proofs, negatives, plates, dies, artwork and so on), the cost of paper, printing, and binding, royalties paid to authors, and an inventory adjustment, or write-down, representing the loss in sales potential (and hence, asset value) of books that have been produced but not yet sold or otherwise disposed of.

The second major category of cost is usually called *Operating Expenses* (item 5 in the table). This category includes editorial expenses, production expenses (principally the labor costs incurred in supervising the production process as opposed to the materials costs which are included under *Cost of Books Sold*), advertising expenses, marketing, fulfillment (order processing, billing, shipping and warehousing) and general and administrative expenses.[3] The difference between the two cost

[3]It is customary to list the expenses separately on the statement, but it will suffice in this example merely to show one amount representing the total of all the expenses named.

TABLE 7.3.1 Statement of Annual Income and Expense for a Typical Publishing Firm, 1976 and 1977

	1976		1977	
	Dollars	Per cent of net sales	Dollars	Per cent of net sales
1. Gross sales	$10,273,900	111.3	$11,359,500	110.7
Returns and allowances	($ 1,043,100)	11.3	$ 1,097,900	10.7
2. Net sales	$ 9,230,800	100.0	$10,261,600	100.0
3. Cost of books sold:				
Plant costs	$ 807,200	8.7	$ 976,000	9.5
Paper, printing, binding	$ 1,740,300	18.9	$ 1,799,700	17.5
Royalties	$ 1,162,400	12.6	$ 1,180,700	11.5
Inventory adjustment	$ 644,000	7.0	$ 645,700	6.3
Total cost of books sold	$ 4,353,900	47.2	$ 4,602,100	44.8
4. Gross margin on sales (Net sales minus cost of books sold)	$ 4,876,900	52.8	$ 5,659,500	55.2
5. Operating expenses (Editorial, production, advertising, marketing, fulfillment, general and administrative)	$ 4,833,000	52.3	$ 5,659,700	55.2
6. Other income	$ 299,100	2.5	$ 219,100	2.1
7. Net income from operations (Gross margin on sales minus operating expenses plus other income)	$ 273,000	3.0	$ 218,900	2.1

Source: Machlup, Leeson, and Associates.

categories, *Cost of Books Sold* and *Operating Expenses*, is that the former, which we shall sometimes refer to as *direct* costs, includes costs that can be more readily allocated to individual titles, whereas the latter, which we shall sometimes refer to as *indirect* costs, includes costs that are more in the nature of "overhead" expenses that cannot be readily allocated to individual titles. An understanding of the difference in the treatment of these two types of costs will be of importance in some of the later discussions and hence warrants some elaboration.

The costs of producing a title may either be *expensed* at the time of publication, that is, shown immediately as a cost on the income-and-expense account, or they may be treated as an *investment in inventory* and charged as a cost only as copies of the titles are sold or otherwise disposed of. There is a variation on this second possibility, that the costs will be considered an *investment in inventory* and amortized independently of the rate of sale according to some formula or arbitrary rule of thumb.

Certain categories of costs are more likely than others to be *expensed*. For example, it would be too costly for the publisher to allocate to particular titles most of the items falling under the category *Operating Expenses* (indirect costs) and to defer charging the expenses against income until these books are actually sold. The complications that would be involved in making the cost allocations, in keeping the records and carrying detailed inventory accounts for each title separately and, finally, in showing the expense on the income-and-expense account in the years in which the books are actually sold, would be awkward and the accounting cost would be high.[4]

Costs that fall under the category *Cost of Books Sold* (direct costs), on the other hand, are more easily allocable to individual titles and, hence, are more likely to be treated as *investments in inventory* to be charged as costs on the income-and-expense account only as copies of the titles are sold — or written off if judged to be of uncertain salability. Plant costs, however, are apt to receive different treatment from different categories of publishers. If the expected life of a title, say an adult-trade title, is only a year, it is prudent accounting practice to "expense" all of the plant cost; if a title is expected to sell for several years, as, for example, an elhi (elementary-high school) text, it might be considered

[4]People in the production department, for example, work at any one moment on a particular book, but in the course of a day they usually work on several books; it would probably be too bothersome for them to record the minutes or hours spent during a day on this or that particular book. Hence the entire cost of the production department is treated as an unallocated operating expense.

more appropriate to regard the plant cost as an *investment in inventory* and to amortize it only gradually, either in proportion to sales or in a few installments over a few years.

With this preparation let us return to Table 7.3.1 to observe the arrangement of categories and the financial entries on an actual income-and-expense statement. The data on the table are expressed in both dollar amounts and as percentages of net sales, the latter providing a more convenient means of comparing from one year to the next the relative size of *Gross Margin on Sales* and *Net Income from Operations* and of the distribution of costs among the various categories.

By observing the table for the year 1976, it can be seen that this publisher had *Net Sales* of $9,230,800, a figure obtained by subtracting *Returns and Allowances* from the *Gross Sales* figure of $110,273,900. *Cost of Books Sold* totaled $4,353,900 (47.2 per cent of *Net Sales*), while *Gross Margin on Sales* was $4,876,900 (52.8 per cent of *Net Sales*). *Operating Expenses* were $4,833,000 (52.3 per cent of *Net Sales*) and *Other Income* amounted to $229,100 (2.5 per cent of *Net Sales*). Finally, *Net Income from Operations* totaled $273,000 (3.0 per cent of *Net Sales*). *Net Income from Operations* is seen to be a residual, the dollar amount that remains after total costs shown for the year are subtracted from total revenue.[5]

Using Annual Data To Assess Profitability

It may seem reasonable to base an analysis of profitability on annual accounting records such as the one just described. One might, for example, collect income-and-expense statements from a number of publishers and observe their combined net incomes over a period of years to see if profits have been rising, falling, or showing little change. Such a study would undoubtedly shed some useful light on current and past trends in

---

[5]There is, of course, still another cost category not shown here but usually found on the statements of for-profit publishers: federal, state, and local income taxes. Since both for-profit and not-for-profit publishers are the topic of this inquiry and since ignoring taxes will have no effect on the arguments of the analysis, *Net Income from Operations* will be considered the appropriate "bottom line" for all publishers.

profitability of individual firms, groups of firms or of the industry as a whole.[6]

There is, after all, a great advantage in fashioning an analysis around data that are likely to be compiled by publishers on a regular basis. The cost and effort involved in gathering and reporting on existing financial data are far below the cost and effort required to devise alternative analytical methods, to gather the required raw data, and finally, to derive the sought-after results. Data needed for an untried analytical technique may be either unavailable altogether or extremely difficult to cull from whatever records and reports the publisher may keep. The types of data useful to a business enterprise are likely to differ substantially from the types of data needed to test the researcher's hypothesis or statistical model.

Nevertheless, if it can be demonstrated that under certain circumstances the net-income figures reported on income-and-expense statements may not accurately reflect the profitability of a publishing operation, then there would be sufficient reason to seek alternative methods of analysis.

WHY ANNUAL FINANCIAL DATA MAY BE MISLEADING

What was said in the preceding section about the accounting treatment of the "cost of books sold," especially of "plant costs," and the expensing of certain costs of production as general "operating expenses" has implications which deserve further discussion. They relate chiefly to the analysis of the net-income calculations in years in which the ratios of sales from the backlist and sales from the list of new publications diverge substantially from the norm. If these ratios are ab-

---

[6]The annual *Industry Statistics* of the Association of American Publishers contains operating data, or income-and-expense data, for samples of publishers from several categories of publishing including trade and religious, technical, scientific, business, medical and other professional, mass-market paperback and elementary, high school, and college text books. The drawbacks to the data published in *Industry Statistics* is that from one year to the next the composition of the samples change, which renders unreliable any time-series analyses of the data.

normally high or abnormally low for two or three years in a row, the figures on the bottom line and the ratio of net income to net sales will convey a misleading picture of the economic health of a firm or even a sector of the industry.

Costs Expensed in the Year Incurred

If all the costs involved in producing books — from the procuring of the manuscripts for publication to the shipment of printed and bound copies — could be allocated to individual titles and deferred (not shown as costs on the income-and-expense statement) until the time when the books are sold or otherwise disposed of,[7] the closest possible relationship would be established between the realization of income from the sale of the product (book) and the realization of the cost involved in producing the product. Under such circumstances, the net-income figures derived from income-and-expense accounts would probably convey a somewhat more reliable picture of the profitability of book publishing.[8]

Unfortunately, a large proportion of the total cost of producing a book, those listed under *Operating Expenses* in the preceding section, are not allocated to individual titles, but rather "expensed" as soon as they are incurred. This clearly upsets the relationship between the realization of income and the incurrence of cost. Thus, a substantial portion of sales proceeds reported for a year is received for books produced one, two or more years earlier, and for which costs incurred for editing, production management, perhaps even composition,

---

[7]Each copy of a title would receive a "per-unit" asset value equal to the total cost allocated to the production of the title divided by the number of copies produced. This per-unit value would not be charged as a cost on the accounts until the year in which the copy of the title is sold and revenue received. ". . . or otherwise disposed of" refers to copies of books that, because of age, can no longer be sold at full price. Such copies may have to be "remaindered" (sold very inexpensively to a wholesaler or some other intermediary) or destroyed; if and when either of these actions are taken, the full per-unit value will have to appear as a cost on the income-and-expense account.

[8]We state that the picture of profitability conveyed would be only "somewhat more reliable" rather than wholely reliable because costs and revenues of titles of different ages would still be neither properly discounted nor adjusted to account for price inflation. A discussion of the importance of these two types of adjustments in the derivation of an economically sound notion of profits is presented in Chapter 7.5.

etc., were expensed at the time of their publication. For example, some of the costs that should have been charged against sales made in 1977 were actually charged against sales and incomes in 1976, 1975, or earlier. On the other hand, some of costs charged in 1977 were not incurred for books sold in 1977, but for books that will be sold in 1978, 1979, or later.

Only on the basis of a simplifying assumption would the costs expensed in a given year be equal to the costs associated with sales for that year. This simplifying assumption is that the *past expenses* for producing the books sold in the *current year* are exactly equal to the *current expenses* made for producing books expected to be sold in the *future*. It is apparent that such an assumption could not be seriously entertained during periods of inflation in costs and prices, during periods of large changes in the ratio of sales coming from the backlist, or during periods when the number of books published annually by the firm is increasing or decreasing significantly.

Costs that are likely to be expensed in the year they are incurred (rather than deferred until income from sales is realized) constitute a substantial proportion of the total costs shown on income-and-expense reports. For instance, a sample of ten publishing houses from which financial data have been obtained show operating expenses that ranged from 44 per cent to 67 per cent of net sales for the year 1975.

Costs Deferred Until Income is Realized

It is necessary to add a few important qualifications to those contained in footnote 8 concerning a claim made in the preceding section. There it was stated that "If all costs involved in producing books . . . could be allocated to individual titles and deferred until the time when the books are sold . . . net income figures derived from income-and-expense accounts would probably convey a somewhat more reliable picture of the profitability of book publishing."

By and large, the costs of composition, paper, printing, and binding — the costs usually shown under the heading *Cost of Books Sold* — are handled by most publishers in this manner; they are allocated to individual titles and treated as an investment in inventory to be deferred as a cost on the income-and-expense account until copies of the title are sold. Thus, if we could disregard for the moment the need to discount and deflate costs and revenues we might suggest an alternative method for analyzing profits. Instead of observing the net-income figure on the financial statements, we might observe *Gross Margin on Sales* (*net sales* minus *cost of books sold*). The latter figure, it could be argued, while providing only a partial picture of incomes and costs, would at least be free of the potential distortions caused by the treatment of operating expenses.

Regrettably, the gross-margin-on-sales figure is subject to another kind of distortion and, under certain conditions and assumptions concerning the valuation of inventory and the technique used to write down these values over time, may also mislead the uninitiated or incautious observer.

Inventory Valuation and Write Down

The usual accounting procedure is to divide the sum of plant costs, and the costs of paper, printing, and binding by the number of copies of the title produced to obtain a measure of manufacturing cost per copy.[9] This "unit cost" is also the "unit inventory value," the amount that is listed under *Cost of Books Sold* whenever a copy of the title is sold. As long as copies continue to sell, the corresponding unit manufacturing costs are shown as expenses on the income-and-expense account in whichever year the sales take place. If a time comes when copies remaining in stock can no longer be sold, their inventory value has to be "written off," and shown as an inventory adjustment, lest the publisher hold assets of questionable liquidity at values which may not be realizable in the market.

In reality, there are a variety of methods of inventory valuation and write down. It has already been mentioned that some publishers expense composition costs when the title is published and hence do not include that cost as part of the inventory value; others may amortize plant costs by some rule that has nothing to do with the rate of sale of copies of the title; some may seek to "write off" the value of inventory as soon as possible while others may seek to postpone writing off inventory values for longer periods of time. There are many reasons for choosing different techniques — the type of book being published, the field or subject area, the intended readers, the preferences of management, etc. — but this does not mitigate the problems involved in trying to interpret gross-margin or net-income figures when the techniques being applied are not known, or when the figures for different firms using different techniques are mixed together.

In order to see how serious the variations in *Gross Margin on Sales* (and, hence on *Net Income*) would be if different methods of inventory valuation and write down were applied under otherwise identical circumstances, we obtained from

---

[9]To be more concise, the phrase "manufacturing cost" will be used as a synonym for "plant costs and the costs of paper, printing, and binding."

twenty publishing houses, including commercial publishers and university presses, descriptions of the methods they use to establish accounting values for books held in inventory and of the procedures they use to write down or write off these inventory values over the lives of the books. The findings of an experiment in which identical (though simulated) data on sales and costs were applied to six of these methods tend to support the suspicion that under certain conditions the reported *Gross Margin on Sales* may vary significantly from one method to the next.

Here are a few examples of valuation and write-down methods currently in use:

1. Books are held in inventory at full-cost value (plant cost, paper, printing, and binding costs) for five years; in the sixth year the full value of stock remaining is written off.

2. Books are given full-cost value. Each year the value of the number of unsold copies in stock that exceeds twice the number of the year's unit sales is written off.

3. Plant costs are expensed in the year of publication. Inventory value is based on paper, printing, and binding costs and is written down as follows: remaining stock is valued at 100% of that cost in the first year, 50% in the second year, 30% in the third year, 20% in the fourth year, and zero value thereafter.

4. Fifteen per cent of plant costs is expensed in the year of publication. The stock of books in inventory is given the remaining value plus the costs of paper, printing, and binding. If unit sales fall below 250 copies and the book is more than three years old, the inventory value is completely written off.

5. Plant costs are amortized over a six-year period. Inventory value is based on paper, printing, and binding costs, which are written off only at the end of the sixth year.

6. Books are held at full-cost value with no write downs during the first year of life. Annually, stock in excess of three times the current year's unit sales (number of copies sold) is written off. Any value remaining after six years is written off completely.

7. Plant costs are amortized over a three-year period. Inventory value is based on paper, printing, and binding costs. Annually, stock in ex-

cess of three years' anticipated sales is written off.

8. Books are held at full-cost value. A committee of editors, sales managers, and other staff consider the sales potential of books on an individual basis and establish the amount to be written off accordingly.

9. Inventory value is based on paper, printing, and binding costs. Plant cost is amortized over a period of two months for certain types of books and over five years for others. Twice a year, a title-by-title assessment is made and the number of copies that can be sold over the following five years is estimated. Whatever value remains in excess of this amount is written off.

For any of the above methods of inventory valuation and write down an annual figure for *Gross Margin on Sales* can be derived from the following information on each title published:

(1) manufacturing costs (with plant costs and the cost of paper, printing, and binding separately given)

(2) the number of copies of the title printed

(3) the net selling price, or revenue actually received for each copy sold, and

(4) the number of copies sold each year.

To construct an income-and-expense statement, the accountant follows the rules prescribed by the chosen method of valuation and write down. Whenever a title is produced, a unit-inventory value is calculated which may, for example, be equal to total manufacturing costs divided by the number of copies printed. Alternatively, if the valuation method being used requires that the composition costs be "expensed" immediately, the unit inventory value would be equal to the costs of paper, printing, and binding only, divided by the number of copies printed. Each time a copy of the title is sold, the revenue received is listed on preliminary accounting ledgers under "net sales," and, at the same time, the off-setting cost, or unit inventory value, is listed under the heading "cost of books sold."

Whenever the rule or method of writing down the value of inventory dictates, the unit inventory value of each copy remaining in stock is adjusted downward and the amount of the reduction is listed on the preliminary ledger under "inventory adjustment." Based on the size of the write down, a new unit value is imputed to the copies of the title remaining in stock and this value becomes the unit inventory value charged when copies are sold in the future.[10] The same procedure is followed for all titles.

At the end of the 12-month accounting period, the income-and-expense account is made up by summing the individual entries under each of the three categories, net sales, manufacturing costs, and inventory adjustment. *Gross Margin on Sales* is then calculated by subtracting the two aggregated cost figures from the total revenue figure.[11]

The sales and cost figures for any year will, of course, include titles of a variety of vintages. Some titles will be from the current list, others from the backlist. Some titles will be carried at their full-cost value at the time of sale, others at only partial value, or in some cases, even zero value because of the write downs of previous years. In some instances, the prices charged for titles of earlier vintages will have been raised above their original prices and hence contribute more revenue to the net-sales figure.

TESTS ON SIMULATED DATA - AN ILLUSTRATION

The procedure just described will now be employed to calculate gross margins on annual income-and-expense statements using simulated data and a computer program.[12] The purpose is

---

[10]There are, of course, other factors that normally have to be considered in the valuation of inventory, such as reprintings of titles that sell very well or decisions to retain some portion of inventory as unbound "sheets" to be bound only as the need arises. Such considerations do not substantially affect the thrust of the analysis and hence will not be discussed.

[11]The gross-margin calculation described here excludes royalties which are customarily included under *Cost of Books Sold*. Omitting this category will have no effect on the essential threads of the argument.

[12]The computer program, written in Fortran, had six subroutines, one for each of the valuation-and-write-down methods

to observe under controlled conditions whether, or to what extent, the calculated *Gross Margin on Sales* would vary if all assumptions about manufacturing costs, number of copies printed, and number of copies sold remained the same, while the method of inventory valuation and write down changes.

The first six valuation-and-write-down methods described above were applied to five separate sets of data, each embodying varying assumptions about (1) growth in the size of the publication program (number of titles published), (2) inflation in costs and prices, and (3) changes in the proportion of annual sales coming from the backlist. The results of the tests are given in Table 7.3.2.

All Tests

The imaginary publisher whose financial accounts are shown in the table has been in business since the early 1960's. From that time until 1973 the following conditions are presumed to have prevailed:

(1) 100 new titles were published every year.

(2) 10,000 copies of each title were produced with plant costs totaling \$6,240 and paper, printing, and binding costs totaling \$4,160 (hence,

---

involved in the tests. It might at first blush seem unnecessary to go to the trouble of writing and debugging an elaborate computer program to perform the seemingly simple calculations described in the text. The number of computations involved, however, is formidable. Each of the five tests displayed in Table 7.3.2 is based on simulated data for the years 1961-1975. As far as the computer was concerned, however, there was only "one" title published in each of these 15 years. (The final results were "scaled" by multiplying through by 100 to make the examples more realistic.) Even with only one title per year, some 750 calculations are required to obtain results for each of the six methods, or 4,500 calculations per test. Thus, the five tests on Table 7.3.2 represent 22,500 calculations. If each calculation took only 15 seconds, it would have taken over 93 hours of constant work to produce the results. Even with a 2 per cent rate of error, some 450 errors of unknown seriousness would have been part of the results. The computer completed the task in a few seconds and made no computational errors.

TABLE 7.3.2 Financial Statements of Incomes and Expenses and Resulting Gross Margins Derived Using Five Separate Sets of Simulated Data and Six Different Methods of Inventory Valuation and Write Down

	All tests	Test 1 No change in conditions			
	1972	1973	1974	1975	Three year average
Method 1					
Net sales	$3,900,000	$3,900,000	$3,900,000	$3,900,000	
Manufacturing costs	$1,039,900	$1,039,900	$1,039,900	$1,039,900	
Inventory adjustment	$ 0	$ 0	$ 0	$ 0	
Gross margin	$2,860,100	$2,860,100	$2,860,100	$2,860,100	$2,860,100
Method 2					
Net sales	$3,900,000	$3,900,000	$3,900,000	$3,900,000	
Manufacturing costs	$1,039,900	$1,039,900	$1,039,900	$1,039,900	
Inventory adjustment	$ 0	$ 0	$ 0	$ 0	
Gross margin	$2,860,100	$2,860,100	$2,860,100	$2,860,100	$2,860,100
Method 3					
Net sales	$3,900,000	$3,900,000	$3,900,000	$3,900,000	
Manufacturing costs	$ $947,200	$ $947,200	$ $947,200	$ $947,200	
Inventory adjustment	$ 92,700	$ 92,700	$ 92,700	$ 92,700	
Gross margin	$2,860,100	$2,860,100	$2,860,100	$2,860,100	$2,860,100
Method 4					
Net sales	$3,900,000	$3,900,000	$3,900,000	$3,900,000	
Manufacturing costs	$1,039,900	$1,039,900	$1,039,900	$1,039,900	
Inventory adjustment	$ 0	$ 0	$ 0	$ 0	
Gross margin	$2,860,100	$2,860,100	$2,860,100	$2,860,100	$2,860,100
Method 5					
Net sales	$3,900,000	$3,900,000	$3,900,000	$3,900,000	
Manufacturing costs	$ $975,800	$ $975,800	$ $975,800	$ $975,800	
Inventory adjustment	$ 64,100	$ 64,100	$ 64,100	$ 64,100	
Gross margin	$2,860,100	$2,860,100	$2,860,100	$2,860,100	$2,860,100
Method 6					
Net sales	$3,900,000	$3,900,000	$3,900,000	$3,900,000	
Manufacturing costs	$1,039,900	$1,039,900	$1,039,900	$1,039,900	
Inventory adjustment	$ 0	$ 0	$ 0	$ 0	
Gross margin	$2,860,100	$2,860,100	$2,860,100	$2,860,100	$2,860,100
Gross margins					
Average	$2,860,100	$2,860,100	$2,860,100	$2,860,100	$2,860,100
Standard deviation	0	0	0	0	0
Ratio: Standard deviation / Average	0	0	0	0	0

(continued)

TABLE 7.3.2, continued

	All tests	Test 2 Growth in the publication program			
	1972	1973	1974	1975	Three year average
Method 1					
Net sales	$3,900,000	$4,134,000	$4,485,000	$4,863,300	
Manufacturing costs	$1,039,900	$1,102,300	$1,195,900	$1,296,800	
Inventory adjustment	$ 0	$ 0	$ 0	$ 0	
Gross margin	$2,860,100	$3,031,700	$3,289,100	$3,566,500	$3,295,800
Method 2					
Net sales	$3,900,000	$4,134,000	$4,485,000	$4,863,300	
Manufacturing costs	$1,039,900	$1,102,300	$1,195,900	$1,296,800	
Inventory adjustment	$ 0	$ 0	$ 0	$ 0	
Gross margin	$2,860,100	$3,031,700	$3,289,100	$3,566,500	$3,295,800
Method 3					
Net sales	$3,900,000	$4,134,000	$4,485,000	$4,863,300	
Manufacturing costs	$ 947,200	$1,034,600	$1,128,200	$1,222,600	
Inventory adjustment	$ 92,700	$ 92,700	$ 101,000	$ 110,200	
Gross margin	$2,860,100	$3,006,700	$3,255,800	$3,530,500	$3,264,300
Method 4					
Net sales	$3,900,000	$4,134,000	$4,485,000	$4,863,300	
Manufacturing costs	$1,039,900	$1,108,600	$1,203,700	$1,305,100	
Inventory adjustment	$ 0	$ 0	$ 0	$ 0	
Gross margin	$2,860,100	$3,025,400	$3,281,300	$3,558,200	$3,288,300
Method 5					
Net sales	$3,900,000	$4,134,000	$4,485,000	$4,863,300	
Manufacturing costs	$ $975,800	$1,038,200	$1,128,700	$1,224,500	
Inventory adjustment	$ 64,100	$ 68,200	$ 74,100	$ 80,500	
Gross margin	$2,860,100	$3,027,600	$3,282,200	$3,558,300	$3,289,400
Method 6					
Net sales	$3,900,000	$4,134,000	$4,485,000	$4,863,300	
Manufacturing costs	$1,039,900	$1,102,300	$1,195,900	$1,296,800	
Inventory adjustment	$ 0	$ 0	$ 0	$ 0	
Gross margin	$2,860,100	$3,031,700	$3,289,100	$3,566,500	$3,295,800
Gross margins					
Average	$2,860,100	$3,025,800	$3,281,100	$3,557,800	$3,288,200
Standard deviation	0	9,200	11,800	11,200	11,200
Ratio: Standard deviation / Average	0	<0.01	<0.01	<0.01	<0.01

(continued)

TABLE 7.3.2, continued

	All tests	Test 3 Inflation in costs and prices			
	1972	1973	1974	1975	Three year average
Method 1					
Net sales	$3,900,000	$4,350,000	$4,845,000	$5,200,500	
Manufacturing costs	$1,039,900	$1,159,900	$1,225,900	$1,344,900	
Inventory adjustment	$ 0	$ 0	$ 0	$ 0	
Gross margin	$2,860,100	$3,190,100	$3,619,100	$3,855,600	$3,554,900
Method 2					
Net sales	$3,900,000	$4,350,000	$4,845,000	$5,200,500	
Manufacturing costs	$1,039,900	$1,159,900	$1,225,900	$1,344,900	
Inventory adjustment	$ 0	$ 0	$ 0	$ 0	
Gross margin	$2,860,100	$3,190,100	$3,619,100	$3,855,600	$3,554,900
Method 3					
Net sales	$3,900,000	$4,350,000	$4,845,000	$5,200,500	
Manufacturing costs	$ $947,200	$1,115,200	$1,135,600	$1,280,700	
Inventory adjustment	$ 92,700	$ 92,700	$ 108,700	$ 111,100	
Gross margin	$2,860,100	$3,142,100	$3,600,700	$3,808,700	$3,517,200
Method 4					
Net sales	$3,900,000	$4,350,000	$4,845,000	$5,200,500	
Manufacturing costs	$1,039,900	$1,171,900	$1,229,500	$1,356,200	
Inventory adjustment	$ 0	$ 0	$ 0	$ 0	
Gross margin	$2,860,100	$3,178,100	$3,615,500	$3,844,300	$3,546,000
Method 5					
Net sales	$3,900,000	$4,350,000	$4,845,000	$5,200,500	
Manufacturing costs	$ $975,800	$1,095,800	$1,155,800	$1,270,800	
Inventory adjustment	$ 64,100	$ 72,100	$ 75,800	$ 83,800	
Gross margin	$2,860,100	$3,182,100	$3,613,400	$3,845,900	$3,547,100
Method 6					
Net sales	$3,900,000	$4,350,000	$4,845,000	$5,200,500	
Manufacturing costs	$1,039,900	$1,159,900	$1,225,900	$1,344,900	
Inventory adjustment	$ 0	$ 0	$ 0	$ 0	
Gross margin	$2,860,100	$3,190,100	$3,619,100	$3,855,600	$3,554,900
Gross margins					
Average	$2,860,100	$3,178,800	$3,614,500	$3,844,300	$3,545,800
Standard deviation	0	17,000	6,500	16,600	13,300
Ratio: Standard deviation / Average	0	0.01	<0.01	<0.01	<0.01

(continued)

TABLE 7.3.2, continued

	All tests	Test 4 Change in the pattern of sales			
	1972	1973	1974	1975	Three year average
Method 1					
Net sales	$3,900,000	$1,950,000	$1,170,000	$1,287,000	
Manufacturing costs	$1,039,900	$ $519,900	$ $311,900	$ $343,100	
Inventory adjustment	$ 0	$ 0	$ 0	$ 0	
Gross margin	$2,860,100	$1,430,100	$ 858,100	$ 943,900	$1,077,400
Method 2					
Net sales	$3,900,000	$1,950,000	$1,170,000	$1,287,000	
Manufacturing costs	$1,039,900	$ $519,900	$ $231,100	$ $164,000	
Inventory adjustment	$ 0	$ 727,900	$ 866,600	$ 895,500	
Gross margin	$2,860,100	$ 702,200	$ 72,300	$ 227,500	$ 334,000
Method 3					
Net sales	$3,900,000	$1,950,000	$1,170,000	$1,287,000	
Manufacturing costs	$ $947,200	$ $739,200	$ $697,600	$ $701,300	
Inventory adjustment	$ 92,700	$ 92,700	$ 196,700	$ 254,900	
Gross margin	$2,860,100	$1,118,100	$ 275,700	$ 330,800	$ 547,900
Method 4					
Net sales	$3,900,000	$1,950,000	$1,170,000	$1,287,000	
Manufacturing costs	$1,039,900	$ $597,900	$ $421,100	$ $447,700	
Inventory adjustment	$ 0	$ 0	$ 0	$ 0	
Gross margin	$2,860,100	$1,352,100	$ 748,900	$ 839,300	$ 980,100
Method 5					
Net sales	$3,900,000	$1,950,000	$1,170,000	$1,287,000	
Manufacturing costs	$ $975,800	$ $455,800	$ $268,600	$ $291,500	
Inventory adjustment	$ 64,100	$ 116,100	$ 237,400	$ 353,500	
Gross margin	$2,860,100	$1,378,100	$ 664,000	$ 642,000	$ 894,700
Method 6					
Net sales	$3,900,000	$1,950,000	$1,170,000	$1,287,000	
Manufacturing costs	$1,039,900	$ $519,900	$ $242,600	$ $182,800	
Inventory adjustment	$ 0	$ 623,900	$ 797,300	$ 849,300	
Gross margin	$2,860,100	$ 806,200	$ 130,100	$ 254,900	$ 397,100
Gross margins					
Average	$2,860,100	$1,131,100	$458,183	$539,700	$ $705,200
Standard deviation	0	285,500	310,000	284,600	290,800
Ratio:					
Standard deviation					
	0	0.25	0.68	0.53	0.41

(continued)

TABLE 7.3.2, continued

	All tests	Test 5 A combination of changes			
	1972	1973	1974	1975	Three year average
Method 1					
Net sales	$3,900,000	$2,071,500	$1,513,500	$1,939,900	
Manufacturing costs	$1,039,900	$ $552,100	$ $390,100	$ $501,900	
Inventory adjustment	$ 0	$ 0	$ 0	$ 0	
Gross margin	$2,860,100	$1,519,400	$1,122,400	$1,438,000	$1,359,900
Method 2					
Net sales	$3,900,000	$2,071,500	$1,513,500	$1,939,900	
Manufacturing costs	$1,039,900	$ $552,100	$ $284,200	$ $256,600	
Inventory adjustment	$ 0	$ 952,900	$1,231,500	$1,530,000	
Gross margin	$2,860,100	$ 566,500	($2,200)	$ 153,300	$ 239,200
Method 3					
Net sales	$3,900,000	$2,071,500	$1,513,500	$1,939,900	
Manufacturing costs	$ $947,200	$ $946,300	$ $998,300	$1,230,200	
Inventory adjustment	$ 92,700	$ 92,700	$ 253,800	$ 358,000	
Gross margin	$2,860,100	$1,032,500	$ 261,400	$ 351,700	$ 548,500
Method 4					
Net sales	$3,900,000	$2,071,500	$1,513,500	$1,939,900	
Manufacturing costs	$1,039,900	$ $946,300	$ $556,600	$ $703,500	
Inventory adjustment	$ 0	$ 0	$ 0	$ 0	
Gross margin	$2,860,100	$1,125,200	$ 956,900	$1,236,400	$1,106,200
Method 5					
Net sales	$3,900,000	$2,071,500	$1,513,500	$1,939,900	
Manufacturing costs	$ $975,800	$ $487,900	$ $343,500	$ $437,000	
Inventory adjustment	$ 64,100	$ 145,200	$ 322,000	$ 525,200	
Gross margin	$2,860,100	$1,438,400	$ 848,000	$ 977,700	$1,088,000
Method 6					
Net sales	$3,900,000	$2,071,500	$1,513,500	$1,939,900	
Manufacturing costs	$1,039,900	$ $552,100	$ $299,300	$ $282,800	
Inventory adjustment	$ 0	$ 816,700	$1,126,800	$1,425,600	
Gross margin	$2,860,100	$ 702,700	$ 87,400	$ 231,500	$ 340,500
Gross margins					
Average	$2,860,100	$1,064,100	$ $545,700	$ $731,400	$ $780,400
Standard deviation	$ 0	348,900	444,200	507,200	423,600
Ratio: Standard deviation / Average	0	0.33	0.81	0.69	0.54

Source: Machlup, Leeson, and Associates.

unit costs were $1.04). Each copy sold produced revenues of $3.90 for the firm.

(3) All 10,000 copies of each title were sold in 4 years; 6,000 copies in the first year, 3,000 in the second, 700 in the third and 300 in the fourth.

Each of the five tests in Table 7.3.2 reflects the impact on *Gross Margin* of a change in one or more of these assumptions beginning in the year 1973. Because no changes occurred prior to 1973, the results for 1972 and before are the same for all tests and are shown in the first column of the table.

Test 1 - No Change in Conditions

The first test extends the three conditions listed above for an additional three years. The results illustrate clearly that with no change in the number of new titles published, in the cost of producing a title, or in the rate of sale, the same *Gross Margin* is obtained regardless of the valuation/write-down method used. It can be seen that the distribution of costs between the categories "manufacturing costs" and "inventory adjustment" is not the same for all methods, but that the total remains constant. This situation would continue indefinitely, as long as the underlying conditions do not change. In such unlikely circumstances, the *Gross Margin* figures would be perfectly comparable among publishers and greater confidence could be placed in an analysis of profitability based on such figures. In reality, however, these underlying conditions change all the time, and although the magnitude of the changes, their timing, and distribution among publishers cannot be measured at any reasonable cost, the certainty of their effect on calculated *Gross Margins* can at least be demonstrated in principle.

Test 2 - Growth in the Publication Program

In the second test the number of titles published begins growing by 10 titles per year starting in 1973. From Table 7.3.2 it can be seen that this causes an immediate, though only slight divergence in the *Gross Margins* calculated with different inventory methods. The results using Methods 1, 2, and 6 do not differ from one another at all, but the results based on Methods 3, 4, and 5 do differ.

The average *Gross Margins* for all six methods, as well as their standard deviations and the ratio of the latter to the former, are shown at the bottom of the table.[13] The magnitude of the change in the underlying conditions imposed in Test 2 obviously cause insignificant variation in the *Gross Margin* figures. The standard deviations range from $9,200 to $11,800 in relation to an average of over $3,000,000, in each case resulting in a ratio of the standard deviation to the average of less than .01, which is hardly an indication of wide divergence.

Test 3 - Inflation in Costs and Prices

In the third test, the original assumption about 100 new titles per year is reinstated, but costs and prices per title are increased in 1973 and thereafter. The schedule of increases is as follows:

	Plant costs	Paper, printing, and binding costs	Average net selling price
1972 and before	$6,240	$4,160	$3.90
1973	$7,440	$4,960	$4.65
1974	$7,500	$5,000	$5.10
1975	$8,520	$5,680	$5.38

Under these conditions, calculated *Gross Margins* again diverge beginning in 1973, but again by only insignificant amounts. The standard deviation as a proportion of the average gross margin is below .01 in 1974 and 1975, and just equal to .01 ($17,000/$3,178,800) in 1973.

---

[13] Standard deviation, calculated by the formula $\sigma = \sqrt{\frac{\Sigma(X-\bar{X})^2}{N}}$, is a measure of the dispersion of the elements (the X's) of a collection of numbers (N of them) around their average ($\bar{X}$). For samples of numbers of the same general order of magnitude, the larger the calculated standard deviation, the more scattered the elements. When comparing the dispersion of collections of numbers of very different orders of magnitude, however, it is desirable to "standardize" the standard deviation. For example, a standard deviation of 10 shows greater dispersion of individual elements in relation to an average of 2.5 than does a standard deviation of 10,000 to an average of 1,000,000. When these standard deviations are divided by their averages, the resulting ratios, 4 and .01, demonstrate this fact.

Test 4 - Change in the Pattern of Sales

In the fourth test, the only change imposed on the original conditions is a shift in the pattern of sales for each title. Instead of selling all 10,000 copies in four years, the rate of sale is reduced to a constant 1,000 copies per year. This is tantamount to suddenly increasing the proportion of sales coming from backlist titles. In fact, this shift in the rate of sale brought about a change in the proportion of unit sales coming from the backlist from .40 in 1972 and before to .80 in 1973, .67 in 1974, and .70 in 1975.

Unlike the effect of the changing conditions in Tests 2 and 3, the effect of a change in the pattern of sales on the *Gross Margin* figures calculated by the six methods shown in Table 7.3.2 is very significant. In the first year of the change, 1973, *Gross Margins* range from a high of $1,430,100 to a low of $702,200, a difference equal to more than 50 per cent of the higher figure. The standard deviation for the six figures that year is $285,500, a significant magnitude in relation to the average *Gross Margin* of $1,131,100. In 1974 and 1975 the individual *Gross Margins* are even more widely disbursed around the average as indicated by the ratios of the standard deviation to the average for these years (.68 and .53, respectively). Even for the three year average (calculated to see if annual differences will smooth out over longer periods) the variations caused by applying the different methods are still very notable: the *Gross Margins* range from $1,077,400 to $334,000 and the standard deviation is 41 per cent of the average.

The results of Test 4 would indicate that a shift in the pattern of sales over the life of a title could lead to very misleading conclusions about profits based on income-and-expense accounts.

Test 5 - A Combination of Changes

The final test combines all three changes imposed individually in Tests 2, 3, and 4. In Test 5, beginning in 1973, the number of new titles published grows by 10 each year, costs and selling prices rise according to the schedule shown for Test 3 above, and the pattern of sales shifts as in Test 4. These changes occur simultaneously, producing the results shown in the last panel (Test 5) of Table 7.3.2.

A remarkable result observed here is that of complementarity, meaning that the variations in *Gross Margins* in this Test 5 are greater than the sum of the variations in *Gross Margins* observed separately for each of the preceding tests. For example, the differences between the largest and smallest *Gross Margins* calculated for Tests 2, 3, and 4 are $33,300, $18,400, and $785,800 respectively, for a total of $837,500. In Test 5 this difference is $1,124,600. Furthermore, the ratios of the standard deviation to the average in Test 5 are substantially above what one might have expected by observing these ratios for each of the preceding tests.

At any rate, Test 5 clearly reinforces the claim that income-and-expense accounts can be misleading. If one were to observe the profit performance of a firm or group of firms using Method 1 or Method 4, for example, a far different picture would be painted than if the same firms facing the same underlying conditions had used instead Method 2 or Method 6.

To sum up, this exercise demonstrates that the choice of inventory method can have a significant effect on calculated gross margins, and hence on net profits, suggesting that analyses of profitability based on annual income-and-expense accounts may be misleading. The exercise provides no hints or guidelines concerning which among the several methods are preferable, either from the point of view of the publishing community or of the researcher.

Qualifications

A few arguments have to be considered before the above demonstrations are accepted as cogent.

It may be argued, for example, that the illustrations pertain to an individual case and that, if the financial statements from a sufficiently large number of publishers are aggregated, the resulting "average" profits will be indicative of the true economic health of the industry. This, however, need not be the case at all. An average so derived will be biased by the diversity of write-down methods subsumed in its calculation, but the extent and direction of the bias would probably never be known. Furthermore, variations in the characteristics of books, particularly with respect to the number of years a book is expected to sell, prompt publishers within certain categories, such as textbook publishers, publishers of professional books, trade-book publishers, university presses and so on, to adhere to similar (though still not identical) methods of write down. Again, comparisons of profitability among these broad categories of publishers are not founded on common accounting principles. If, for example, most university presses happen to use Method 2 and most commercial publishers of professional books happen to use Method 4, comparisons of aggregated profit figures would not result in sound conclusions about the relative profitability of these two types of publishing.

A second argument against the validity of the demonstrations relates to the plausibility of the magnitudes of the changes introduced in each of the tests. By themselves, Tests 2 and 3, involving increases in the number of titles published and increases in costs and prices, respectively, resulted in small variations in *Gross Margins* among the six inventory methods. The average annual rates of change in the underlying variables were 9 per cent for the number of titles and 14 per cent for prices and costs, neither of which can be considered unreasonably rapid increases.

The changes introduced in Tests 4 and 5 produced significant variations among the *Gross Margin* figures, variations attributable primarily to the shift in the proportion of sales coming from the backlist. To show that the magnitude of the changes introduced in these two tests are also plausible, the changes in the proportion of unit sales from the backlist observed in Tests 4 and 5 are compared in Table 7.3.3 with actual data on changes in these proportions obtained from five publishing divisions of a large commercial publishing house.

As a consequence of the rate of sale of books chosen for the simulations, the change in the proportion of sales coming from backlist titles is most dramatic between 1972 and 1973 with the ratio jumping from .40 to .80 for Test 4 and from .40 to .78 for Test 5. To show that a change of such magnitude is not unusual we may compare it with the changes observed for some divisions of the real publishing firm. The ratio for Division E, for example, falls precipitously from .73 to .32 between 1972 and 1973, and then shoots up again to .48 and then .53 in the following two years. Changes for some of the other divisions are certainly on a par with those of Tests 4 and 5 over the period 1973-1975.

It is not being claimed that the magnitudes shown for this single publisher are representative of the population of publishers; nor is it being claimed that the magnitudes and changes used in the tests are the norm. The illustration is only presented to show that the results observed in the earlier tests are based on reasonable assumptions.

IMPLICATIONS FOR AN ANALYSIS OF PROFITABILITY

The discussions so far have centered on two aspects of annual income-and-expense records that argue against their suitability for assessing profits in book publishing: the effect on reported net income of (1) the practice of expensing immediately a good portion of the costs of producing a title and thereby breaking the link between the realization of income and the incurrence of costs and (2) the effects of different methods of inventory valuation and write down. To these may be added two additional observations.

TABLE 7.3.3 Proportion of Total Unit Sales Coming from Backlist Titles for Five Divisions of a Large Commercial Publisher and for Tests 4 and 5 of Table 7.3.2 (Total Number of Titles in Parentheses)

	1972	1973	1974	1975
Publishing divisions				
A.	.83 (32)	.63 (30)	.74 (57)	.96 (63)
B.	.90 (255)	.81 (272)	.92 (297)	.87 (281)
C.	.72 (1,839)	.74 (1,996)	.81 (2,079)	.82 (2,039)
D.	.50 (236)	.53 (285)	.71 (318)	.66 (385)
E.	.73 (351)	.32 (1,120)	.48 (1,323)	.53 (1,748)
Average, weighted by number of titles	.72 (2,713)	.51 (3,733)	.70 (4,074)	.70 (4,516)
Simulated data				
Test 4	.40 (100)	.80 (100)	.67 (100)	.70 (100)
Test 5	.40 (100)	.78 (110)	.67 (120)	.67 (130)

Source: Machlup, Leeson, and Associates.

Additional Observations

The first pertains to the necessity of being able to observe the profitability of different fields or subject areas. It is, after all, very likely that the various fields of knowledge have had different experiences with regard to sales and costs, yet this could never be uncovered by studying income-and-expense records. Although most publishers carry titles in a variety of fields, few, if any, maintain (or distribute outside their own firm) any financial statistics on a field-by-field basis. Some may group monthly or annual sales figures this way, but rarely do any maintain corresponding cost figures.

The final comment on financial data pertains to their failure to convey any information on physical magnitudes. Annual reports can show in current dollars, or in dollars adjusted for inflation, changes over the years in gross sales, net sales, costs of various kinds and net incomes, but they provide no information about numbers of titles, numbers of copies printed, numbers of copies sold and so on. To be in the dark regarding changes in such magnitudes while at the same time speaking about trends in profits is a risky analytical procedure. To know, for example, that the sales revenue of a publisher increased by, say, 20 per cent from one year to the next owing to an increase in the number of copies of books sold would imply something very different about the health of the firm than if the increase in dollar sales was accomplished in spite of, say, a decline in physical sales. The importance of knowing the physical magnitudes behind the financial magnitudes is sufficiently obvious to require no further elaboration.

Concluding Remarks

The preceding discussions and demonstrations were not offered as conclusive evidence that an illuminating analysis of the profitability of book publishing cannot be based on income-and-expense statements. Rather, the objective has been to point out some of the sources of significant error inherent in annual financial data and thereby establish a basis for proposing alternative methods of studying profitability in this industry. This task has been accomplished. We will in the following chapters seek to shed light on trends in sales, costs, and profits in publishing by applying an alternative analytical technique — cohort analysis.

CHAPTER 7.4

COHORT ANALYSIS

Arguments presented in the preceding chapter were intended to cast doubt on the advisability of basing analyses of trends in profits in book publishing on annual financial data. Whether or not those arguments were sufficiently compelling to provide a "justification" for the development of an alternative analytical technique is a question that need not be given further consideration. After all, it would be counterproductive to seek to postpone the development of new methods of analysis merely because existing methods have not yet been discredited or shown conclusively to be inadequate or obsolete. Thus, we shall proceed with a discussion of cohort analysis, an analytical technique, novel to the study of the economics of book publishing, that was developed to try to overcome some of the drawbacks that seem to be inherent in analyses based on annual records of sales and costs.

THE TECHNIQUE

The term "cohort" is commonly found in demographic and other statistical studies that typically focus on the behavior and influence over time of groups of individuals who were born during a specified period. Those born during the "baby boom" following the Second World War, for example, constitute a cohort that has moved through time, exerting along the way noticeable and often-cited influences on such things as patterns of consumer demand and of enrollments first in elementary schools, then in secondary schools, then in colleges and universities, and ultimately in the adult labor force. This baby-boom cohort was approximately ten years old in the mid-to-late 1950's, twenty years old in the mid-to-late 1960's and is about thirty years old today. Similarly, a cohort analysis may entail defining and studying the composition, behavior, and influence over time of the cohort of those born during the five years prior to World War II, or those born between 1955 and 1961, or those born in the year 1978.

Analogously, cohort analysis in book publishing focuses on the comparative performance over a number of years, in terms of costs and sales, of cohorts of books (groups of individual book titles) of different vintage, or years of "birth," in different subject areas, with different levels of readership and major sales outlets.

Cohorts of Titles by Vintage

As applied to a study of book publishing, cohort analysis is a method of observing changes over time in any number of variables (gross margins, total number of copies of books sold, average number of copies sold per title, plant costs per page, list price charged per word, to name just a few) that may provide clues about trends in profitability. The data, however, are separated according to the year of publication rather than — as in the customary approach — according to the year in which sales take place.

Suppose, for example, we wanted to look at the changes that have occurred in average number of copies of books sold per title for a sample of publishers over the period 1968-1975. This important variable is frequently cited as a gauge of the health of book publishing. The usual procedure would be to obtain, from the members of the sample, data on total number of copies of books sold for each of the years in question and then to divide these totals by the number of titles available for sale in each year. The results obtained would be a series of observations of annual data with each observation derived from a cross section of titles, some newly published, some one year old, some two, three, four or more years old.

In cohort analysis no annual averages of the mixed bag of books are calculated. Instead, all data are re-grouped according to the year of publication of the title to which they pertain. The sought-after averages are then calculated for each group, or vintage. In this way one can observe the performance of successive vintages — the 1968 vintage, the 1969 vintage, the 1970 vintage and so on — rather than of successive agglomerations of annual data comprised of unknown mixtures of titles of several vintages, as is the case with conventional analysis. A comparative analysis of the experiences of different cohorts of titles based on observations of the life history of the members of each as they move together through time would seem to constitute a promising alternative to, or at the very least an instructive supplement to, conventional analyses.

Advantages

A cohort analysis of costs, sales, and profits in book publishing has several important advantages over conventional analysis. As noted above it is usually not possible when using conventional analysis to tell whether changes in a particular variable observed over a number of years are due to current changes in conditions that affect mostly new titles or merely to shifts over the years in the relative weights of titles of different vintage comprising the sample. To cite one example, it is quite possible for a decline in the average number of copies sold per title "observed" by looking at annual data to have nothing whatever to do with a deterioration in the sales potential for titles of either new or backlist books. If publishers have decided to keep old titles in print for longer periods of time, the relative share of titles, the sales of which have dwindled to just a few copies per year, increases. Thus, the denominator of the fraction Total Number of Copies Sold ÷ Number of Titles Available for Sale increases far more than the numerator, which causes a decline in the calculated average number of copies sold per title. This decline occurs irrespective of any changes in conditions in the markets for books. Cohort analysis would clearly show that this decline was only a fallacy of composition.

A related advantage of cohort analysis pertains to the absence of the problems found to plague annual financial data, problems that were discussed at some length in Chapter 7.3. These include, first, the absence of synchronization between the incurrence of costs in the publication of books and the realization of revenues from the sale of books and, secondly, the effects on reported profits of the application of different methods of inventory valuation and write down. Neither of these problems exist in cohort analysis. In the first place, all costs incurred and all revenues received are associated exclusively with the cohort of titles to which they belong. Hence, calculations of gross margins or of net profits on a cohort-by-cohort basis would, unlike annual data, not be muddled by the inclusion of revenues received for the sale of books of earlier vintages or costs incurred in the production of titles whose sales will occur only in future years. In the second place, cohort analysis does not have to comply with the requirements of accepted accounting practices and hence avoids the need to assign values to inventories of books in order to spread costs over the lives of the titles. In the calculations made in cohort analysis, all costs are included as soon as, and whenever, they are incurred over the lives of titles in the cohort. Likewise, all revenues are shown as soon as, and whenever, they are received. Hence, to calculate the gross margin of a cohort of titles that is three years old, one need only subtract from all revenues received over that period all costs incurred over the same period. These streams of costs and revenues, each spread over a period of three years in this example, will first have to be expressed in equivalent magnitudes, that is, discounted to adjust for the rate of interest and deflated to adjust for price inflation; but unlike the case with conventional analysis, such adjustments can be made quite easily in cohort analysis. These considerations are discussed in greater detail in Chapter 7.5. Costs, of course, will be concentrated at the beginning of the life of the titles and revenues will be spread out over the years, but this creates no problem as long as comparisons of gross margins among cohorts refer to equivalent spans of years.

Disadvantages

There are a few disadvantages to cohort analysis and these ought to be mentioned in order to avoid an unintended impression that the proposed technique is offered as a flawless alternative to conventional analysis.

Perhaps the most serious limitation is a problem that involves not the concepts or the technique but the application of data to the concepts. This problem is that there exist virtually no readily available data in cohort form. Neither publications of industry associations nor publications of the statistical divisions of government agencies contain data on sales or costs for a succession of years on titles grouped according to year of publication.[1] All of the data used in this cohort analysis had to be collected first-hand from the internal records and confidential reports of a sample of publishing firms. As a consequence the samples are small and may not provide findings that can be considered representative of book publishing as a whole. In the future, industry-wide, or sector-wide cohort analyses cannot be performed unless special efforts are mounted to collect the required data or unless those who regularly collect and publish data on this industry see some merit in including cohort data along with the statis-

---

[1]To the extent that such publications contain annual series of data, such as number of titles published or number of copies sold, that pertain only to new titles, it can be said that they contain cohort data. Even these data, however, are sparse and of limited usefulness for the types of analyses proposed in this study. A single year's history of titles that may continue to sell and incur reprinting costs over a number of years may not by itself be sufficiently informative.

tical series which they make available. Nevertheless, the techniques of cohort analysis are well suited for use by individual firms that may wish to study various aspects of their own economic performance over the years.

As was just mentioned, the necessity of having to go out and collect the data on our own has imposed an additional problem, one whose seriousness cannot easily be ascertained. This relates to the size of the samples of titles used in the analyses and the degree to which findings based on these samples can be considered representative of the larger population of titles published.

Publishers, being unaccustomed to receiving requests for complete life histories of individual titles, including all manufacturing costs incurred, royalties paid, list prices established, number of copies sold, revenues received, number of pages published, number of words per page, to name just a few, were usually not prepared to accommodate the collectors of these data. Without exception, the information had to be laboriously culled from several different ledgers, computer print-outs, and file cards that were usually spread out over a variety of departments of the publishing firm, some easily accessible, others already sent to the archives kept in some far-off warehouse. Consequently, a great deal of time was required to collect all desired data for each title. These conditions imposed a serious constraint on the total number of titles included in the sample. More will be said in subsequent sections about the size and composition of the samples obtained.

One final problem to be mentioned pertains to the desirability in a cohort analysis of being able to observe the life histories of titles of each vintage over several years in succession. To study only the first year's activity of titles of different vintages would yield a possibly very distorted picture of costs and sales. Comparing the first three or four years of life of each cohort would be far more illuminating. The drawback is that the longer the period over which titles are observed, the more distant in the past will be the most recent vintage that can be observed and analyzed. For example, in an analysis that compares the first three years' history of cohorts of books of different vintage, the most recent cohort that can be studied would be composed of titles that are already three years old. No comparative analyses could be done on cohorts of titles that were published two years ago unless only a two years' history were considered for all vintages of titles and no analyses of last year's titles could be done unless only a single year of history was considered. Clearly, in planning the analyses to be undertaken in a study of cohorts of books one is confronted by a tradeoff between the span of years that can be observed for each cohort and the age of the most recent vintage of titles that would qualify for inclusion in the analysis.

For categories of titles that have a comparatively long active life — as do, for example, textbooks or scholarly titles published by university presses — this problem would be more imposing than for other categories of titles, such as popular adult trade books, whose active lives are comparatively short. The importance of the trade-off is also likely to be greater for analyses of sales than for costs since by and large most costs are incurred during the first year of life of a title whereas sales usually continue for several years.

THE DATA

The empirical results presented in the following chapters are derived from two separate sets of cohort data collected from a sample of book publishers expressly for this study. The first and most comprehensive set contains data on the life histories of a sample of 746 individual book titles published between 1968 and 1975 by a total of 20 publishers — 9 commercial firms and 11 university presses. This set is the one that was designed at the outset to provide the data deemed necessary to conduct the cohort analyses and will serve as the basis for the bulk of empirical findings presented.

The other set of data was devised along the way, partly as a result of an unanticipated opportunity to expand the analysis with a minimum of effort and partly as a result of the occasionally baneful "what if we tried. . ." syndrome prevalent in such research undertakings. This second set contains data on all of the titles published between 1961 and 1975 by a medium-size university press and will provide the basis for a case study of a single firm.

The common characteristic of both sets of data is, of course, the manner in which the data are grouped: according to year of publication of the titles to which they pertain.

Data Sought for Each Title

An effort was made to obtain several types of data for each of the 746 titles in the sample. Table 7.4.1 contains a list of the data sought and shows from which of three potential sources values could be obtained.

Data on costs of production and on sales could only be obtained from the records of those publishers who agreed to participate in this undertaking. Other data, such as the functional category of the book (college textbook, scholarly monograph, etc.), subject area, number of pages, and average number of words per page, could best be gathered by examining copies of each title. Ultimately, after a very time-consuming search that entailed visiting the collections of four library systems having together more than 17 separate branches, copies were located and examined for some 700 of the titles. Data on the list prices established for the titles at the time of publication and on the year-to-year increases in their prices were most conveniently obtained from *Publisher's Trade List Annual*, a publication of the R.R. Bowker Company that contains the individual catalogs, or lists of titles available for sale, of a large number of book publishers in the United States.

TABLE 7.4.1 Data Sought for Each of the 746 Individual Book Titles in the Cohort Sample

Data obtained from publishers' records	*Data obtained by examining copies of each title*
1. Year of publication	*13. Functional category (e.g., college text, elhi text, scholarly monograph, etc.)*
2. Month of publication	*14. Subject area (e.g., physical sciences, economics, literature, etc.)*
3. Type of cover — hardbound, paperbound	*15. Number of pages*
4. Plant costs (composition, typesetting)	*16. Average number of words per page*
5. Cost of paper	
6. Cost of printing	*Data obtained from publishers' catalogs or trade lists*
7. Cost of binding	*17. Original list price*
8. Royalties paid to authors	*18. Annual changes in list prices*
9. Number of copies printed	
10. Number of copies bound	
11. Number of copies sold in each year of life	
12. Dollar revenues received in each year of life	

Source: Machlup, Leeson, and Associates.

Data were sought for each year of life of the titles from time of publication to 1975, the most recent year for which data were available when they were collected. Some of the data, of course, such as year of publication, month of publication, and type of cover, do not change from one year of a title's life to the next, and thus have to be collected only once per title. Other data, such as number of copies sold, dollar revenues received, and list prices charged, must be collected for each year of a title's life.

For titles in the sample published as early as 1968, data for the list of variables in Table 7.4.1 had to be obtained for eight successive years, 1968 through 1975, a total of 144 values. For those titles published in, say, 1973, only three years of data had to be gathered, a total of 54 values. For all 746 titles, therefore, some 56,000 values were sought.

The second set of data, the one pertaining to all titles published between 1961 and 1975 by a medium-size university press, is roughly similar to the list given in Table 7.4.1. The only important difference is the exclusion of those variables the values of which would have to be derived from sources other than the publisher's own records. It was decided to do without these additional data because the cost in terms of time required to collect them would have been prohibitive.

Selecting the Sample of Book Titles

Titles belonging to the cohort sample of 746 titles were chosen on the basis of three criteria: (1) subject area, (2) the intended audience or type of reader, and (3) the availability of data. Owing primarily to the third criterion, the availability of data, it would not have been feasible to select titles strictly in conformance with the rules of scientific sampling. The experience gained in gathering the data bore out this claim and demonstrated clearly that any attempt to select a random sample of titles in advance would only have resulted in countless unfulfilled requests for data. The procedures actually used were, perhaps, more pragmatic than "scientific," but they were nevertheless effective in providing at reasonable cost a fairly large sample of detailed data on the life histories of book titles.

All publishers, both commercial and university press, who publish scholarly and scientific books intended primarily for learned audiences, were eligible to participate in this study. From among these, cooperation was actually solicited from approximately 50 firms. Some of these were selected because they had recognized the need for a study of book publishing and had offered enthusiastic support; others were selected because they specialized in the publication of books in particular subject areas that were needed to round out the samples. The 50 candidates were asked to allow a small team of researchers to visit their premises to collect the needed data. Twenty of the firms eventually agreed to cooperate in the cohort analysis. For each of these firms a sample of approximately 40 titles published between 1968 and 1975 — hence five each for every one of the eight years — was selected from their annual catalogs. Data were collected from one publisher at a time. As each publisher was covered, titles to be included in the sample for the next publisher were selected on the basis of the composition of the evolving sample up to that point.

Composition of the Sample

A summary of the composition of the cohort sample is presented in Table 7.4.2. The table shows how many of the 746 titles were published in the years 1968-1975, how many were published by commercial publishers and how many by university presses, how many were hardbound and how many paperbound, and how many belong to each of three broadly defined subject categories. The number of titles in each vintage ranges from a low of 89 for the year 1975 to a high of 100 for 1971.

Type of Publisher — Every title in the sample was published either by a commercial, for-profit firm or by a not-for-profit university press. It is necessary to make such a distinction in an analysis of profitability, because the financial objectives and editorial leanings of these two types of publishers are quite different. In general it may be said that commercial firms aspire to attain annually some acceptable level of accounting profits from their operations. University presses on the other hand, which are by charter not-for-profit institutions, may aspire only to break even financially and may even find it acceptable to operate at a deficit, provided, of course, the deficit is of a magnitude that can be covered by funds allocated by special endowments or by the parent university, or donoated by outside sponsors or benefactors. While both types of publishers may publish titles of high intellectual or scholarly merit and both may have an occasional best-seller, university presses are more likely than commercial publishers to accept for publication manuscripts that treat very specialized topics and attract an extremely limited audience. Often such titles can only be published at a financial loss. One may expect, therefore, to observe significant differences in the sales performances and profits of cohorts of books published by these two types of firms.

The upper portion of Table 7.4.2 shows that for each vintage titles published by university presses account for slightly more than half of the titles in the sample, and commercial firms for less than half. This distribution is a direct result of the number of each type of publisher that agreed to participate in the study — 11 university presses and nine commercial firms.

Type of Cover — It would seem apparent from the center portion of Table 7.4.2 that the emphasis of the study is on titles published in hard cover. The table shows that the num-

TABLE 7.4.2 Number of Titles in the Cohort Sample for Each Vintage, 1968 through 1975, Broken down by Type of Publisher, Type of Cover, and Major Subject Area

	1968		1969		1970		1971		1972		1973		1974		1975	
	Number	Per cent	Number	Per cent	Number	Per cent	Number	Per cent	Number	Per cent	Number	Per cent	Number	Per cent	Number	Per cent
Type of publisher																
University press	49	52.1	51	53.7	55	60.4	53	53.0	48	51.1	50	54.9	48	52.2	49	55.1
Commercial	45	47.9	44	46.3	36	39.6	47	47.0	46	48.9	41	45.1	44	47.8	40	44.9
Total	94	100.0	95	100.0	91	100.0	100	100.0	94	100.0	91	100.0	92	100.0	89	100.0
Type of cover																
Hardbound	77	81.9	78	82.1	74	81.3	81	81.0	76	80.9	68	74.7	73	79.3	71	79.8
Paperbound	17	18.1	17	17.9	17	18.7	19	19.0	18	19.1	23	25.3	19	20.7	18	20.2
Total	94	100.0	95	100.0	91	100.0	100	100.0	94	100.0	91	100.0	92	100.0	89	100.0
Major subject areas																
Natural sciences	21	22.3	25	26.3	20	22.0	31	31.0	22	23.4	23	25.3	23	25.0	23	25.8
Social sciences	42	44.7	38	40.0	46	50.5	51	51.0	41	43.6	40	44.0	48	52.2	46	51.7
Humanities	31	33.0	32	33.7	25	27.5	18	18.0	31	33.0	28	30.7	21	22.8	20	22.5
Total	94	100.0	95	100.0	91	100.0	100	100.0	94	100.0	91	100.0	92	100.0	89	100.0

Source: Machlup, Leeson, and Associates.

ber of hardbound titles in the sample ranges from a low of 68 in 1973 to a high of 81 titles in 1971. In percentage terms, they account for no fewer than 74.7 per cent of the titles for any of the eight vintages.

There are, regrettably, a few serious problems involved with trying to draw a meaningful distinction between hardbound and paperbound titles. Many titles are available in both types of covers, published either simultaneously or a few years apart, by one publisher or by two different publishers. Among other things, this makes it extremely difficult, if not impossible, to impute the costs of production to one edition or the other. This is particularly true for plant costs which may go into producing a single set of printing plates from which copies in both hardcover and softcover may be run off. If, for example, a publisher were this year to publish the hardbound version of a title, plant costs would be shown on the record books for that title. If, a few years later, the publisher were to publish a paperbound version of the same title, the original printing plates could be used to print the copies and zero plant costs would be entered on the record books for the paperbound version.

The treatment of sales poses another problem. Depending upon the strategy of the marketing division of the publishing firm, the hardbound and paperbound versions of the same title may be considered close substitutes, one competing with the other for sales in the same market; or they may be viewed as being two different non-competing products, one intended for sale, in say, the library market (hardbound version) and the other in the college market (paperbound version). They are sometimes considered different titles when the paperbound version is not published until after the hardbound version has exhausted its sales potential at the price established; or they may be treated as two different titles because they are published at different times by different publishers. Alternatively, some will argue that there are no circumstances under which the two should be considered different titles. In principle, this may be a defensible position, but for the researcher who must collect and analyze data it would impose far too many insoluble problems.

We have found no completely satisfactory solution for this problem. When the data were being collected there was usually no way of knowing for sure when, or even if, a title already available in hard cover had also become available in soft cover. Most publishers maintain separate records of sales for hardbound and paperbound books. Checking and cross-checking the publishers' records to try to determine if each title chosen for the sample was available in one type of cover or in both types proved to be incredibly time-consuming. Nevertheless, an attempt was made to identify simultaneous editions. Of the 746 titles in the sample, 526 were determined to be available only in hardcover, 80 only in papercover, 72 were found to be the hardbound version of a simultaneous edition and 68 the paperbound version of a simultaneous edition. The reliability of these figures is, however, questionable.

Subject Area — An attempt was made to obtain a fairly uniform distribution of titles in three major subject groupings: (1) natural sciences, technology, and mathematics, (2) social sciences, and (3) humanities. Titles were actually classified in one of 24 more detailed subject categories. These 24 are listed below under their major subject heading.

Classifying each of these 24 subject areas under one of only three major headings entails a few rather arbitrary decisions about where to place some of the fields. For example, medical sciences, which includes psychiatry, is classified under natural sciences, technology, and mathematics, while psychology is found under social sciences; history is classified here under social sciences, yet it might just as well have been classified under humanities.

Natural sciences, technology, and mathematics	*Social sciences*	*Humanities*
1. Life sciences	*9. Psychology*	*19. Philosophy and religion*
2. Physical sciences	*10. Economics*	*20. Language and linguistics*
3. Environmental sciences	*11. Business administration*	*21. English composition*
4. Mathematics	*12. Political science*	*22. Literature*
5. Statistics	*13. Law*	*23. Music*
6. Engineering	*14. History and archaeology*	*24. Art and art history*
7. Medical sciences	*15. Geography*	
8. Other applied sciences	*16. Anthropology and sociology*	
	17. Education	
	18. Home economics	

The third section of Table 7.4.2 shows the number of titles in the cohort sample in each of the three major subject categories. Titles in the social sciences account in each year for the majority of titles, slightly less than half. Titles in the humanities and in the natural sciences, technology, and mathematics each account for roughly one-quarter of the sample. This distribution resulted to some degree from the concerted effort to include titles in all 24 subject areas, to some degree to the fact that the major subject area that has the biggest representation, social sciences, also has the largest number of subfields subsumed in it, and in some part to the fact that the publishers in the sample published relatively more titles in the social sciences and humanities than in the natural sciences, technology, and mathematics.

CHAPTER 7.5

GROSS MARGINS AS SEEN BY CONVENTIONAL ANALYSIS AND BY COHORT ANALYSIS

The discussion in Chapter 7.4 presented in general terms the notion of cohort analysis as a method of analyzing economic trends in book publishing. The remainder of Part 7 will elaborate on those generalizations both by describing particular methods of analyzing costs, revenues, profits and several other characteristics of book publishing and by providing some tentative empirical results.

THEORETICAL CONSIDERATIONS

In this chapter we shall describe a method of calculating gross profits, or gross margins, that is free of many of the deficiencies inherent in conventional analyses (pointed out in Chapter 7.3). Actual data on costs and revenues obtained for cohorts of titles will be used to demonstrate how the method can be used by individual firms or for industry-wide analyses. Unfortunately, the small sample of titles available for the calculations will not permit any acceptable "findings" regarding trends in gross margins over the years. However, they will provide some useful illustrations.

Defining Profit and Profit Rates

In general terms, profit may be defined as the arithmetic difference between the capitalized value of a stream of revenues received from the sale of a good or service and the capitalized value of the stream of costs incurred in the production of the good or service, with this difference expressed in terms of dollars of equivalent purchasing power. The "good" or "service" under consideration in this study is the individual book title. "Capitalized values" are annual streams of costs or revenues where both annual receipts and annual payments (strictly speaking, each individual receipt or payment) have been "discounted," using an appropriate rate of interest, back to the year of publication. "In terms of equivalent purchasing power" refers to the need to express the calculated profits in dollar values that have been adjusted for changes in the price level. Such an adjustment is necessary to render meaningful comparisons of profits among titles of different vintages, that is, among titles published in different years; and also comparisons of profits among titles, published in the same year, the sales of which may extend over different periods so that receipts in later years are received in dollars of different purchasing power.

Profit *rates* are ratios obtained by dividing the profit figure calculated by the method described above by either total capitalized revenues or total capitalized costs. Either of these magnitudes can be used as the denominator, the former providing a measure of the rate of return on sales, the latter a measure of the rate of return on investment.

For any given dollar amount of profits, the profit rate bears an inverse relationship to the dollar amount of revenues received or of costs incurred. For example, $100 in profits made on a good or service that costs $2,500 to produce represents a profit rate of 4.0 per cent, while $100 in profits made on a good or service that costs $25,000 to produce represents a profit rate of only 0.4 per cent. The former venture, while bestowing upon the producing firm the same dollar amount of profits as the latter venture, can, nevertheless, be considered more profitable in the sense that it requires a smaller total investment, thereby freeing funds, $22,500 in this example, that could be used for other productive undertakings.

In the conventional financial statements prepared by book publishers, profit rates are customarily expressed as a ratio of dollar profits to dollar sales. The income-and-expense statement displayed in Table 7.3.1 of Chapter 7.3, for example, expresses both gross dollar profits and net dollar profits as ratios to net dollar sales. It is important to point out, however, that the revenues and costs reported on the conventional financial statements are neither capitalized values nor values adjusted for changes in the price level. Indeed, it is not possible to make these necessary adjustments, because the aggregate sales and costs figures reported for any given year on such statements are composed of an unknown mixture of the sales and costs of individual titles of several different vintages. Hence, the resulting profits and profit rates do not conform with the definition of profits given here which are based on traditional economic theory. The adjustments required to take account of the rate interest and price changes cannot be made unless titles, or groups of titles, have first been separated according to their year of publication — as is done in cohort analysis.

Net Profit Versus Gross Profit

Net profit of a book title is the difference between *all* costs incurred in producing and distributing the title and all revenues received from its sale. *All* costs include direct as well as indirect costs. Direct costs include the cost of composition (typesetting), the cost of paper, printing, binding, and royalties paid to authors, that is, costs that can be attributed unequivocally to the production of a specific title. Indirect costs, on the other hand, are costs that cannot be easily associated with particular titles and include such items as general and administrative expenses, some editorial costs, promotional and marketing expenses, order fulfillment, and so on. Hence, on a conceptual plane, one can think of the net profit of an individual title as total dollar revenues received from selling copies of the title, minus total direct costs, minus whatever proportion of total indirect expenses the firm had to incur in producing the title.

In practice, some publishers may attempt to allocate indirect expenses by assigning to the costs of producing a particular title some percentage of the salaries of the staff in the editorial department, production department, promotion and selling department, some fraction of the salaries of managers and executives of the firm, and some fraction of the total cost of office supplies, office space, electricity and so on. Unfortunately, such attempts at allocation have to rely on arbitrary rules of thumb and formulas that cannot capture with any known degree of reliability the costs incurred in the publication of a given title.

Rather than attempting to measure net profits, it would therefore be preferable to confine the analysis to the measurement of gross profits, that is, the difference between sales revenues and direct manufacturing costs only — composition, paper, printing, and binding. If one title has a larger gross profit than another, it can be considered more profitable in the sense that it is able to defray a greater amount of the total indirect expenses incurred by the firm. To remain consistent with the terms introduced in Chapter 7.3, we shall use from now on the phrase "gross margin" in place of "gross profit." When referring specifically to the dollar value of gross margin, the phrase "absolute gross margin" will be used; when referring to the ratio of this dollar value to sales revenues or to direct costs, the phrase "relative gross margin" will be used.

Capitalizing the Flows of Costs and Revenues

The definition of profits given earlier in the chapter may be reformulated to read as follows: "Gross margin" of a book title is the arithmetic difference between the capitalized value of the stream of sales revenues received over the life of the title and the capitalized value of the stream of *direct* costs incurred in the production of the title, all expressed in terms of dollars of equivalent purchasing power.

A full appreciation of this definition of gross margin hinges on an understanding of the concept of capitalized values and on the method of expressing monetary magnitudes in units of equivalent purchasing power.[1]

At 5 per cent interest, $100 received today is equivalent to $105 received one year from today or to $110.25 received two years from today or to $115.76 received three years from today, and so on. Each of these three amounts, or *future* values, when expressed in terms of *present* values equals $100 and the arithmetic manipulation used to find present values is called discounting for a single payment and capitalizing for a series of payments.[2]

Discounting and capitalizing are essential operations in calculating the gross margins of book titles because some of the costs that go into producing a title and a good portion of the revenue received from its sale are not realized in the first year of life of the title, but are spread out over a number of years.

Adjusting for Price Changes

A second adjustment has to be made before meaningful comparisons can be made among dollar amounts spent or received in different years: an adjustment for changes in the value of the dollar, that is, in price levels. If, for example, over a five-year period, the price of the goods and services usually purchased with the revenues received from selling books should rise by, say, 20 per cent, then a dollar received in the fifth

---

[1]A thorough discussion of the concepts involved in discounting and capitalizing streams of costs and revenues can be found in E.J. Mishan, *Cost-Benefit Analysis* (New York: Praeger Publisher, Inc., 1971), especially Part IV, "Investment Criteria."

[2]The general formula used to express the net (capitalized) present value of streams of costs and revenues spread over future periods is

$$\sum_{t=0,\,n} \frac{R_t}{(1+r)^t} - \sum_{t=0,\,n} \frac{C_t}{(1+r)^t}$$

where n = number of periods, R_t = revenue received in future period t, C_t = cost incurred in future period t, and r = the rate of interest, or rate of discount. A few words about the selection of an appropriate rate of discount are given in a subsequent section of the text.

year of life of a title could buy less, some 17 per cent less in real terms, than a dollar received in the first year.[3]

A third adjustment is needed if comparisons of gross margins are to be made among titles or cohorts of titles of different vintages: the various gross margins have to be expressed in terms of a single constant dollar value. This constitutes a second adjustment for changing price levels. Even if gross margins are properly calculated according to the method described above, that is, using discounted, deflated cost and revenue figures, the results for each vintage will still be expressed in terms of the *current* dollar values of the year of publication. Hence, for titles published in 1968 gross margins will be expressed in terms of *current* 1968 dollars, while for titles published in 1971 gross margins will be expressed in *current* 1971 dollars, gross margins for titles published in 1975 will be expressed in terms of *current* 1975 dollars, and so on. In order to compare these *current* dollar values, all must be converted, again using an appropriate index of prices, to constant dollar values of a chosen year, say, in terms of constant 1978 dollars.

To repeat, three adjustments are required for calculating economically sound gross margins. The flows of costs and revenues upon which the calculations are based have to be discounted back to the year of publication and they have to be deflated to adjust for rising prices that occur over the life of the title. Finally, to facilitate comparisons among titles published in different years, the gross margins must all be expressed in terms of constant dollars of equivalent purchasing power.

---

[3]The formual used to deflate dollar values is similar to that used for discounting. If, in the formula given in footnote 2, we regard r as the annual rate of inflation rather than the rate of discount and R and C as the nominal dollar values of revenues and costs in each period t, then the formula would provide the sought-after deflated dollar value. A few words about the selection of an appropriate price deflator are given in a subsequent section of the text.

It should be pointed out that there is no logical necessity for capitalizing values *back* to the year of publication or for expressing nominal dollar amounts in terms of the purchasing power of the dollar prevailing in the year of publication. The streams of costs and revenues could just as well be brought *forward*, that is, stated in terms of the value of any chosen future year. As long as all values are adjusted to the same date, that is, capitalized and deflated to an earlier date or compounded and inflated to a later date, the choice of the year is arbitrary.

Internal Rates of Return

In this study we have chosen a method of analysis in which gross margins are calculated by finding the arithmetic difference between the discounted and deflated flows of direct costs and sales revenues for cohorts of books. The dollar values obtained in these calculations, designated "absolute gross margins," measure the amount of revenue in excess of (or short of) direct costs that accrue to the cohort of titles involved. A second step involves calculating "relative gross margins" by finding what percentage absolute gross margins are of either direct costs or of revenues. We thus present three measures, all based on present discounted values, with which to compare the performances of the various cohorts under study.

An alternative measure might have been tried, one that would express the relative performances of cohorts in terms of their internal rates of return.[4] This method, as applied to cohort analysis, would entail calculating the rate of discount that would equate the present value of the stream of revenues with the present value of the stream of direct costs of the books: the higher the internal rate of return, the more profitable the cohort at the gross margin.[5]

We chose not to do the numerous additional calculations that would have been required to calculate internal rates of return, largely because they would not have provided additional information in the analysis; they merely provide an alternative way to compare the performances of cohorts.

---

[4]There are still other methods of evaluating alternative investment opportunities, or in the language of this study, of evaluating the comparative performances of different cohorts of books. These include the "pay-off period," that would provide a measure of the period of time (number of years) in which direct costs expended on the books would be fully recovered; the "average rate of return" in which the sum of revenues over the years of life of the cohort of books is divided by the number of years and then expressed as a percentage of the initial outlay; and the "net average rate of return," in which the sum of the differences between costs and revenues over the years is divided by the number of years and then expressed as a percentage of initial outlays. These methods are discussed by Mishan in *Cost-Benefit Analysis* along with the weaknesses inherent in each. Essentially these pertain to the failure of the methods to take proper account of distribution of costs and revenues over time.

[5]The internal rate of return is calculated by setting equal to zero the formula given in footnote 2 and solving for r. This is also discussed in some detail by Mishan.

EMPIRICAL RESULTS: GROSS MARGINS IN CONVENTIONAL ANALYSIS

By way of introduction to the empirical results on calculations of gross margins for cohorts of titles, it will be helpful to return briefly to one of the topics discussed in Chapter 7.3: the methods of calculating gross margins on conventional income-and-expense accounts. This will serve primarily to clarify the relationship between cohort analysis and conventional analysis and will provide, incidentally, additional support for a conclusion drawn in the earlier chapter, that analyses of the economic health of a book publishing firm or of sectors of the industry based on annual financial data may be misleading.

A medium-size university press was able to provide, on a title-by-title basis, life histories of the direct costs incurred and revenues received for a large majority of the titles published between 1961 and 1975. With the help of specially written computer programs these data were used to compute (1) annual gross margins for the press as they would appear on a typical income-and-expense statement, and (2) gross margins for cohorts of the titles that conform with the definitions of profit set down earlier in this chapter.

Conventional Analysis Revisited

In Chapter 7.3 it was demonstrated with the use of simulated data that under certain assumptions regarding growth in the number of titles published annually by a firm, inflation in costs and prices, and changes in the proportion of sales coming from the backlist, calculated gross margins would vary significantly for different methods of inventory valuation and write down. Six inventory methods (described in Chapter 7.3) were used in that demonstration. The same six methods have been used again here to calculate conventional gross margins. This time, however, the data are not simulated, but are actual costs and sales for titles of the cooperating university press.

The absolute and relative gross margins resulting from these calculations are displayed in Table 7.5.1 for the years 1970 to 1975. Note that since Net Dollar Sales are the same for all methods they are shown only once, at the top of the table. Recall that "Net Dollar Sales" minus "Manufacturing Costs" minus "Inventory Adjustment" equals "Gross Margin." To save space, the manufacturing costs and inventory adjustments are not shown for any of the six methods — only the gross margins are shown.

Judging from the standard deviations and the ratios of standard deviations to the average shown in Table 7.5.1, the variations among gross margins calculated from these real data are every bit as pronounced as were the variations for the

TABLE 7.5.1 A Single University Press — Net Dollar Sales, Gross Margins in Dollars, and Gross Margins as a Per Cent of Net Sales, for a Medium-Size University Press, 1970-1975, Calculated in the Conventional Manner from Actual Data Using Six Different Methods of Inventory Valuation and Write Down (Dollar Values Expressed in Current Dollars)

	1970	1971	1972	1973	1974	1975	Per cent change 1970-1975
Net dollar sales	$342,800	$417,100	$466,900	$300,000	$356,300	$319,700	
Gross margins calculated using:							
Method 1 - Gross margin in dollars	$165,600	$174,100	$260,900	$155,900	$132,800	$ 92,300	-44.3
As a per cent of net sales	48.3	41.7	55.9	52.0	37.3	28.9	
Method 2 - Gross margin in dollars	$ 72,200	$ 63,000	$217,500	$118,100	$204,800	$154,600	+114.1
As a per cent of net sales	21.1	15.1	46.6	39.4	57.5	48.4	
Method 3 - Gross margin in dollars	$ 73,700	$ 79,000	$238,400	$136,900	$186,500	$141,900	+92.5
As a per cent of net sales	21.5	18.9	51.1	45.6	52.3	44.4	
Method 4 - Gross margin in dollars	$144,100	$160,600	$213,500	$ 80,600	$110,700	$142,700	-1.0
As a per cent of net sales	42.0	38.5	45.7	26.7	31.1	44.6	
Method 5 - Gross margin in dollars	$138,800	$153,200	$212,200	$133,400	$161,400	$127,000	-8.5
As a per cent of net sales	40.5	36.7	45.4	44.5	45.3	39.7	
Method 6 - Gross margin in dollars	$ 84,900	$ 85,800	$197,300	$106,500	$195,600	$161,800	+90.6
As a per cent of net sales	24.8	20.6	42.3	35.5	54.9	50.6	
Average of the gross margins	$113,200	$119,300	$223,300	$121,900	$165,300	$136,700	
Standard deviation	$ 37,400	$ 44,300	$ 20,700	$ 24,100	$ 34,100	$ 20,200	
Standard deviation/average	0.33	0.37	0.09	0.20	0.21	0.15	

Source: Machlup, Leeson, and Associates.

simulated data in Table 7.3.2. Compare, for example, the annual gross margins of Method 1 with the annual gross margins of Method 3. Method 1 produces an absolute gross margin in 1970 of $165,600, and in 1975 of only $92,300, a decline over the period of 44.3 per cent. For the same data, Method 3 produces an absolute gross margin in 1970 of only $73,700 and in 1975 of $141,900, for an *increase* over the period by 92.5 per cent.

Not surprisingly, the relative gross margins, that is, absolute gross margins expressed as percentages of net dollar sales, also vary dramatically from one method to the next. For Method 1, the relative gross margin (that is, relative to net dollar sales) falls from 48.3 per cent in 1970 to 28.9 per cent in 1975; for Method 3 it rises from 21.5 per cent in 1970 to 44.4 per cent in 1975.

The conclusion suggested by this demonstration based on observed real-world data is similar to the conclusion drawn from the earlier demonstration based on simulated data: if we attempt to assess the profitability of this publisher, we would draw very different conclusions depending on the inventory method he happens to use.

Conventional Analysis Dissected

Let us now select one of the six inventory methods, Method 1, and take a closer look at what lies behind the sales figures and gross margins shown in Table 7.5.1.

The annual dollar amounts shown on conventional income-and-expense accounts are composed of costs and sales of titles of several vintages of earlier years, not only of the current vintage. Hence, in Table 7.5.1, some portion of net dollar sales of $342,800 shown for 1970 are from sales of titles published in 1970, in 1969, in 1968, and in earlier years. Similarly, some percentages of manufacturing costs and of inventory adjustments (neither of which are actually shown on Table 7.5.1) were incurred for titles published prior to 1970 and some percentages were incurred for titles published during that year, with sales distributed over subsequent years.

Table 7.5.2a shows for Inventory Method 1 the vintage-by-vintage composition of total sales revenues, Table 7.5.2b shows total manufacturing costs, and Table 7.5.2c shows total inventory write-offs for the accounting years 1970-1975. Finally, Table 7.5.2d shows the totals as they might appear on the income-and-expense account of the university press.

It can be seen from Tables 7.5.2a through 7.5.2c that there were, for example, 58 titles published by this press in 1970. In their first year of life these titles contributed $142,000 in sales revenue, 41.4 per cent of the total net sales of $342,800 for that year. In their second year of life, 1971, the 58 titles of vintage 1970 contributed $94,000 in sales

TABLE 7.5.2a *A Single University Press — Net Dollar Sales of a Medium-Size University Press, 1970-1975, Derived Using a Selected Method of Inventory Valuation and Dissected to Show the Composition of Total Amounts by Vintage*

Vintage year of publication	Number of titles	Sales revenues from titles of each vintage received in: 1970	1971	1972	1973	1974	1975
1961	15	$ 6,300	$ 6,600	$ 6,000	$ 3,500	$ 8,500	$ 3,600
1962	15	$ 8,900	$ 9,500	$ 12,100	$ 7,900	$ 8,100	$ 4,900
1963	43	$ 21,200	$ 17,700	$ 18,300	$ 12,500	$ 11,500	$ 10,300
1964	35	$ 19,400	$ 16,900	$ 16,400	$ 18,000	$ 14,800	$ 12,400
1965	41	$ 15,900	$ 13,800	$ 10,800	$ 9,800	$ 14,800	$ 7,900
1966	32	$ 9,800	$ 9,800	$ 12,800	$ 10,600	$ 15,600	$ 10,300
1967	27	$ 14,800	$ 11,300	$ 9,300	$ 7,600	$ 8,100	$ 7,200
1968	30	$ 26,700	$ 19,300	$ 16,500	$ 12,500	$ 13,000	$ 11,200
1969	41	$ 77,800	$ 34,600	$ 27,000	$ 22,100	$ 25,000	$ 22,700
1970	58	$142,000	$ 94,000	$ 39,500	$ 21,700	$ 29,700	$ 20,600
1971	68	-	$183,600	$175,900	$ 43,800	$ 41,300	$ 27,500
1972	41	-	-	$122,300	$ 59,600	$ 25,200	$ 19,000
1973	16	-	-	-	$ 70,400	$ 48,000	$ 15,900
1974	30	-	-	-	-	$ 92,700	$ 72,400
1975	28	-	-	-	-	-	$ 73,800
Totals	520	$342,800	$417,100	$466,900	$300,000	$356,300	$319,700

See TABLE 7.5.2d, "Net Dollar Sales"→

(continued)

TABLE 7.5.2b A Single University Press — Manufacturing Costs of a Medium-Size University Press, 1970-1975, Derived Using a Selected Method of Inventory Valuation and Dissected to Show the Composition of Total Amounts by Vintage

Vintage year of publication	Number of titles	Manufacturing costs of titles of each vintage charged on the income-and-expense account in:					
		1970	1971	1972	1973	1974	1975
1961	15	$ 1,100	$ 900	$ 900	$ 400	$ 600	$ 400
1962	15	$ 1,600	$ 1,400	$ 1,600	$ 1,200	$ 800	$ 700
1963	43	$ 3,500	$ 2,900	$ 2,300	$ 1,700	$ 1,500	$ 1,800
1964	35	$ 4,600	$ 3,700	$ 2,800	$ 3,000	$ 4,800	$ 3,200
1965	41	$ 4,700	$ 2,300	$ 2,000	$ 2,900	$ 1,700	$ 1,100
1966	32	$ 3,700	$ 5,500	$ 1,100	$ 1,700	$ 2,400	$ 1,000
1967	27	$ 3,900	$ 2,900	$ 3,100	$ 1,400	$ 800	$ 700
1968	30	$ 7,400	$ 5,800	$ 8,200	$ 3,900	$ 2,400	$ 1,300
1969	41	$ 24,900	$ 10,800	$ 7,500	$ 6,000	$ 9,300	$ 1,900
1970	58	$ 80,000	$ 37,700	$ 15,100	$ 14,700	$ 22,400	$ 13,400
1971	68	-	$ 97,200	$ 78,500	$ 16,000	$ 22,800	$ 12,200
1972	41	-	-	$ 52,400	$ 21,200	$ 10,400	$ 9,100
1973	16	-	-	-	$ 29,200	$ 17,700	$ 7,300
1974	30	-	-	-	-	$ 43,800	$ 27,500
1975	28	-	-	-	-	-	$ 38,900
Totals	520	$135,400	$171,100	$175,500	$103,300	$141,500	$120,500

See TABLE 7.5.2d, "Manufacturing Costs"⟶

(continued)

TABLE 7.5.2c A Single University Press — Inventory Write-offs of a Medium-Size University Press, 1970-1975, Derived Using a Selected Method of Inventory Valuation and Dissected to Show the Composition of Total Amounts by Vintage

Vintage year of publication	Number of titles	Inventory write-offs for titles of each vintage charged to the income-and-expense account in: 1970	1971	1972	1973	1974	1975
1961	15	$ 0	$ 100	$ 100	$ 1,400	$ 100	$ 1,800
1962	15	$ 2,700	$ 0	$ 0	$ 900	$ 300	$ 2,700
1963	43	$ 0	$ 7,600	$ 0	$ 2,600	$ 700	$ 1,300
1964	35	$ 0	$ 2,300	$ 0	$ 900	$ 1,600	$ 3,400
1965	41	$39,100	$ 0	$ 800	$ 6,900	$ 1,400	$ 0
1966	32	$ 0	$61,900	$ 0	$ 1,900	$ 2,000	$ 0
1967	27	$ 0	$ 0	$29,600	$ 0	$ 1,700	$ 7,600
1968	30	$ 0	$ 0	$ 0	$26,200	$ 0	$ 4,800
1969	41	$ 0	$ 0	$ 0	$ 0	$74,200	$ 0
1970	58	$ 0	$ 0	$ 0	$ 0	$ 0	$ 85,300
1971	68	-	$ 0	$ 0	$ 0	$ 0	$ 0
1972	41	-	-	$ 0	$ 0	$ 0	$ 0
1973	16	-	-	-	$ 0	$ 0	$ 0
1974	30	-	-	-	-	$ 0	$ 0
1975	28	-	-	-	-	-	$ 0
Totals	520	$41,800	$71,900	$30,500	$40,800	$82,000	$106,900

See TABLE 7.5.2d, "Inventory Adjustment" →

(continued)

TABLE 7.5.2d Total Net Dollar Sales, Manufacturing Costs and Inventory Write-offs Derived in Tables 7.5.2a Through 7.5.2c, Shown as They Would Appear on the Income-and-Expense Account

	1970	1971	1972	1973	1974	1975
Net dollar sales	$342,800	$417,100	$466,900	$300,000	$356,300	$319,700
Manufacturing costs	$135,400	$171,100	$175,500	$103,300	$141,500	$120,500
Inventory adjustment	$ 41,800	$ 71,900	$ 30,500	$ 40,800	$ 82,000	$106,900
Absolute gross margin	$165,600	$174,100	$260,900	$155,900	$132,800	$ 92,300
As a per cent of net sales	48.3	41.7	55.9	52.0	37.3	28.9

Source: Machlup, Leeson, and Associates.

revenue, some 22.5 per cent of total net sales of $417,100 for 1971. In the subsequent four years of their lives the 58 titles belonging to the 1970 cohort contributed $39,500 (8.5 per cent of 1972 sales), $21,700 (7.2 per cent of 1973 sales), $29,700 (8.3 per cent of 1974 sales), and $20,600 (6.4 per cent of 1975 sales). Analogously, each of the other vintages, going back to 1961, contributed something to total net sales in each of the years 1970-1975, though obviously, for any given accounting year, each vintage is in a different year of its own life.

This example elucidates the relationship between cohort analysis and conventional analysis. Each annual total reported on the summary income-and-expense statement in Table 7.5.2d is composed of a cross section of contributions from the extant titles of the current and of previous cohorts shown individually in Tables 7.5.2a through 7.5.2c.

The distribution of *sales* revenues over the years of life of each vintage does not change from one inventory method to the next. The distributions of manufacturing costs and inventory write-offs, however, do vary among methods, thus accounting for the observed variations in gross margins. The distribution among vintages of these two categories of costs are shown in Tables 7.5.2b and 7.5.2c. These results were obtained by carrying out the directive of Inventory Method 1, which states that, "books are held in inventory at full-cost value (plant cost, paper, printing, and binding cost) for five years; in the sixth year the full value of stock is written off."[6] An additional rule also has to be devised for handling the cost of reprinting of titles. The rule adopted here is that whenever there is a reprinting, inventory values are recalculated for the title at that time, as explained below, and the full value of stock is written off five years after the reprinting instead of five years after the initial year of publication.

In deriving the matrices of values in parts a, b, and c of Table 7.5.2, the 520 titles published by the cooperating university press between 1961 and 1975 were processed one at a time by the computer program (just as the accounting department would have to do in practice). To perform the calculations, the computer program required the following data for each title: year of publication, plant costs, paper, printing, and binding costs, number of copies printed, number of copies sold, and sales revenues received in each year of the title's

---

[6]See Chapter 7.3 for a list of other inventory methods used by the accounting departments of publishing firms.

life; also, for the years in which reprintings occurred, the paper, printing, and binding costs, and the number of copies reprinted.[7]

The following is a description of the algorithm used in deriving the results shown in the various parts of Table 7.5.2, and will serve to explain how individual entries were obtained.

(1) Consider the data for a single title. Compute a unit inventory value by dividing the sum of plant costs, paper, printing, and binding costs by the number of copies of the title printed. (If, for example, the sum of these costs equals \$3,000 and 2,000 copies of the title are produced, unit inventory value equals 3,000 ÷ 2,000, that is, \$1.50 a copy.)

(2) For each year of life of the title, record first net dollar sales under the appropriate calender year on the matrix of sales revenue (Table 7.5.2a); and, second, on the matrix of manufacturing costs, the inventory value corresponding to the number of copies sold (Table 7.5.2b). (For example, if the title is published in 1970 and sales are \$2,000 in the first year, \$1,000 in the second year, and \$500 in the third then these three sales figures are added to the sales matrix under the years 1970, 1971, and 1972, respectively. If unit sales, that is, number of copies of books sold, corresponding to these dollar amounts are 1,000 copies, 500 copies, and 25 copies, then the inventory values recorded under the appropriate years in the matrix of manufacturing costs would be 1,000 × \$1.50 = \$1,500, 500 × \$1.50 = \$750, and 250 × \$1.50 = \$425, respectively.)

(3) After five years, that is, in the sixth year of the title's life, all of its remaining inventory value is written off — shown under the appropriate year on the matrix of inventory write offs (Table 7.5.2c). (For example, if all but 200 copies of the title have been sold by the sixth year, then 200 × 1.50, that is, \$300, is the remaining inventory value and hence the amount written off in the sixth year of life.

(4) If the title is reprinted, no matter in which year of its life, unit inventory values are recalculated.

---

[7]Plant costs are essentially the fixed costs of preparing the plates from which copies of a title are run off. Hence, there are no plant costs for reprintings if the original plates are used.

The first step is to add to the inventory value of existing stock, the paper, printing, and binding costs incurred in producing the new stock. This value is then divided by the total number of copies, newly printed and previously existing. Write-offs are then re-scheduled for the sixth year after the reprinting. (For example, if 500 new copies of the 1970 title are printed in, say, 1972, the third year of its life, at a cost of $500 — equivalent to a unit cost of $1.00 per copy, $.50 below the unit cost of the initial printing, owing, primarily, to the absence of plant costs — and if there are at that time 250 copies remaining from the initial printing, each having an inventory value of $1.50, then the new *total* inventory value equals $925, that is, $500 for the cost of the reprinting plus $425, $1.50 per copy × 250, for the value of existing stock. The new *unit* inventory value equals $1.23, $925 divided by the total of 750 copies. Write-offs are then re-scheduled for the title for the year 1977.).

(5) Return to Step (1) and repeat the procedure until all 520 titles have been considered.[8]

In this manner the computer program processed each of the 520 titles published by the university press and yielded the matrices displayed in Tables 7.5.2a through 7.5.2c. These three tables show, respectively, sales by cohorts, manufacuturing costs by cohort, and write-offs by cohort. The seemingly strange configuration of entries in the matrix of write-offs is primarily the result of titles that have been reprinted at some time during their lives. If none of the titles had been reprinted, all entries would be zero, except, of course, for the diagonal containing the values of the write-offs occurring in the sixth year of life of each cohort.

Another interesting feature of the results displayed here is that some of the titles published as early as 1961 registered sales through 1975. The positive entries for the 1961 cohort and subsequent years under manufacturing costs and inventory write-offs indicate that some of these sales are accounted

---

[8]The procedure just described is, admittedly, not formulated in strict conformance with the parlance of the accounting profession. Such a formulation would require the use of a series of "T" accounts, one each for inventory, sales, manufacturing costs and inventory write-offs. Every charge, or debit on one of these accounts would have to be offset by a credit on some other account. We do not believe the clarity of the exposition has been compromised to any great extent by describing the procedure in less technical language.

for by titles that were reprinted along the way. Were this not the case, entries for the 1961 cohort in the two cost matrices would be zero. According to the rules of Method 1, the inventory values of these 1961 titles would have been completely written off in the year 1966. Nevertheless, the practice followed by university presses of keeping titles in stock year after year, regardless of their rates of sale, is demonstrated in these results.

To complete the derivation of the conventional income-and-expense report, we sum the entries in each column of the first three parts of Table 7.5.2 and show the totals in Table 7.5.2d. Then for each year we subtract from sales revenues (Net Dollar Sales), both Manufacturing Costs and Inventory Adjustment (write-offs). Had we used one of the other five methods of inventory valuation and write down rather than Method 1, we would have obtained one of the other series of gross margins shown in Table 7.5.1. The application to the same sample of titles of one of the other methods would have resulted in a different configuration of manufacturing costs and of inventory write-offs, leading to different values of gross margins.

Conventional Analysis Abandoned

Gross margins calculated in the manner just described do not conform with the more economically sound definition of gross margin developed earlier in this chapter. That is, they are not calculated by comparing the capitalized and deflated flow of revenue received from the sale of a particular title, or group of titles, with the capitalized and deflated costs of the titles. Rather, they compare, in any given accounting year, the sum of sales revenues of a cross section of titles of various vintages with the sum of a cross section of prorated fractions of the costs of producing the titles, with the distributions of the fractions of total costs over the life of each title determined almost arbitrarily by the inventory method chosen. Thus, gross margins calculated in the conventional manner clearly distort the association between particular costs and the returns to these costs, that is, the dollar returns realized as a direct consequence of having incurred the costs.

It is likely, moreover, that the fraction of total costs actually charged in any given accounting year are historical costs and not replacement costs, meaning they are expressed in terms of the purchasing power of money prevailing when the titles were initially produced, rather than in terms of the purchasing power of money prevailing when the titles are actually sold. As a consequence, the real value of gross margins would be overstated during periods of price inflation. Revenues, on the other hand, are usually "inflated" to keep pace with economy-wide price increases, since it is a common practice for publishers to raise the list prices of given titles over the years of their lives.

This brings to a close the discussion of conventional gross margins. The remainder of the chapter will be devoted to discussions of the empirical results obtained in calculating gross margins for cohorts of titles.

EMPIRICAL RESULTS: GROSS MARGINS IN COHORT ANALYSIS

Data on direct costs incurred and sales revenues received over the lives of the 520 titles published between 1961 and 1975 by the university press that served as a case study earlier in this chapter will presently be used to calculate gross margins true to the definition given in the section above on "Capitalizing the flows of Costs and Revenues." In addition, gross margins will be calculated using cohort data on a sample of over 650 titles published between 1968 and 1975 by 20 publishing firms.

Generalizing the Results

A few words of warning are in order regarding the representativeness of the empirical results presented below. Results for the single university press are interesting because they constitute a case study that will serve to demonstrate how the preferred method of calculating gross margins can be used by individual publishers. While the numerical results observed for this particular publisher provide a reliable summary of his own experiences with regard to gross margins, it goes without saying that they can in no way be used to make generalizations about gross margins of publishers in general, or even of university presses.

Even the 650 titles published by 20 publishing firms will provide only the most tenuous basis for generalizations about trends in gross margins for the population of publishers. The sample is simply too small and hence the results of the calculations could be changed significantly by including or omitting just one or two titles that happen to have had extraordinarily large or small sales or costs. Nevertheless, a few interesting observations can be made from the data and they make the presentation of the empirical results a worthwhile exercise.

Choice of Price Deflator and Discount Rate

In reducing the theoretical procedures to practice, we must try to select an appropriate price deflator and an appropriate rate of discount for deflating and capitalizing the actual flows of costs and revenues of each title, or group of titles, for which gross margins are to be calculated. Deciding on the most appropriate rates is not a trivial matter. Numerous price deflators or price indexes, are available for converting current dollars of various years into constant dollars of a chosen base year; each of the deflated values obtained by using any of these deflators would convey a somewhat different meaning. Likewise, there is a wide choice of interest rates but no general consensus on which, if any, would be the most appropriate to serve as the rate of discount or capitalization.

The "Implicit Gross Product Originating Deflator for Printing and Publishing Industries" was chosen here as the most relevant deflator, because it reflects the price increases of a large proportion of the goods and services regularly purchased by book publishers as inputs to their production processes. Values of both the Wholesale Price Index and the Consumer Price Index are probably weighted by the prices of too great a proportion of goods and services that have little to do with the way publishers spend their gross or net incomes. For example, if it were the case that all profits are regularly distributed as dividends to stockholders, then it could possibly be argued that the Consumer Price Index would be a more appropriate deflator; it would convert the nominal dollar values to constant dollar values expressed in terms of the goods and services that are more likely to be purchased by the owners of the business. Usually, however, commercial publishers retain a good portion of their earnings to maintain or expand their publishing programs. Besides, none of the "earnings" of university presses are distributed as dividends since they are not-for-profit organizations; university presses are an important component of the cohort analysis.

With regard to the rate of discount it would seem prudent for this analysis to select one that would give some indication of what publishers might have expected in the way of returns if they had decided to invest their funds elsewhere, rather than using them to publish books. This admits a rather broad range of candidates from which to select. For example, does one choose an interest rate that would reflect the returns on investing in the best possible alternative, irrespective of the term of the investment, or one that would reflect the return only on investments that would tie up funds for periods of time equivalent in length to those required for publishing a book? Does one select an interest rate characteristic of very risky ventures or of investments relatively free of risk? Does one use an interest rate somewhat below those of alternative ventures that promise purely financial return? It may be suggested that publishers are likely to count as part of their returns a feeling of satisfaction from their role as disseminators of knowledge beneficial to society. The choices made by individual publishers would probably vary according to their preferences.

With these difficulties in mind, we have chosen to use as the discount rate the prime rate of interest charged by banks on loans to businesses. Such a rate should provide some indication of the opportunity cost associated with publishing books.

It should be noted that the results obtained in the calculations of gross margins would be different if, instead, a higher or lower rate were chosen. In general, for a given stream of values obtained in future periods, lower rates of discount would result in larger present values. Furthermore, the farther in the future a given amount is to be received, the greater will be the difference in present values calculated by two different rates.[9] To cite an extreme example, the present value of $100 received one year from the present is $99.01 at a rate of interest of 1 per cent and $66.67 at a rate of interest of 50 per cent, a difference of $32.34. However, the present value of $100 received seven years hence is $93.27 at the rate of interest of 1 per cent and only $5.85 at the rate of 50 per cent, a difference of $87.42. This shows how much the calculated values of gross margins would vary, not only as a direct result of using different rates of interest in discounting the values but also in consequence of differences in the profiles, or distributions of the sales and costs over the years of life of the various cohorts.

Table 7.A.1 in the appendix gives values of both the price deflator and interest rate used.

Interpreting the Numerical Results

In the tables that follow, gross margins for various cohorts of titles are presented both in terms of absolute dollar amounts and as percentages of sales revenues or of direct costs.

In order to compare the absolute gross margins for cohorts containing different numbers of titles, results are expressed as averages per title. Indeed, it would be very awkward try-

---

[9]Rather than speaking of the rate of discount we speak here of the rate of interest, a parameter used in the formulas for both compounding and discounting. In compounding, the rate of interest, r, is contained in the formula $FV_t = PV\ (1 + r)^t$, where PV is the given initial (present) value, t the number of periods of compounding, and FV the resulting future value; hence (1 + r) is actually the rate of compounding. In discounting, the same rate of interest, r, is contained in the formula as $PV = \frac{FV_t}{(1 + r)^t}$, where FV is the given future value, t the number of periods of discounting, and PV the resulting present value; hence $\frac{1}{(1 + r)}$ is actually the rate of discount.

ing to compare an absolute gross margin of, say, $65,000 for a cohort containing 20 titles with the absolute gross margin of $115,500 for another cohort containing 33 titles. It is much more meaningful to compare the average gross margins per title; $3,250 and $3,500, respectively.

It was explained earlier that absolute gross margins become relative gross margins when they are expressed as percentages either of sales revenue or of direct costs. The emphasis in the results presented below will be on the latter of these two percentages, that is, on absolute gross margin as a percentage of direct cost. For purposes of illustration both percentages have been calculated for the single university press. In general, however, it would probably be more confusing than enlightening to try to display and discuss in every case both measures of relative gross margin. Direct costs incurred was chosen as the preferred denominator because the resulting percentage figure bears a close resemblance to the rate of return on investment, a notion fundamental to the concept of profit.

As a guide for interpreting the numerical results presented in the tables below, it may be helpful to summarize briefly what each of the ranges of magnitudes of the gross margins tell us about the economic performance of the titles involved. Consider the four situations shown for a cohort of imaginary titles in the following table:

	Examples			
	(1)	*(2)*	*(3)*	*(4)*
Discounted and deflated revenues	*$15,000*	*$20,000*	*$25,000*	*$40,000*
Discounted and deflated direct costs	*$20,000*	*$20,000*	*$20,000*	*$20,000*
Absolute gross margin	*($ 5,000)*	*($ 0)*	*$ 5,000*	*$20,000*
Relative gross margins:				
Absolute gross margin as a percentage of revenues	*(33.3%)*	*0.0%*	*20.0%*	*50.0%*
Absolute gross margin as a percentage of direct costs	*(25.0%)*	*0.0%*	*25.0%*	*100.0%*

In Column (1) the discounted and deflated flow of revenue equals $15,000, and the discounted and deflated flow of direct costs equals $20,000, for a *negative* absolute gross margin of $5,000. This, as a percentage of revenues, is negative 33.3 per cent and, as a percentage of costs, is negative 25.0 per cent. (Throughout the exposition negative numerical values are given in parentheses.) In Column (2), where revenues are just equal to costs, all three expressions of gross margins are zero. Whenever revenues exceed costs, as in Column (3), all three expressions for gross margins are positive, and whenever revenues are twice as large as costs, as in Column (4), gross margin as a percentage of revenues equals 50 per cent and as a percentage of direct costs equals 100 per cent. These results may be summarized by saying that whenever gross margins expressed as absolutes or as relative magnitudes, are negative, titles have not even covered their own direct costs. Whenever gross margins are near zero in magnitude, the titles to which the figures pertain are just breaking even, at least in the sense that they have earned sufficient revenue to cover their own direct costs. Whenever gross margins are positive, the titles to which they pertain have covered their own costs and are then helping to defray some portion of the firm's indirect expenses.

It is not possible to establish with very much precision how far above zero the relative gross margin (in terms of direct costs) has to be before the titles contained in the cohort have covered not only their direct costs, but have generated also sufficient revenue to cover the *indirect* costs associated with their production. This may be looked upon as a higher-order break-even point, the point at which *all* costs, direct and indirect, have been covered and above which contributions are being made to a firm's *net* profits.

We may obtain a very rough idea of the order of magnitude of such a higher-order break-even point by observing historical data on how much of total costs of publishing has been accounted for by the components of direct cost (composition, paper, printing, and binding) and how much by the components of indirect cost (editorial expenses, production, advertising, marketing, shipping & warehousing, general and administrative expenses.) Having argued at length in previous sections that annual figures obtained from conventional income-and-expense accounts are likely to be misleading, we shall not use annual data to calculate the sought-after ratio. Instead, we shall compare for a small sample of publishers the sum of direct costs incurred over the eight year period 1968-1975 with the sum of all costs, direct and indirect, incurred over the same period. The figures are presented in Table 7.5.3.

The first column of the table displays for four university presses and four commercial firms, all of which are contributors of data for this cohort analysis, direct costs reported on annual income-and-expense accounts over the eight year

TABLE 7.5.3 Cumulative Direct Costs and Total Costs Reported on Annual Income-and-Expense Accounts over the Period 1968-1975 by Four University Presses and Four Commercial Publishers, and the Resulting Relative Gross Margins that Would be Required to Cover Total Costs (Dollar Values Expressed in Constant 1977 Dollars)

		Direct costs 1968-1975	Total costs 1968-1975	Relative gross margin (absolute gross margin as a percentage of direct costs) required to cover all costs, direct and indirect [(total cost) - (direct cost)] ÷ direct cost
University press				
	No. 1	$ 4,389,000	$ 13,861,000	215.8
	No. 2	$ 8,792,000	$ 23,169,000	163.5
	No. 3	$ 9,801,000	$ 33,861,000	238.8
	No. 4	$17,391,000	$ 47,424,000	172.7
Total		$40,373,000	$117,658,000	191.4
Commercial publisher				
	No. 1	$ 7,750,000	$ 22,166,000	186.0
	No. 2	$ 11,406,000	$ 37,834,000	231.7
	No. 3	$ 22,907,000	$ 74,950,000	227.2
	No. 4	$193,778,000	$621,664,000	220.8
Total		$235,841,000	$756,614,000	220.8

Source: Machlup, Leeson, and Associates.

period 1968-1975. The second column displays the corresponding total costs reported by these publishers over the same period. The annual costs reported for each of the individual eight years were first converted to constant 1975 dollars and then summed over the years.

The two cost figures can be used to calculate the relative gross margin (absolute gross margin as a percentage of direct costs) that would have to be attained in order to cover all costs, direct and indirect, that is, the relative gross margin above which net dollar profits would be positive. Since such a point is attained when dollar revenues from the sale of books equal total costs, the latter figure may be substituted for the former in the formula otherwise used to calculate relative gross margins {(revenues) - (direct costs)}÷ direct costs; the resulting percentage will be the higher-order break-even point sought. Such a calculation was done for each of the individual firms and for the totals shown for the four university presses and the four commercial publishers, with the resulting percentages displayed in the third column of the table.

These percentages can be relied upon to do little more than provide a very rough idea of how large relative gross margins have to be before revenues cover total cost. For the university presses in the sample, the required percentage ranges from a low of 163.5 per cent to a high of 238.8 per cent; for the commercial publishers from 186.0 per cent to 237.1 per cent. The weighted averages for the two types of publishers, 191.4 per cent and 220.8 per cent, respectively, are both in the neighborhood of 200 per cent. From these results we may distinguish, though somewhat arbitrarily, three zones, or ranges of values, for the relative gross margins in terms of direct costs. If the relative gross margin is less than 175 per cent we can, based on the sample data presented, be reasonably confident that revenues received for a cohort of titles is less than total costs incurred, and hence the titles have not yet reached the higher-order break-even point; if the relative gross margin lies between 175 per cent and 275 per cent, the titles are approaching or have reached the higher-order break-even point; and if the relative gross margin is above 275 per cent, revenues exceed total costs and the titles have reached and perhaps surpassed the higher-order break-even point.

The Single University Press

Table 7.5.4 contains absolute and relative gross margins for cohorts of titles published over the period 1961-1975 by the university press for which conventional income-and-expense accounts had been calculated in an earlier section. For purposes of illustration relative gross margins are expressed in two ways: absolute (dollar) gross margin as a per cent of

TABLE 7.5.4 Titles of a Single University Press--Capitalized and Deflated Gross Margins, as Average Absolute Dollar Amounts per Title, and as Percentages of Revenues and Percentages of Direct Costs for Cohorts of Titles Published by a Medium-Size University Press, 1961-1975 (Dollar Values Expressed in Constant 1977 Dollars)

		First year of life			First 2 years of life			First 4 years of life			First 6 years of life		
Vintage year	Number of titles	Absolute	Per cent of revenues	Per cent of direct costs	Absolute	Per cent of revenues	Per cent of direct costs	Absolute	Per cent of revenues	Per cent of direct costs	Absolute	Per cent of revenues	Per cent of direct costs
1961	15	($ 810)	(16.3)	(14.0)	$1,520	20.2	25.3	$4,410	42.3	73.4	$5,685	47.6	91.0
1962	15	($5,030)	(111.6)	(52.7)	($1,515)	(18.9)	(15.9)	$ 705	6.6	7.0	$1,930	15.5	18.3
1963	43	($2,785)	(83.7)	(45.6)	($ 805)	(14.7)	(12.8)	$1,235	15.5	18.4	$2,620	27.0	37.0
1964	35	($2,820)	(67.4)	(40.3)	($ 685)	(10.6)	(9.5)	$1,215	13.8	15.9	$2,400	22.6	29.2
1965	41	($1,820)	(54.4)	(35.2)	$ 25	0.4	0.4	$1,340	19.1	23.2	$2,135	27.0	37.0
1966	32	($4,830)	(105.7)	(51.4)	($2,970)	45.1	(31.1)	($1,680)	(21.0)	(17.3)	($1,175)	(13.5)	(11.9)
1967	27	($1,260)	(24.4)	(19.6)	$1,085	13.7	15.9	$2,240	23.1	30.0	$3,065	29.1	41.1
1968	30	($1,845)	(33.5)	(25.1)	$1,440	15.8	18.7	$2,895	26.2	35.5	$3,900	32.3	47.7
1969	41	($1,545)	(24.9)	(19.9)	$1,100	12.4	14.1	$2,670	24.8	33.0	$3,590	30.2	43.3
1970	58	($3,535)	(94.3)	(48.5)	($1,620)	(27.0)	(21.3)	($ 375)	(5.1)	(4.9)	$ 305	3.8	3.9
1971	68	($3,460)	(87.5)	(46.7)	($ 125)	(1.6)	(1.6)	$ 990	11.2	12.6	-	-	-
1972	41	($1,545)	(36.4)	(26.7)	$ 270	4.4	4.6	$1,105	15.4	18.2	-	-	-
1973	16	($1,735)	(28.6)	(22.2)	$1,550	16.4	19.6	-	-	-	-	-	-
1974	30	($1,880)	(48.3)	(32.6)	$ 440	6.9	7.4	-	-	-	-	-	-
1975	28	($2,685)	(91.9)	(47.9)	-	-	-	-	-	-	-	-	-

Source: Machlup, Leeson, and Associates.

revenues received from the sale of the books and absolute gross margin as a per cent of direct costs incurred.

In the year 1961, the press published 15 titles. In their first year of life these titles had, on the average, received in sales revenue $810 less than the direct costs that had been incurred to produce them. This is what the ($810) entry under the heading "Absolute" tells us. The negative dollar amount is 16.3 per cent of revenues received in the first year of life and 14.0 per cent of direct costs incurred in the first year.[10]

After two years of life the 15 titles of the 1961 cohort had, on average, a positive dollar gross margin of $1,520. The titles had covered their direct costs and were already making some contribution to indirect costs. The absolute gross margin is 20.2 per cent of revenue, which equals $7,525 (i.e., absolute gross margin ÷ revenues = relative gross margin, that is, $1,520 ÷ revenues = .202, or revenues = $7,525) and 25.3 per cent of direct cost of $6005. After the first four years of life the absolute gross margin for the average title was $4,410, 42.3 per cent of revenues and 73.4 per cent of direct costs, and after the first six years of life the average gross margin had increased to $5,685, which is 47.6 per cent of revenues and 91.0 per cent of direct costs.

Since all of the absolute gross margins on the table are expressed in constant 1977 dollars and all have been calculated using flows of costs and revenues that were properly capitalized and deflated, the results for cohorts of different vintages are comparable. Hence, it can be seen that the performance of the average title in the 1961 cohort was better than the performances of titles in any other cohort, with one possible exception. The 1973 cohort of 16 titles had, in the first two years of life, an absolute gross margin of $1,550 which is slightly above the gross margin of $1,520 in the first two years of life of the 1961 cohort.

The most dismal performance of any of the 15 cohorts shown for this publisher was registered by the 32 titles published in 1966, though the 58 titles of the 1970 cohort did not fare very much better. The average title in the 1966 group had not even after six years of life covered direct costs. This fact is made apparent by the negative entries appearing all the way across the table for that vintage. After six years of life,

---

[10]Actually, it is not the first full year of life that is being considered for each title in the cohort since some titles are published toward the beginning of the year and others toward the middle or end of the year. Titles released for sale just before the end of the year are likely to show larger negative gross margins than those released earlier in the year since the former would not have very much time to accumulate revenues from sales.

direct costs incurred still exceeded revenues received, and by a substantial $1,175 for the average title. The 1970 cohort, on the other hand, had at least reached, and slightly surpassed, the lower-order break-even point, the point at which sufficient revenues have been earned to cover direct costs.

In the first year of life none of the 15 cohorts shown had attained their break-even point. In the first two years of life, eight of fourteen cohorts had attained their lower-order break-even point, and in the first four years of life ten out of the twelve cohorts shown had attained their lower-order break-even point. By the end of four years of life, several of the cohorts seem to have had similar experiences. The absolute and relative gross margins for the 1963, 1964, and 1965 cohorts are all very much alike. After four years of life the absolute gross margins for the average title in these three cohorts was $1,235, $1,215, and $1,340 respectively, and after six years of life $2,620, $2,400, and $2,135. Titles in the 1967, 1968, and 1969 cohorts also had similar experiences, although as a group they seem to be about two years ahead of the 1963, 1964, and 1965 cohorts. Values attained after six years by the three cohorts of earlier vintage had already been attained after only four years by the three cohorts of more recent vintage. Comparing all of the cohorts after two years of life would suggest that the 1961, 1967, 1968, 1969 and 1973 cohorts were comparatively good vintages for this publisher and that the 1962, 1966, and 1970 cohorts were comparatively poor vintages.

Earlier, a few rough criteria, specified in terms of relative gross margins, were established to aid in estimating the point at which a cohort of titles had reached what was there termed the "higher-order break-even point," the point at which sufficient revenues had been earned to cover total costs. The university press whose cohort data are shown in Table 7.5.4 was not part of the sample of presses used to establish those criteria because it was unable to supply annual income-and-expense data for the entire period 1968-1975. However, the press was able to provide annual data for the 1971-1975 period. Direct costs (adjusted for inflation) over that period were equal to $1,137,000 and total costs were equal to $3,346,900. Hence, the resulting relative gross margin (in terms of direct costs) that would have to be attained by titles of this publisher in order to cover *total* costs associated with their publication was 194.4 per cent. Even after six years of life, none of the cohorts of titles published by the press over the period 1961-1970 came even close to that mark. The 1961 cohort shows the largest relative gross margin of all the 10 cohorts after six years of life, 91.0 per cent — less than half the margin required to reach the higher-order break-even point.

The reasons for the different performances of titles of different vintage are not revealed by the gross margins themselves. These reasons would be revealed only by closer examination of the individual titles — their prices, subject areas, the audience of readers for which they are intended, and so forth. Such a detailed investigation is beyond the scope of this analysis but could be performed by the individual publisher after cohort analysis has been used to measure the performances of the various vintages.

The Sample of 746 Titles

Gross margins for the cohorts of titles contained in the sample of 746 titles published by 11 university presses and 9 commercial firms are presented in Tables 7.5.5 through 7.5.8 The formats of these tables are slightly different from the format of Table 7.5.4 on the single university press; they contain gross margins for the vintages 1968-1975 only, and not for the longer period 1961-1975; they contain only one measure of relative gross margin, absolute gross margin expressed as a percentage of direct costs, rather than two measures; and they display results for the first year, first two years and first four years of life of the titles of each vintage, but not for the first six years as was the case for the single university press.

Of the 746 titles in the cohort sample, 658 have all of the data on costs and sales needed for calculating gross margins. This subsample of 658 titles is composed of 314 commercial titles and 344 university-press titles. The 314 commercial titles include 12 titles of various vintages with unusually large dollar sales and 8 titles with unusually small dollar sales.[11]

---

[11]The order of magnitude of the 20 unusual values vis-à-vis the rest of the sample is illustrated by the following example. In the sample of 42 titles of vintage 1971, one title had sales revenue of only $73 in the first year of life, while two other titles had sales revenues of $277,189 and $285,358 in their first year of life. Thus, revenues range from $73 to $285,358, and the average revenue per title for the 42 titles is $43,015. If the three extreme values are excluded, the sample size falls to 39, revenues range from a low of $290 to a high of $71,560 and the average revenue per title falls to $25,185, a very steep drop. Gross margin in the first year of life for the sample of 42 titles is $22,375 and for the 39 titles, only $7,970, a tremendous difference owing to just three titles. All 12 unusually large values in the group of 314 commercial titles are above $75,000, and all 8 unusually small values are below $100. It can be presumed that the small values are the result of the titles in question being released shortly before the end of the year of their publication, leaving little time in which to accumulate sales revenues in the first year of life.

Should we exclude from the sample the titles that have unusual values? One can offer arguments both in favor of including and in favor of excluding them. If, on the one hand, we acknowledge the lottery-like nature of book publishing, where a good portion of the titles published are apt to be only marginally profitable and where only a minority are likely to become highly profitable, then we would argue for including the extreme values in the analysis. After all, if it is only the occasional bestseller that makes some types of book publishing economically viable, then the effect of such titles on the profits of firms ought not be omitted from a study of profitability. If, on the other hand, we want to observe the economic performances of titles in the mainstream of publishing, then we would argue for excluding the extreme values from the analysis, particularly where the sample size is very small, as is the case here. Rather than choose in favor of one or the other of these alternatives, we shall present both sets of gross margins: one that includes titles with unusual values of sales revenue and one that excludes them.

Table 7.5.5 presents capitalized and deflated gross margins for (1) the entire sample of 314 commercial titles, (2) the reduced sample of 294 commercial titles, excluding the 20 titles with unusual values, and (3) the sample of 344 university press titles.

Of the eight cohorts in the sample of 314 commercial titles, all but one, the 41 titles published in 1973, show positive values for average gross margins in the first year of their lives, meaning that within one year, they had already generated revenue sufficient to cover direct costs and had consequently attained their lower-order break-even points. The 1971 cohort turned in the best performance with an absolute gross margin for the average title of $22,375 and a relative gross margin of 108.4 per cent. The 1968 and 1970 cohorts had just barely broken even in their first year of life, with relative gross margins of 3.6 and 3.0, respectively. After two years of life, each of the seven cohorts, 1968-1974, for which a minimum of two years of data are available, registered fairly healthy average gross margins. The relative gross margin of 182.5 per cent attained after two years by the 44 titles published in 1974, surpasses the 175 per cent level designated earlier as the lower boundary of the region in which the higher-order break-even point is likely to be reached. The relative gross margin of the 1971 cohort of titles, 171.8 per cent, is very close to the 175 per cent mark. After four years of life, three of the five cohorts for which four years of data are available had relative gross margins that lie within the range of the higher-order break-even point.

The second panel of Table 7.5.5 contains average gross margins for the smaller sample of 294 commercial titles. The number of titles omitted from each of the eight cohorts varies from only one in 1968, 1972, and 1973, to five for the 1974 cohort. Changes in the values of the average gross margins

TABLE 7.5.5 Titles of Commercial Publishers and University Presses--Capitalized and Deflated Gross Margins, as Average Absolute Dollar Amounts per Title and as Percentages of Direct Costs, for Two Overlapping Samples of Titles Published by 9 Commercial Publishers, and for a Sample of Titles Published by 11 University Presses, 1968-1975 (Dollar Values in Constant 1977 Dollars)

	Entire sample of 314 commercially published titles						
		First year of life		First 2 years of life		First 4 years of life	
Vintage year	Number of titles	Absolute	Per cent of direct cost	Absolute	Per cent of direct cost	Absolute	Per cent of direct cost
1968	37	$ 775	3.6	$21,910	85.7	$42,285	147.6
1969	39	$ 6,945	40.5	$23,215	115.2	$43,055	188.6
1970	32	$ 500	3.0	$14,980	85.5	$24,740	136.7
1971	42	$22,375	108.4	$41,260	171.8	$58,455	230.8
1972	40	$ 2,600	18.3	$19,100	119.2	$35,420	204.0
1973	41	($ 1,030)	(7.3)	$14,540	91.4	-	-
1974	44	$11,750	81.2	$31,155	182.5	-	-
1975	39	$11,440	51.1	-	-	-	-
All cohorts combined:							
Weighted average		$ 7,450	41.3	$24,215	124.2	$41,615	184.4
Number of titles	314	314	314	275	275	190	190

(continued)

Table 7.5.5, continued

	Sample of 294 commercially published titles (excludes 12 titles with extremely large dollar sales and 8 titles with extremely small dollar sales)						
		First year of life		First 2 years of life		First 4 years of life	
Vintage year	Number of titles	Absolute	Per cent of direct cost	Absolute	Per cent of direct cost	Absolute	Per cent of direct cost
1968	36	($1,050)	(5.1)	$20,225	82.9	$40,645	147.4
1969	36	$2,140	13.5	$15,910	87.7	$29,120	145.2
1970	30	($2,790)	(17.4)	$ 5,590	33.2	$17,105	98.1
1971	39	$7,970	46.3	$22,655	119.5	$35,465	174.1
1972	39	$ 460	3.4	$16,135	105.5	$32,100	192.5
1973	40	($ 850)	(6.0)	$15,085	93.7	-	-
1974	39	$1,235	10.0	$11,750	90.5	-	-
1975	35	$ 590	4.2	-	-	-	-
All cohorts combined:							
Weighted average		$1,085	7.6	$15,610	89.5	$31,440	154.3
Number of titles	294	294	259	259	259	180	180

(continued)

TABLE 7.5.5, continued

Vintage year	Number of titles	Sample of 344 university-press titles: First year of life: Absolute	First year of life: Per cent of direct cost	First 2 years of life: Absolute	First 2 years of life: Per cent of direct cost	First 4 years of life: Absolute	First 4 years of life: Per cent of direct cost
1968	43	$ 585	4.9	$5,970	48.7	$9,065	71.9
1969	45	($2,550)	(25.1)	$2,380	23.1	$4,965	47.6
1970	45	($2,060)	(20.7)	$1,160	11.4	$3,520	34.1
1971	44	($2,625)	(24.2)	$1,455	13.0	$5,430	47.7
1972	42	$ 525	5.7	$4,795	50.8	$6,445	65.6
1973	44	$ 520	5.7	$4,165	43.4	-	-
1974	39	($ 360)	(4.2)	$2,590	28.6	-	-
1975	42	($2,025)	(25.0)	-	-	-	-
All cohorts combined:							
Weighted average		($1,025)	(10.6)	$3,195	31.1	$5,850	53.1
Number of titles	344	344	344	302	302	219	219

Source: Machlup, Leeson, and Associates.

brought about by excluding the extreme values are significant. In the diminished sample three of the cohorts failed to reach the lower-order break-even point in the first year of life. The 1973 cohort, the only one to show a negative average gross margin in the first year of life in the larger sample, registered a slight gain (because the one title excluded from that sample had extremely *small* dollar sales in the year of its publication), from negative $1,030 to negative $850. For the remaining cohorts the effect of excluding titles with extremely large sales overwhelmed the effect of excluding titles with extremely small sales and their average gross margins consequently fell. The 1968 and 1970 cohorts that had just barely broken even in the larger sample are now below the lower-order break-even point with gross margins of negative $1,050 and negative $2,790, respectively. The remaining five cohorts each show substantially lower gross margins. Not surprisingly, the effects on average gross margin of excluding the extreme values is sustained over the lives of the cohorts. After two years of life none of the cohorts have approached the region of the higher-order break-even point, and after four years of life only the 1972 cohort has crossed the lower boundary of that region.

The effect upon the value of average gross margin of excluding titles with extreme values of dollar sales is illustrated more strikingly by the gross margins for all years considered collectively. These values are shown near the bottom of Table 7.5.5. Since gross margins for the cohorts of each of the eight years are calculated using capitalized and deflated values and are all expressed in constant 1977 dollars, data for all the years can be lumped together to obtain a measure of average gross margin for the sample as a whole. Thus, for the combined sample of 314 commercially published titles, absolute gross margin after one year of life averages $7,450, and relative gross margin 41.3 per cent; for the combined sample of 294 commercially published titles that excludes extreme values, absolute gross margin averages only $1,085, and relative gross margin 7.6 per cent, a very large difference. The difference between the two samples persists but becomes slightly less severe when the first two and the first four years of life are considered. This is because 10 of the 20 extreme values in all eight cohorts happened to be in one of the three most recent cohorts. When these cohorts are dropped from the combined sample, which is implicit in a calculation that focuses on sales for four years of life, the effects of the omission of extreme values drop out too.

A short digression concerning an important point demonstrated by this exercise is in order. The size of the samples used in the analysis are obviously too small to permit us to draw conclusions regarding trends in the profitability of book publishing in general. If the values of gross margin for each cohort can be affected so dramatically by just one or two titles, then the inferential power of the findings must be viewed with skepticism. The weakness of the particular empirical results presented here, however, in no way impugns the cogency of the analytical technique used in their derivation. The inadequacy of the data can be attributed both to a failure to give proper consideration at the outset of the research to the problems imposed by large variations in the costs and sales among individual book titles and to the huge expense in terms of time and money involved in culling the required data from the large variety of working files, bookkeeping records, and confidential reports compiled and maintained in different ways by each of the 20 cooperating publishers. With the lessons learned from this study and the apparent trend in publishing toward computerizing data on sales and costs, neither of these problems should impose a constraint on an individual firm interested in using cohort analysis as a method of studying the economic performance of its own titles. Even sector-by-sector or industry-wide analysis would be feasible if conducted under the aegis of one of the professional associations of the book-publishing industry.

Returning to the discussion of the data, we see average gross margins for the sample of 314 university-press titles in the third panel of Table 7.5.5. In general, the values for these titles are noticeably lower than the values for the commercial publishers. In the first year of life, five out of the eight cohorts failed to earn enough revenues to cover direct costs and consequently have negative values of average gross margin. The remaining three cohorts just barely managed to cover direct costs in the first year of life with positive relative gross margins of 4.9 per cent of direct cost in 1968 and 5.7 per cent in both 1972 and 1973.

After two years of life the average gross margins for all seven vintage years, 1968 to 1974, are positive. The dollar values range from a low of $1,160 for the 1970 cohort to a high of $5,970 for the 1968 cohort. The respective relative gross margins range from a low of 11.4 per cent for the 1970 cohort to a high of 50.8 per cent for the 1972 cohort. Compared with the single university press discussed earlier, the title under discussion here has much healthier average gross margins. For the single press, all of the eight cohorts 1968-1975 had negative gross margins in the first year of life, and two out of seven still had negative gross margins in the second year of life. Though it may be nothing more than coincidence, it is interesting to note that for both samples, the 1970 cohort had, by far, the poorest performance of all.

After four years of life absolute gross margins for the sample of university-press titles in Table 7.5.5 ranged from a low of $3,520 in 1970 to a high of $9,065 in 1968, and relative gross margins ranged from 34.1 to 71.9 per cent, for the same two cohorts. These are rather modest performances when compared either with the results for the commercially published titles or with the relative gross margins estimated earlier in the chapter as deliniating the range in which the higher-order break-even point is likely to be reached. After four years of life none of the cohorts shown on the table have relative gross margins above 75 per cent, and consequently they would have a long way to go before even approaching 175 per cent, the lower boundary of the higher-order break-even point.

A convenient comparison of the overall performance of the university press titles with the overall performance of the commercial titles can be made by referring to the average gross margins for all titles combined, the figures presented across the bottom of Table 7.5.5. Looking at the gross margins after four years of life for titles of the five cohorts 1968-1972 combined, we see that the average of the absolute gross margins for 190 commercially published titles (including extreme values) is $41,615; for 180 commercially published titles (excluding extreme values) it is $31,440; but, for 219 university-press titles the absolute gross margin is only $5,850. The relative gross margins for these three samples are 184.4 per cent, 154.3 per cent, and 53.1 per cent, respectively.

Another point that warrants mention is the fact that there were no titles with unusually large values of dollar sales in the sample of 344 university press titles. Unlike commercial firms, for which a few high sellers managed to raise the average gross margins of the sample of titles significantly, the university presses received no exceptionally large pay-offs in their publishing "lotteries."

Comparisons among Broad Subject Areas

One of the advantages of cohort analysis is that titles can be grouped according to subject area. This enables the publisher or researcher to conduct studies of the profitability of book publishing on a field-by-field basis. While it is very likely that different fields have had different experiences regarding profits, these differences could never be unraveled using conventional analysis, where financial data on titles of numerous subject areas are invariably tossed together.

As an illustration of cohort analysis by field, a new set of gross margins have been calculated for the samples of titles presented in Table 7.5.5. This time, however, the titles are grouped under one of three major subject areas — natural sciences, social sciences, or humanities. A list of the subfields contained under each of these three headings was provided in Chapter 7.4, but for the sake of convenience we shall repeat the list here.[12]

---

[12]Classifying each of these 24 fields, or subject areas, under one of only three major headings entails a few rather arbi-

Natural sciences, technology, and mathematics	*Social sciences*	*Humanities*
1. Life sciences	*9. Psychology*	*19. Philosophy and religion*
2. Physical sciences	*10. Economics*	*20. Language and linguistics*
3. Environmental sciences	*11. Business administration*	*21. English composition*
4. Mathematics	*12. Political science*	*22. Literature*
5. Statistics	*13. Law*	*23. Music*
6. Engineering	*14. History and archaeology*	*24. Art and art history*
7. Medical sciences	*15. Geography*	
8. Other applied sciences	*16. Anthropology and sociology*	
	17. Education	
	18. Home economics	

It would, of course, be more illuminating to calculate gross margins for each of the 24 sub-fields rather than just for the major subject areas. Once again, however, the sample size is not large enough to allow such a detailed analysis.

Table 7.5.6 contains gross margins by major area for the 314 commercial titles, including the 20 titles with extreme values of dollar sales. Of the 314 titles, 108 belong to the natural sciences, 152 belong to the social sciences, and 54 belong to the humanities. Table 7.5.7 contains gross margins by field for the smaller sample of 294 commercially published titles *excluding* the 20 titles with extreme values. Here the number of titles in the natural sciences, social sciences, and humanities are 103, 141, and 50, respectively. Table 7.5.8 contains gross margins by field for the 344 university-press titles, 46 in the natural sciences, 175 in the social sciences, and 123 in the humanities.

In Table 7.5.6, several cohorts among the three major subject areas have rather large gross margins. The 1974 cohort

---

trary decisions about where to place some of the fields. For example, medical sciences, which includes psychiatry, is classified here under natural sciences, technology, and mathematics, while psychology is found under social sciences; history is classified here under social sciences, yet it might just as well have been classified under humanities.

TABLE 7.5.6 Titles of Commercial Publishers by Subject Area--Capitalized and Deflated Gross Margins, as Average Absolute Dollar Amounts per Title and as Percentages of Direct Costs, for a Sample of 314 Commercially Published Titles (Including Extreme Values) Broken Down by Major Subject Areas, 1968-1975 (Dollar Values in Constant 1977 Dollars)

		Natural sciences					
		First year of life		First 2 years of life		First 4 years of life	
Vintage year	Number of titles	Absolute	Per cent of direct cost	Absolute	Per cent of direct cost	Absolute	Per cent of direct cost
1968	12	($ 1,475)	(5.6)	$20,350	70.6	$33,810	115.8
1969	14	$ 5,695	36.5	$12,945	81.3	$20,690	123.7
1970	10	$ 780	6.2	$ 5,355	42.5	$ 8,220	65.2
1971	15	$ 5,065	31.3	$17,745	104.6	$27,270	150.4
1972	10	$ 1,110	8.6	$11,540	82.8	$19,150	125.5
1973	17	($ 1,565)	(8.7)	$16,545	80.2	-	-
1974	17	$31,050	168.3	$62,770	264.8	-	-
1975	13	$ 4,375	53.3	-	-	-	-
All cohorts combined:							
Weighted average		$ 6,620	41.4	$23,410	112.3	$22,590	119.4
Number of titles	108	108	108	95	95	61	61

(continued)

Table 7.5.6, continued

Vintage year	Number of titles	Social sciences: First year of life: Absolute	First year of life: Per cent of direct cost	First 2 years of life: Absolute	First 2 years of life: Per cent of direct cost	First 4 years of life: Absolute	First 4 years of life: Per cent of direct cost
1968	15	$ 5,870	22.5	$35,195	105.7	$69,945	176.9
1969	15	$10,710	48.0	$38,760	133.2	$75,625	221.1
1970	18	$ 500	2.4	$23,420	107.5	$37,035	162.4
1971	23	$22,845	100.0	$42,920	160.7	$63,550	224.2
1972	18	($ 145)	(0.9)	$20,830	118.6	$44,540	232.6
1973	20	($ 410)	(3.5)	$14,155	108.4	-	-
1974	23	($ 550)	(4.3)	$12,015	87.5	-	-
1975	20	$19,710	60.4	-	-	-	-
All cohorts combined:							
Weighted average		$ 7,590	29.1	$26,165	117.7	$57,455	204.9
Number of titles	152	152	152	132	132	89	89

(continued)

Table 7.5.6, continued

Vintage year	Number of titles	Humanities: First year of life – Absolute	Humanities: First year of life – Per cent of direct cost	Humanities: First 2 years of life – Absolute	Humanities: First 2 years of life – Per cent of direct cost	Humanities: First 4 years of life – Absolute	Humanities: First 4 years of life – Per cent of direct cost
1968	10	($ 4,040)	(40.1)	$ 3,865	38.4	$ 11,000	94.5
1969	10	$ 3,015	26.3	$ 14,300	113.3	$ 25,540	176.3
1970	4	($ 185)	(1.7)	$ 1,045	9.8	$ 10,715	100.8
1971	4	$84,600	341.1	$119,930	343.8	$146,120	418.8
1972	12	$ 7,970	59.9	$ 22,800	147.9	$ 35,305	214.9
1973	4	($ 1,885)	(19.4)	$ 7,950	78.9	-	-
1974	4	$ 440	5.9	$ 6,850	84.9	-	-
1975	6	($ 670)	5.0	-	-	-	-
All cohorts combined:							
Weighted average		$ 7,650	35.5	$ 20,800	111.7	$ 35,410	184.1
Number of titles	54	54	54	48	48	40	40

Source: Machlup, Leeson, and Associates.

of 17 titles in natural sciences has, in the first year of life, an absolute gross margin of $31,050 and a relative gross margin of 168.3 per cent. After only two years of life the relative gross margin is 264.8 per cent, well in the range of the higher-order break-even point. In the social sciences, the 23 titles of the 1971 cohort register a relative gross margin of 100.0 per cent in the first year of life, 160.7 after two years, and 224.2 per cent after four years of life. The 1969 and 1972 cohorts in the social sciences are both off to slow starts, with the latter having a negative gross margin in the first year of life. After four years, however, both of these cohorts have relative gross margins above 200 per cent. The most spectacular performance for any cohort in Table 7.5.6 is the 1971 cohort in the humanities. For these four humanities titles, average absolute gross margin per title after only one year of life is $84,600, and relative gross margin is 341.1 per cent! These two magnitudes grow over time, reaching, after four years of life, $146,120 and 418.8 per cent, respectively.

With the exception of the 1972 cohort in the social sciences, the high performances of these cohorts can be attributed to the few titles with unusually high sales. This is borne out by the lower gross margins displayed in Table 7.5.7. After dropping two of the 17 titles from the 1974 cohort in the natural sciences, the average absolute gross margin per title falls from $31,050 (Table 7.5.6), to $2,810 (Table 7.5.7), and the relative gross margin falls from 168.3 per cent to 24.0 per cent. One of the exceptional titles is in the field of environmental science and had dollar sales of $351,600 in its first year of life. The other is in the field of medical science and had dollar sales of $142,500 in the first year.

The exceptional title in the humanities that contributed so much to the average gross margin of $84,600 for the 1971 cohort shown in Table 7.5.6 is in the field of philosophy and religion and had dollar sales of $277,200 in the first year of its life. After excluding this title, the average gross margin for the three titles that remain in the cohort shown on Table 7.5.7 falls to $3,410 and the relative gross margin falls from 341.1 per cent of direct costs in the first year to 47.7 per cent. Nonetheless, these three remaining titles manage to attain an average gross margin of $21,950 after four years of life for a relative gross margin of 307.3 per cent, the highest relative gross margin of any of the cohorts in any of the three major areas shown on Table 7.5.7.

Gross margins for the combined cohorts of titles, that is, for the titles of *all* eight vintages considered collectively, are shown in the next-to-the-last row of Tables 7.5.6 and 7.5.7. These values give an overall indication of the comparative performance of the titles in each of the three major fields or subject areas. Again, because of the small sample, the results cannot be generalized with any confidence.

TABLE 7.5.7 Titles of Commercial Publishers by Subject Area--Capitalized and Deflated Gross Margins, as Average Absolute Amounts per Title and as Percentages of Direct Costs, for a Sample of 294 Commercially Published Titles (Excluding Extreme Values) Broken Down by Major Subject Areas, 1968-1975 (Dollar Values in Constant 1977 Dollars)

	Natural sciences						
		First year of life		First 2 years of life		First 4 years of life	
Vintage year	Number of titles	Absolute	Per cent of direct cost	Absolute	Per cent of direct cost	Absolute	Per cent of direct cost
1968	11	($7,655)	(33.9)	$14,690	58.0	$27,660	107.5
1969	14	$5,695	36.5	$12,945	81.3	$20,690	123.7
1970	9	$3,245	27.5	$ 8,395	71.1	$11,845	100.3
1971	14	$5,960	35.5	$18,865	107.7	$28,715	153.1
1972	10	$1,110	8.6	$11,540	82.8	$19,150	125.5
1973	17	($1,565)	(8.7)	$16,545	80.2	-	-
1974	15	$2,810	24.0	$ 9,925	83.7	-	-
1975	13	$4,375	40.7	-	-	-	-
All cohorts combined:							
Weighted average		$1,860	16.6	$13,645	81.9	$22,310	124.4
Number of titles	103	103	103	90	90	58	58

(continued)

Table 7.5.7, continued

Vintage year	Number of titles	Social sciences: First year of life: Absolute	First year of life: Per cent of direct cost	First 2 years of life: Absolute	First 2 years of life: Per cent of direct cost	First 4 years of life: Absolute	First 4 years of life: Per cent of direct cost
1968	15	$5,780	22.5	$35,200	105.7	$69,945	176.9
1969	14	($3,380)	(18.7)	$17,840	77.8	$37,210	145.0
1970	17	($6,600)	(33.9)	$ 5,175	24.7	$21,395	97.2
1971	22	$9,870	52.3	$26,450	123.1	$41,610	179.5
1972	18	($ 145)	(0.9)	$20,830	118.6	$44,540	232.6
1973	19	$ 5	0.1	$15,290	115.0	-	-
1974	20	$ 210	1.5	$14,100	95.2	-	-
1975	16	($2,010)	(14.9)	-	-	-	-
All cohcrts combined:							
Weighted average		$ 805	3.0	$19,160	96.2	$42,455	168.3
Number of titles	141	141	141	125	125	86	86

(continued)

Table 7.5.7, continued

Vintage year	Number of titles	Humanities					
		First year of life		First 2 years of life		First 4 years of life	
		Absolute	Per cent of direct cost	Absolute	Per cent of direct cost	Absolute	Per cent of direct cost
1968	10	($4,040)	(40.1)	$ 3,865	38.4	$11,000	94.5
1969	8	$5,585	44.6	$17,730	129.8	$29,750	186.1
1970	4	($ 185)	(1.7)	$ 1,045	9.8	$10,715	100.8
1971	3	$3,410	47.7	$12,525	175.3	$21,950	307.3
1972	11	$ 870	7.5	$12,640	98.8	$23,520	169.4
1973	4	($1,885)	(19.4)	$ 7,950	78.9	-	-
1974	4	$ 440	5.6	$ 6,850	84.9	-	-
1975	6	($ 670)	(4.6)	-	-	-	-
All cohorts combined:							
Weighted average		$ 270	1.9	$ 9,555	84.8	$19,875	156.2
Number of titles	50	50	50	44	44	36	36

Source: Machlup, Leeson, and Associates.

Looking at the gross margins for the combined cohorts of titles of commercial publishers shown near the bottom of Table 7.5.6 — gross margins that include the titles with extreme values — we see that average gross margins in the first year of life and the first two years of life have remarkably similar values both in terms of absolute dollar amounts, and as percentages of direct costs. In the first year of life, average absolute gross margins are, for the titles in the natural sciences, social sciences, and humanities, $6,620, $7,590, and $7,650, respectively, and the corresponding relative gross margins are 41.4 per cent, 29.1 per cent, and 35.5 per cent. After two years of life average absolute gross margins for the three fields are $23,410, $26,155, and $20,800 and the relative gross margins corresponding to these dollar amounts are 112.3 per cent, 117.7 per cent, and 111.7 per cent. By the end of the four years of life the performances of the titles begin to diverge. The social sciences have the highest values with an average absolute gross margin of $57,455 and a relative gross margin of 204.9 per cent. Humanities titles are next with an absolute gross margin of $35,410, or 184.1 per cent of direct costs, and titles in the natural sciences occupy third place after four years of life with a combined absolute gross margin for the average title of $22,590, or 119.4 per cent of direct costs.

The average gross margins for the combined cohorts of titles of commercial publishers *excluding* the titles with extreme values, shown in Table 7.5.7, are as expected, below the gross margins that include the extreme values. Nevertheless, the ranking of the three major subject areas after four years of life is the same as in Table 7.5.6. We find the largest relative gross margin in the social sciences with 168.3 per cent of direct costs; the second highest in the humanities, with 156.2 per cent; and the lowest in the natural sciences with 124.4 per cent.

Table 7.5.8 presents the analogous figures for books published by university presses. In the first year of life, five out of eight cohorts have negative gross margins in the natural sciences and the social sciences, while six out of eight cohorts have negative values in the humanities. After two years of life one cohort in the natural sciences (1969) and one cohort in the humanities (1970) remain negative; all others are positive. After four years of life only the 1969 cohort of titles in the natural sciences is still negative. Overall, the ranking of the three major areas is different from the rankings observed for the books published by commercial publishers. Average gross margins for the combined cohorts after four years of life are highest for the natural sciences with an average dollar value of $10,165, or 72.3 per cent of direct costs. Titles in the social sciences are next with the average absolute gross margin reaching $6,470 after four years of life, or 59.5 per cent of direct costs; and titles in the

TABLE 7.5.8 Titles of University Presses by Subject Area--Capitalized and Deflated Gross Margins, as Average Absolute Amounts per Title and as Percentages of Direct Costs, for a Sample of 344 University-Press Titles Broken Down by Major Subject Areas, 1968-1975 (Dollar Values in Constant 1977 Dollars)

		Natural sciences					
		First year of life		First 2 years of life		First 4 years of life	
Vintage year	Number of titles	Absolute	Per cent of direct cost	Absolute	Per cent of direct cost	Absolute	Per cent of direct cost
1968	5	$6,075	49.1	$ 9,665	78.2	$11,950	96.7
1969	5	($4,365)	(36.5)	($ 1,320)	(10.7)	($ 490)	(4.0)
1970	5	($3,940)	(30.5)	$ 1,425	10.2	$ 7,705	52.9
1971	8	($4,455)	(31.1)	$ 1,480	10.3	$13,700	92.8
1972	5	$6,055	46.6	$13,175	101.3	$15,840	111.7
1973	5	($5,015)	(45.6)	$ 1,635	14.9	-	-
1974	6	$ 70	1.7	$ 1,295	27.5	-	-
1975	7	($ 855)	(16.8)	-	-	-	-
All cohorts combined:							
Weighted average		($1,025)	(9.6)	$ 3,655	31.2	$10,165	72.3
Number of titles	46	46	46	39	39	28	28

(continued)

TABLE 7.5.8, continued

		Social sciences					
		First year of life		First 2 years of life		First 4 years of life	
Vintage year	Number of titles	Absolute	Per cent of direct cost	Absolute	Per cent of direct cost	Absolute	Per cent of direct cost
1968	22	$1,070	8.7	$7,855	62.7	$12,020	92.2
1969	22	($ 790)	(8.0)	$4,410	43.5	$ 7,245	70.4
1970	25	($1,145)	(12.4)	$2,415	25.9	$ 4,555	48.0
1971	25	($2,555)	(22.9)	$ 380	3.3	$ 2,665	22.7
1972	20	$ 795	8.8	$5,020	54.1	$ 6,655	71.7
1973	20	$ 615	7.1	$3,871	41.9	-	-
1974	19	($1,380)	(12.6)	$2,115	18.0	-	-
1975	22	($2,595)	(29.9)	-	-	-	-
All cohorts combined:							
Weighted average		($ 810)	(35.0)	$3,645	34.8	$ 6,470	59.5
Number of titles	175	175	175	153	153	114	114

(continued)

TABLE 7.5.8, continued

		Humanities					
		First year of life		First 2 years of life		First 4 years of life	
Vintage year	Number of titles	Absolute	Per cent of direct cost	Absolute	Per cent of direct cost	Absolute	Per cent of direct cost
1968	16	($1,795)	(15.3)	$2,220	18.7	$4,100	33.9
1969	18	($4,190)	(42.2)	$ 925	9.3	$3,700	36.7
1970	15	($2,960)	(29.2)	($1,030)	(10.0)	$ 410	4.0
1971	11	($1,450)	(19.0)	$3,865	49.0	$5,695	70.0
1972	17	($1,420)	(17.0)	$2,065	24.1	$3,435	38.4
1973	19	$1,880	19.6	$5,135	53.7	-	-
1974	14	$ 845	11.8	$3,790	52.0	-	-
1975	13	($1,680)	(19.4)	-	-	-	-
All cohorts combined:							
Weighted average		($1,325)	(13.5)	$2,410	27.4	$3,370	34.9
Number of titles	123	123	123	110	110	77	77

Source: Machlup, Leeson, and Associates.

humanities come in last with the average absolute gross margin of $3,370 and relative gross margin of 34.9 per cent.

Expanding the Scope of the Research

Gross margins presented in the several tables of this chapter provide an interesting illustration of the kinds of analysis that can be done by publishers or by industry analysts wishing to obtain a more accurate picture of the profit performance of books than can be obtained from conventional financial statements. Because of the small samples used, it is not possible here to claim "findings" regarding trends in profitability but the technique is nevertheless valid.

Other researches might go beyond the scope of this study, not only by increasing the sample size, but by separating titles into cohorts of finer disaggregation. That is, instead of merely grouping titles by type of publisher — commercial, university press — and by major subject areas — natural sciences, social sciences, humanities — it would probably be far more telling to choose classifications of greater detail, such as "hardbound textbooks in chemistry published by commercial firms and intended for the college audience," or "paperbound monographs in philosophy published by university presses and intended for advanced scholars." Such analyses would be well suited for finding out which are the healthy and which are the not-so-healthy sectors of the publishing industry.

CHAPTER 7.6

BEHIND GROSS MARGINS: MANUFACTURING COSTS AND SELLING PRICES

With cohort data on a sufficiently large number of titles the individual publisher or the industry analyst can calculate gross margins in the manner described in the preceding chapter and thereby shed a good deal of light on the comparative profitability of books of various vintage years, of different types of publishers, of various functional categories, and of different subject areas. Gross margins, however, are essentially the end of the story, the "bottom line" so to speak (or as close to the actual bottom line of net profit as available data and prudent economic analysis will allow us to come) and hence can provide little information about many of the economic factors that lie behind their values. Among these are the levels of output (the number of copies of each title produced) and the selling prices of books decided by editors, production managers, and market analysts in response to prevailing and expected economic conditions, chiefly the costs of production and the perceived demand for the products.

QUESTIONS POSED AND PROCEDURES SELECTED

In this chapter we shall use the cohort data to provide some tentative answers to the following types of questions: How much does it cost, in terms of incremental or direct cost, to produce a single title? What is the relationship between the cost of a book and its list price? How much does it cost for the publisher to produce a word of text? for the reader to buy a word of text? How large are the discounts below list price offered to wholesalers and bookstores as an incentive to carry and sell the books? How rapidly have the list prices of newly published titles risen over the period 1968-1975? To what extent are list prices of existing titles increased over the years of their lives?

As we shall see, answers to these questions provided by the cohort data bring to light some very interesting differences between the publishing operations of the two major types of publishers — university presses and commercial firms — and among titles of the three broad subject areas — the natural sciences, technology, and mathematics; the social sciences; and the humanities.

An Optimistic Note on Sample Size

The discussion of gross margins given in the preceding chapter was amply laced with warnings against any attempt to use the numerical "findings" derived from the cohort sample as a basis for generalizations about the experiences of book publishers in general. It was apparent that with such small samples a mere one or two titles with extremely large or extremely small sales in relation to what might be called the "typical" title could significantly change the central values of the calculated gross margins. In the example cited in footnote 11 of Chapter 7.5, a sample of 42 titles published in 1971 contained one title with sales revenue of only $73 in its first year of life, and two others with first-year sales of more than $277,000. The resulting gross margin in the first year of life for the cohort of titles including the extreme values was $22,375, but without the extreme values only $7,970, a huge difference owing to just three titles.

In this chapter the discussion focuses on costs and prices which, unlike sales, are rarely apt to exhibit large and unpredictable variations in value from one title to the next. There are few surprises waiting for the publisher when he negotiates the cost of composition and printing. Market conditions establish in advance the going rates for such services, and any bid tendered by a supplier that lies too far beyond the range of what is generally known to be reasonable can immediately be rejected by the publisher. The same holds true for the establishment of list prices by the publisher. Even though each title is unique in that its text and graphics are protected by copyright, and hence are not available in any other titles, the existence of close substitutes places stringent limitations on the freedom with which list prices for general classes of books may be set.

All of this is not to say that there are no substantial differences in the costs of producing or in the costs of buying books published by different individual publishers (say, by McGraw-Hill, Scarecrow Press, Princeton University Press), by different types of publishers (university presses, commercial firms), in different subject areas (physics, political science, literature) and for different audiences (juveniles, college students, research scientists). However, the virtual absence of *extreme* values in costs and prices will permit us, even with a small sample size, to observe more clearly the *normal* variations in characteristics among these several classes of titles. Although we still cannot confidently claim any truly general findings, the cohort data on costs and prices seem to exhibit certain regularities that were clearly absent from the analysis of gross margins. It seems obvious that we are on far safer ground in generalizing the results on costs and prices presented in this chapter than we would have been had we attempted to generalize the results of the analyses of gross margins based on samples of comparable size but involving more widely divergent data on sales.

Standard Units of Measurement

A comparison of costs and prices among titles would not be very informative without some attempt to establish standard units of measurement. Knowing, for example, that plant costs for Title A are $7,000 and for Title B only $4,000 is not sufficient by itself to serve as a basis for determining which is more expensive in a meaningful sense. If Title A is 300 pages in length and Title B only 160 pages, then plant costs per page are $20 for the former title and $25 for the latter; on a per-page basis Title A is less expensive than Title B. Similarly, the total cost of paper for a given title may be very different from that for some other title, but without taking account of the number of pages contained in each, or of the number of copies of each printed, a comparison of costs would be rather meaningless. Thus, throughout the chapter, costs and prices will be expressed in standard units of measurement — per copy, per page, per signature (32 pages), per 1,000 words — in order to facilitate comparisons of titles of different vintage years, of different types of publishers and of different subject areas.

The figures displayed in Table 7.6.1 on number of copies printed, number of pages per title, and number of words per title for the sample of 397 titles that will be used in the subsequent analyses serve to demonstrate the need for expressing values in standard units. Note the variations in each of the three characteristics shown, both among titles published in different years and between the products of university presses and commercial publishers. More about the figures in this table will be said presently.

A Sample of Uniform Composition

A second important consideration in providing more meaningful, that is, more comparable results concerns the composition of the samples upon which analyses of various aspects of the costs and prices of titles are based. Since we are interested in comparisons of plant costs, costs of paper, printing, binding, the relationship between direct costs and list prices, and so on, we must select from the entire cohort sample of 746 titles only those for which data on *all* of the relevant vari-

TABLE 7.6.1 Number of Copies Printed per Title, Number of Pages per Title, and Number of Words per Title for 397 Titles (239 by University Presses, 158 by Commercial Publishers) by Vintage Years 1968 to 1975, and All Vintages Combined

Vintage	Number of titles			Number of copies printed per title in first year of life			Number of pages per title			Number of words per title		
	University press	Commercial	All titles	University press	Commercial	All titles	University press	Commercial	All titles	University press	Commercial	All titles
1968	31	23	54	3,430	6,130	4,580	311	389	345	135,600	200,300	163,200
1969	35	24	59	2,860	5,960	4,120	309	446	365	121,300	214,200	159,100
1970	34	16	50	2,940	5,100	3,630	283	440	333	120,300	211,100	149,300
1971	38	20	58	2,720	7,990	4,540	282	392	320	115,000	180,800	137,700
1972	26	20	46	3,180	5,610	4,240	302	311	306	127,500	141,700	133,700
1973	29	25	54	2,820	6,160	4,370	314	330	321	128,500	155,600	141,000
1974	28	17	45	2,400	4,650	3,250	313	310	312	125,400	149,200	134,400
1975	18	13	31	2,300	8,310	4,820	402	429	413	190,500	207,500	197,600
All vintages	239	158	397	2,860	6,190	4,190	309	379	337	129,300	181,600	150,100

Source: Machlup, Leeson, and Associates.

ables have been obtained from the publishers. Had we instead considered one variable at a time, selecting for analysis all titles having data on only that single variable, the sample sizes for each would have been larger owing to the less stringent criteria of selection, but it would be quite unlikely for the size and composition of the sample to remain constant. To study plant costs using one sub-sample of the cohort data, paper costs using another, printing costs using a third, and so on, would result in findings of questionable comparability. Hence it was decided to reject the large sub-samples of titles that would have been available had each variable been considered separately. Instead, a smaller sub-sample of titles, each having data on *all* of the variables of interest, was chosen. The variables in question are: (1) plant costs, (2) paper costs, (3) printing costs, (4) binding costs, (5) number of copies printed, (6) number of copies bound, (7) number of pages, (8) average number of words per page, and (9) list price. Of the 746 titles in the entire cohort sample, 397 have data on all nine of these variables — 239 of university presses and 158 of commercial publishers. We will stay with this uniform sample for most of the discussion that follows. Toward the end of the chapter, however, we will jump to a slightly different, slightly larger sample without adversely affecting the continuity of the analyses.

Copies Printed, Number of Pages, Number of Words

Table 7.6.1 presents for university-press titles, commercially published titles, and for all titles, the average number of copies printed per title, average number of pages per title, and average number of words per title, by the vintage years, or years of publication, 1968 to 1975, and for all eight vintage years combined.

Data on number of copies printed were gathered directly from the records of the cooperating publishers. Data on number of pages and number of words per title could be obtained only by inspecting in various libraries copies of each book. Number of pages includes all pages falling between the first page of the first chapter and the last page of the book. Thus, indices, appendices, and notes are included. It is possible that the word count on pages containing author indexes and perhaps also subject indexes might be below that of ordinary text. It would have been too expensive, however, to take this into account and to inquire whether the cost of composition is significantly lower for a page of index than for a page of text. Title pages, acknowledgments, prefaces, and tables of contents are excluded.

Number of words per title were calculated by taking a sample of the number of words per line on a single page, one that contained only words, no diagrams, tables, footnotes, etc. The average number of words per line was then multiplied by the number of lines, adjusted for breaks between paragraphs. The total number of words for each title was obtained by multiplying number of words per page by the total number of pages. Admittedly, this technique implicitly assumes that all pages are completely filled with words only. This is surely not the case for many titles, particularly in the natural sciences, where special graphics (formulas, tables, equations, etc.) are customary. It would, however, be virtually impossible to measure the amount of special graphics on a given page. In some instances diagrams, charts, figures, or tables, may be very intricate or complicated and hence expensive to compose and print. In other instances they may be relatively simple and inexpensive. There seems to be no way of devising a measure that will accurately reflect such differences. Therefore, in the calculations of average number of words per title used here all of the pages in the book, whether containing special graphics or not, are treated as though they contain only words. This technique provides a measure of the content of books in terms of "equivalent" words, and is probably the most reliable method available for comparing the amount of material published in individual titles.

With regard to number of copies printed in the first year of the book's life the data in Table 7.6.1 suggest that over the period 1968-1975 the 11 university presses that published these 239 titles gradually reduced the size of their average print-runs. The average number of copies printed falls from one year to the next in five out of seven years. Furthermore, average number of copies printed for the 138 titles published in the first four years of the eight-year period, that is, from 1968 to 1971, equals 2,970 while the average for the 101 titles of the four subsequent years is only 2,700, a drop of 9 per cent.

The figures for the commercial publishers also suggest that some reduction has taken place in size of print-runs over the years, but the reductions are not quite as pronounced as they are for the university-press titles. The number of copies printed fell in four out of seven years; the average for the earlier four years is 6,330 and for the latter, 6,043, a difference of less than 5 per cent. It should be noted, however, that the unusually large average of 8,310 copies printed for the 13 titles published in 1975 had much to do with the more gradual reduction observed for commercially published titles. We cannot tell whether the surge in 1975 is indicative of some general resurgence in the size of print-runs for commercial firms or merely an incident of the small sample, but the latter of the two possibilities seems to provide the more plausible explanation.

If a reduction over the years in the average number of copies printed per title could be shown on the basis of conclusive evidence, it would raise several questions regarding the economic health of book publishing. For example, would the reduction in the sizes of the print-runs reflect a gradual adjustment by publishers to shrinking demand by both libraries and individuals confronted with shrinking buying power (budgets and incomes not keeping up with the increases in book prices)? Would this affect books in general or certain types of books in particular, perhaps only in certain subject areas? Would the smaller print-runs be the result of supply conditions rather than demand conditions, for example, an increase in the total number of titles published without a corresponding increase in the total number of books bought, and therefore a reduction in the average number of copies sold per title? Would it be the result of publishers raising dramatically the prices of their books in the hope of obtaining increased revenues? If so, were they successful, or did they perhaps find the markets for their books characterized by price-elastic demand so that revenues actually declined when prices were raised?

The figures in Table 7.6.1 corroborate an almost self-evident generalization: that university presses publish books that cannot reach the sales volume which commercial publishers have to attain if they are to make a profit. One of the raisons d'être of university presses is that they are prepared to publish books with sales potentials insufficient to yield profits. This is the ground on which their status as not-for-profit organizations is justified. The statistical evidence bears out that the average print-runs of books published by university presses are below those of commercially published books. In each of the eight years, the average for university-press titles is below the average for commercially published titles. For all vintages combined, the 239 titles of university presses average 2,860 copies printed per title, less than half the 6,190 copies printed for the average title of commercial publishers.

Number of pages per title and number of words per title for the 397 titles display no notable pattern over the years, but again, there is an obvious difference between the two types of publishers. In every year except one, 1974, the number of pages per title is larger for commercially published titles than for university-press titles and for each of the eight years the number of words per title is larger for the commercially published titles. For the eight vintage years combined, the commercially published books in the sample had an average of 379 pages per title, or 23 per cent more than the 309 pages which were the average for books published by university presses; the former titles had an average of 181,600 words, a full 40 per cent more than the university-press titles with an average of 129,300 words.

Aside from revealing these and similar differences about the books published by the two types of publishers, the figures of varying magnitudes displayed in Table 7.6.1 strongly suggest the desirability of expressing variables in standard units.

The dollar values of costs and prices per standard units that appear in the next several tables are all expressed in constant 1977 dollars. After all, we cannot very well compare costs and prices of different years if they are expressed in terms of noncomparable dollar values. The deflator used is the same as that used in Chapter 7.5 to deflate the flows of costs and revenues in the calculations of gross margins — the "Gross Product Originating" deflator for Printing and Publishing Industries (see Appendix 7A for the source and for the annual values of the GPO deflator). This is an appropriate deflator because it reflects the prices of the goods and services that are likely to be purchased by publishers. Thus, for example, when nominal list prices are converted to constant dollar values using this deflator we will be able to see if the increases in the prices of books kept pace with the increases in the costs of publishing.

PLANT COSTS PER PAGE AND PER 1,000 WORDS OF TEXT

Plant costs were defined in Chapter 7.3 as, "nonrecurring costs such as composition (typesetting), reproduction proofs, negatives, plates, dies, artwork and so on." These are one-time costs that would not have to be incurred again if the title were reprinted from existing plates. Plant costs are the fixed costs of producing a title; they do not vary with the number of copies printed.

By Type of Publisher

Table 7.6.2 presents in constant 1977 dollars plant costs per page of text and plant costs per 1,000 words of text, for the same sample of 397 titles that appears in Table 7.6.1. These figures are averages per title, meaning that costs per page and per 1,000 words calculated for each title individually are given equal weight in the average.

There appears to be some indication that plant costs per page and per 1,000 words declined slightly for the university-press titles over the 1968-1975 period. Plant costs per page were $22 in 1968 and remained above $20 through 1971, but fell to $18 in 1972 and then to $16 for the remaining three years 1973, 1974, and 1975 — all expressed in constant 1977 dollars. Plant costs of the commercially published titles show no particular pattern over the eight-year period. There was a peculiar surge of standard costs in 1971 for both types of publish-

TABLE 7.6.2 Plant Costs per Page and per 1,000 Words of Text in Constant 1977 Dollars for 397 Titles (239 by University Presses, 158 by Commercial Publishers) by Vintage Years 1968 to 1975, and All Vintages Combined

	Number of titles			Plant costs per page			Plant costs per 1,000 words of text		
Vintage	University press	Commercial	All titles	University press	Commercial	All titles	University press	Commercial	All titles
1968	31	23	54	$22	$24	$23	$54	$52	$53
1969	35	24	59	$20	$21	$20	$54	$45	$50
1970	34	16	50	$21	$24	$22	$54	$54	$54
1971	38	20	58	$24	$29	$26	$63	$65	$64
1972	26	20	46	$18	$26	$21	$45	$59	$51
1973	29	25	54	$16	$22	$19	$40	$48	$44
1974	28	17	45	$16	$23	$19	$44	$49	$46
1975	18	13	31	$16	$21	$18	$45	$53	$48
All vintages	239	158	397	$20	$24	$22	$51	$53	$52

Source: Machlup, Leeson, and Associates.

ers; plant costs per page hit highs of $24 for university presses and $29 for commercial publishers, and plant costs per 1,000 words peaked at $63 for university presses and $65 for commercial publishers. We have no explanation for this bulge in the series.

Costs per page of the books of university presses are below those of the commercial publishers in every one of the eight years shown. This consistent inequality does not hold for plant costs per 1,000 words of text. Indeed, in the two years 1968 and 1969, the plant costs per 1,000 words were higher for the university presses than for the commercial publishers; and in 1970 they were the same for both groups, even though on a per-page basis the books of university presses cost less than those of the commercial publishers in each of these years.

The differences in the rankings of the two types of publishers with regard to plant costs in those three years can be the consequence of only one factor, namely, differences in the average number of words per page. Normally, by which we mean in all eight vintage years, the average book of the 239 published by university presses had 401 words per page while the average for the 158 books of commercial publishers was 467 words per page. In 1968, 1969, and 1970, the larger number of words per page in the books of commercial publishers led to the observed results: on a per-page basis the commercial publishers had higher plant costs than university presses in all three years; on a per-1,000-word basis, however, they had, in 1968 and 1969, lower plant costs than university presses and, in 1970, equivalent costs.

In Table 7.6.2, we see that average plant costs per page for titles of all vintages are $20 for university-press titles and $24 for commercially published titles; and per 1,000 words of text, $51 and $53 for the two types of publishers, respectively. It would be worthwhile to try to discover the reasons for these differences. Why are plant costs expressed in standard units generally lower for university-press titles than for commercially published titles? The following hypotheses may be offered tentatively:

Hypothesis 1: The Proportion of Books in the Natural Sciences — Perhaps plant costs can be expected, in general, to be larger for titles in the natural sciences, because of the prevalence of special graphics (formulas, equations, diagrams, etc) that tend to increase composition costs, a major component of plant costs. If the sample of books published by commercial houses contains a larger proportion of titles in the natural sciences than the sample of books by university presses, the observed results would be explained.

Hypothesis 2: The Proportion of Textbooks — Perhaps plant costs are higher for textbooks; since university presses publish a much smaller proportion of textbooks than commercial houses do, the observed results would be explained.

Hypothesis 3: Differences in General Cost Effectiveness — Perhaps plant costs are higher for commercial publishers because of differences in general cost effectiveness: university presses manage to incur smaller plant costs than commercial publishers.

An examination of the statistics of plant costs may support one of these alternative hypotheses — although they are not necessarily mutually exclusive but may be consistent with one another.

By Major Subject Area

Of the 239 university-press titles, 33 are in fields that fall under the general heading of natural sciences, 126 in fields of the social sciences, and 80 in fields of the humanities. (Let us be reminded that in order to condense scores of fields, or scholarly disciplines, into just three major subject groupings some arbitrary, indeed controversial, classifications must be made. See the table and footnote 12 of Chapter 7.5 for a list of the fields belonging to each of the three major subject groupings discussed here.) Of the 158 commercially published titles, 66 fall under the natural sciences, 59 under the social sciences, and 33 under the humanities. Thus, titles in the natural sciences account for only 14 per cent of the total sample of university-press products but almost half, 42 per cent, of the total sample of commercially published titles. In order to test Hypothesis 1, that the higher proportion of titles in the natural sciences explains the higher plant costs per page and per 1,000 words observed for the commercially published titles in Table 7.6.1, we have to separate the titles into the three major subject areas and calculate plant costs per standard units for each. The results in constant 1977 dollars for all vintages combined are as follows:

	University-press titles			*Commercially published titles*		
	Natural sciences	*Social sciences*	*Humanities*	*Natural sciences*	*Social sciences*	*Humanities*
All vintages:						
Plant costs per page	*$22*	*$20*	*$18*	*$23*	*$24*	*$24*
Plant costs per 1,000 words of text	*$56*	*$52*	*$49*	*$51*	*$54*	*$58*
Number of titles	*33*	*126*	*80*	*66*	*59*	*33*

These results seem not to support Hypothesis 1. Plant costs per page and per 1,000 words of text are not uniformly higher for titles in the natural sciences. On both bases, per-page and per-1,000-words, plant costs for titles in the natural sciences, although they are the highest among the three subject areas for the university-press titles, are in fact the lowest among the three subject areas for the commercially published titles. On a per-page basis plant costs are higher in the natural sciences for the commercially published than for the university-press titles, \$23 compared with \$22, but on a per-1,000-word basis they are lower for the commercially published titles, \$51 compared with \$56. A convenient way of demonstrating conclusively that the higher proportion of titles in the natural sciences is not the reason for the higher plant costs observed for the average of commercially published titles is to calculate standardized plant costs giving each subject area equal weight in the average. This is equivalent to taking a straight average of the cost figures in each of the three subject areas. On a per-page basis the unweighted average plant costs for the university-press titles is (\$22 + \$20 + \$18) ÷ 3 = \$20, and for the commercially published titles (\$23 + \$24 + \$24) ÷ 3 = \$24 (by coincidence these unweighted averages are the same as the weighted averages shown for all vintages in Table 7.6.2). On a per-1,000-word basis the unweighted average plant costs for the university-press titles is (\$56 + \$52 + \$49) ÷ 3 = \$52 and for the commercially published titles (\$51 + \$54 + \$58) ÷ 3 = \$54. Thus, even with each subject area given equal weight, plant costs per both standard units of measurement are higher for the commercially published titles. Hypothesis 1 is not supported by our data.

An interesting by-product of this breakdown of plant costs by subject area is the observation that university presses incur the highest plant costs in the natural sciences and the lowest in the humanities whereas the commercial publishers incur the lowest costs in the natural sciences and the highest in the humanities, with plant costs per standard units in the social sciences falling in between for both types of publishers. The data provide no clue to the reasons for these patterns.

Having considered and rejected Hypothesis 1 we may move on to Hypothesis 2.

By Functional Categories of Books

A second explanation that might be offered to account for the differences in plant costs observed for the university-press titles and the commercially published titles is the composition of each of the samples with respect to functional categories of books. Each of the 397 titles falls under one of the following categories:

(1) *Scholarly monographs* - written by research scientists and scholars in a given field, the contents of which generally, but not always, treat a single theme in great depth. The intended audiences for these titles consist primarily of other scientists and scholars and of advanced students involved in research in the same or related fields. Such titles usually contain original contributions to the "state-of-the-art."

(2) *Professional-reference books* - written by research scientists, engineers, and scholars, or by technically qualified practitioners of the state-of-the-art in a given field, the contents of which are generally, but not always, intended for application to problems in industry and government. The intended audiences for these titles consist primarily of technically competent practitioners in the given field.

(3) *College textbooks* - written in most instances by university professors for use in classroom instruction at colleges and universities, the contents of which are intended to provide, on an introductory or advanced level, the foundations for an understanding of accepted knowledge and current issues in a given field. The intended audiences for these titles are college students, both graduate and undergraduate.

(4) *General interest books* - written by scientists, scholars, technically qualified practitioners or laypersons, the contents of which are designed to provide less technical treatments of topics in a given field that are of interest to the general public. The intended audience for these titles is the general public, usually educated readers who possess little or no technical training in the given field.

(5) *Elhi textbooks* - written by educators for classroom use in elementary schools and high schools.

A copy of each of the titles in the cohort sample was inspected to determine which of these functional categories described its contents and intended audiences. Admittedly, a few of the titles exhibited characteristics of more than just one of the five categories listed above. This was particularly true of scholarly monographs and professional-reference books.

In such borderline cases, titles were classified under the category that *best* described their function.[1]

The sample of 397 titles contains 260 scholarly monographs (197 by university presses, 63 by commercial publishers), 16 professional reference books (7 by university presses, 9 by commercial publishers), 91 college texts (18 by university presses, 73 by commercial publishers), 28 general-interest books (16 by university presses, 12 by commercial publishers), and 2 elhi texts (1 by each of the two types of publishers). Plant costs per page and per 1,000 words of text by functional category are shown on the following page for all vintage years combined. The figures are expressed in constant 1977 dollars and are shown separately for university-press titles and commercially published titles.

These results do not provide support for Hypothesis 2. That is to say, the lower plant costs observed for titles of university presses in the sample of 397 titles cannot be attributed to the relative weights given to textbooks in the subsamples of the two types of publishers. Although it is true that there is a larger proportion of textbooks in the sample of commercially published books (73 out of a total of 158, or 46 per cent) than in the sample of university-press books (18 out of a total of 238, or less than 8 per cent), textbooks do not have larger plant costs than titles in the other functional categories. In fact, if we ignore the results for the two elhi texts, we see that of the four remaining functional categories, college texts have comparatively low plant costs. Plant costs per page for the 18 college texts published by university presses are $19, the same as for scholarly monographs and professional-reference books and less than the $25 cost per

---

[1]The Association of American Publishers (AAP) in its annual *Industry Statistics* distinguishes several major categories of books. These include (1) professional; (2) university press; (3) college text; (4) elhi text; (5) subscription reference (encyclopaedias); (6) adult trade; (7) juvenile trade; (8) book clubs; (9) mail-order publications; (10) religious publications; (11) mass market paperback; and (12) all other (which includes maps, standardized tests, and audio-visual materials). Most of these categories lie beyond the scope of this study in which the emphasis is primarily on professional, university press, college text, and on some types of adult trade books. We did not adhere strictly to the AAP categories in classifying the cohort titles, because they were designed primarily to distinguish among types of publishers rather than among types of books. What AAP calls professional publishers or university presses, for example, might publish titles that conform with the definition given above in the text for scholarly monographs.

	Scholarly mono-graphs	Profes-sional-reference	College text	General interest	Elhi text
All vintages					
Plant costs per page					
University press	$19	$19	$19	$25	$14
Commercial	$22	$25	$24	$30	$31
All titles	$20	$22	$23	$27	$23
Plant costs per 1,000 words of text					
University press	$50	$52	$44	$70	$37
Commercial	$49	$57	$51	$83	$73
All titles	$50	$55	$50	$76	$55
Number of titles					
University press	197	7	18	16	1
Commercial	63	9	73	12	1
All titles	260	16	91	28	2

page shown for the 16 general-interest books. For commercial publishers plant costs per page for college texts are $24, less than the $30 for books in the general-interest category and the $25 for professional-reference books, though higher than the $22 for scholarly monographs.

On a per-1,000-word basis, college texts do even better compared with titles in the other functional categories, because they have, on average, more words per page. (Average number of words per page for all titles in the sample are 482 for college texts, 454 for general-interest books, 440 for professional-reference titles, and 408 for scholarly monographs.)

Books published by university presses have lower plant costs per page than those by commercial houses in all five functional categories. They also have lower plant costs per 1,000 words in four of the functional categories. The exception is scholarly monographs for which the commercial publishers manage to eke out a small edge with plant costs of $49 per 1,000 words as against $50 for the university presses.

We are now ready with a conclusion regarding the three hypotheses about relative plant costs. We have just found that there was no empirical evidence for Hypothesis 2 — suspecting the proportion of textbooks. We have previously seen that the statistical data disconfirm Hypothesis 1 — suspecting the proportion of books in the natural sciences. We are left with Hypothesis 3 as the only explanation — although we cannot be sure that no better alternatives could be found by persons more familiar with the conditions of the industry.

RUN-OFF COSTS PER STANDARD UNITS: PAPER, PRINTING, AND BINDING

Plant costs are the "fixed" costs of manufacturing a book, the direct costs incurred prior to the time the printing presses begin turning out copies. Hence, standardized measures of plant costs do not have to take account of the number of copies of the title printed. Plant costs per page or per 1,000 words will be the same for a title whether 500 copies or 15,000 copies are printed. This is not the case with the "variable" costs, sometimes referred to as run-off costs, of manufacturing a book — the costs of paper, printing, and binding. In order to express these costs in standard units, we must take account of the volume of output measured by number of pages and number of copies produced.

Table 7.6.3 presents in constant 1977 dollars standard measures of the costs of paper, printing, and binding for the same sample of 397 titles discussed in previous sections. Paper costs and printing costs are expressed "per signature per copy printed," a signature being a group of 32 pages, or equivalently, 16 leaves of paper. It was decided to use the signature as the unit of measure rather than the individual page, in order to avoid having to deal with very small decimal fractions. Binding costs are expressed "per copy bound."[2]

---

[2]The costs of paper and printing per signature are calculated using the formula:

$$\text{cost of paper (printing) per signature of 32 pages, or 16 leaves} = \frac{\text{total cost of paper (printing)}}{\left[\text{total number of pages per title} \times \frac{\text{number of copies printed}}{32}\right]};$$

note that the expression in the denominator of this ratio takes account both of number of pages and number of copies printed, i.e., of the total output in terms of pages. Binding costs per copy bound are calculated by dividing total costs of binding for each title by the number of copies bound.

TABLE 7.6.3 Paper Cost per Signature per Copy Printed, Printing Cost per Signature per Copy Printed, and Binding Cost per Copy Bound in Constant 1977 Dollars for 397 Titles (239 by University Presses, 158 by Commercial Publishers) by Vintage Years 1968 to 1975, and All Vintages Combined

Vintage	Number of titles			Paper cost per signature per copy printed (16 leaves or 32 pages)			Printing cost per signature per copy printed (32 pages)			Binding cost per copy bound		
	University press	Commercial	All titles	University press	Commercial	All titles	University press	Commercial	All titles	University press	Commercial	All titles
1968	31	23	54	$.055	$.037	$.047	$.092	$.031	$.066	$1.00	$.67	$.86
1969	35	24	59	$.063	$.048	$.057	$.065	$.072	$.068	$1.15	$.71	$.97
1970	34	16	50	$.054	$.037	$.049	$.053	$.023	$.043	$ .86	$.67	$.80
1971	38	20	58	$.045	$.041	$.044	$.058	$.030	$.048	$ .88	$.73	$.83
1972	26	20	46	$.041	$.038	$.040	$.065	$.032	$.051	$ .85	$.59	$.74
1973	29	25	54	$.044	$.032	$.038	$.070	$.038	$.055	$ .91	$.55	$.74
1974	28	17	45	$.044	$.041	$.043	$.052	$.041	$.048	$ .85	$.73	$.80
1975	18	13	31	$.075	$.044	$.062	$.063	$.032	$.050	$1.09	$.58	$.88
All vintages	239	158	397	$.052	$.040	$.047	$.065	$.039	$.054	$ .94	$.65	$.82

Source: Machlup, Leeson, and Associates.

According to the values displayed in Table 7.6.3, paper costs per signature per copy printed are higher for the university-press titles than for the commercially published titles in every one of the eight vintage years shown. Costs for the university-press titles appear to be edging downward between 1969 and 1974 and then shoot up precipitously to $.075 per signature in 1975. There does not appear to be any particular trend in the cost of paper for the commercially published titles. For all vintage years combined, the cost of paper for a 32 page signature of the average university-press title is $.052 and for the average commercially published title only $.040.

Printing costs per signature per copy printed and binding costs per copy bound exhibit similar characteristics. While there may be no discernible trends in values for these two categories of direct manufacturing costs for either the university-press or the commercially published titles, there is a remarkable consistency in the relative values of these costs for the two types of publishers — the costs of both printing and binding incurred by the university presses are larger than the costs incurred by the commercial publishers for every one of the eight vintage years. For all vintage years combined, it cost the university presses $.065 to print one 32 page signature for the average title, while it cost the commercial publishers only $.039; it cost the university presses $.94 to bind one copy of the average title, the commercial publishers only $.65.

Some of this difference in binding cost can be attributed to the fact that there is a lower proportion of paperbound titles in the sample of university-press books than in the sample of commercially published books. Nevertheless, for both types of cover the university presses have higher binding costs. The 219 hardbound titles of university presses in the sample of 239 have an average binding cost of $1.00, while the 114 hardbound titles of commercial publishers in the sample of 158 have an average binding cost of $.81. The 20 paperbound titles of university presses have average binding costs of $.40, while the 44 paperbound titles of commercial publishers have average binding costs of only $.24.

The rather striking differences in run-off costs observed for university-press and commercially published titles in Table 7.6.3 can be summarized in terms of percentages. For the books produced by university presses, the average cost of paper per signature is 30 per cent higher, the average cost of printing per signature is 67 per cent higher, the average cost of binding a hardbound book is 23 per cent higher, and the average cost of binding a paperbound book is 67 per cent higher than for the books produced by commercial publishers.

DIRECT MANUFACTURING COSTS PER STANDARD UNITS: PLANT AND RUN-OFF COSTS COMBINED

The data that we have observed thus far suggest that university presses incur lower plant costs, the fixed component of direct cost, than commercial publishers, but that commercial publishers incur lower run-off costs, the variable component of direct costs. In this section we will observe for the average book of the two types of publishers the combination of both the fixed and variable components of direct manufacturing costs: total direct cost per copy printed, total direct cost per page printed, and total direct cost per 1,000 words printed. The figures expressed in constant 1977 dollars are displayed in Table 7.6.4.

For each of the three standard measures shown and in all eight vintage years, direct manufacturing costs are higher for the books published by university presses than for those of commercial publishers. For two of the three standard measures the largest differences observed between the two types of publishers occur in 1975, when direct costs for university presses were 53 per cent higher on a per-copy basis ($5.17 compared with $3.39) and 100 per cent higher on a per-page basis ($.016 compared with $.008). In the same year, direct costs per 1,000 words were 155 per cent higher for university presses ($.051 compared with $.020), but this is not the largest difference for this standard measure. In 1968, direct costs per 1,000 words were 208 per cent higher for the not-for-profit publishers ($.037 compared with $.012).

For the products of university presses there was a steady decline in direct costs per copy between 1968 and 1973, from $4.67 to $3.94. The trend was reversed in 1974; and then in 1975 cost per copy shot up abruptly to $5.17, the highest value of any of the eight years. Costs per page and per 1,000 words followed the same general pattern, though the declines over the period in these standard measures were interrupted by occasional increases or by unchanged values. The manufacturing costs of commercially published books seem to exhibit no noteworthy trends.

For books of all vintage years combined, direct costs per copy are 23 per cent higher for university presses than for commercial publishers ($4.35 compared with $3.55), direct costs per page are 50 per cent higher for the not-for-profit publishers ($.015 compared with $.010), and direct costs per 1,000 words are 90 per cent higher for the university presses ($.040 compared with $.021). One explanation for this steady progression in the percentage differences in costs between the two types of publishers, from 23 per cent on a per-copy basis, to 50 per cent on a per-page basis, to 90 per cent on a per-1,000-word basis, relates to the "fixed" nature of plant costs and to differences in the number of copies printed, number of pages per title and number of words per page between the books of the

TABLE 7.6.4 Direct Cost per Copy Printed, Direct Cost per Page Printed, and Direct Cost per 1,000 Words Printed in Constant 1977 Dollars for 397 Titles (239 by University Presses, 158 by Commercial Publishers) by Vintage Years 1968 to 1975, and All Vintages Combined

Vintage	Number of titles			Direct cost (plant, paper, printing, binding) per copy printed			Direct cost per page printed			Direct cost per 1,000 words printed		
	University press	Commercial	All titles	University press	Commercial	All titles	University press	Commercial	All titles	University press	Commercial	All titles
1968	31	23	54	$4.67	$3.26	$4.07	$.015	$.009	$.013	$.037	$.012	$.026
1969	35	24	59	$4.57	$4.22	$4.43	$.016	$.011	$.014	$.043	$.022	$.034
1970	34	16	50	$4.35	$3.81	$4.18	$.016	$.009	$.014	$.043	$.022	$.036
1971	38	20	58	$4.22	$4.06	$4.16	$.016	$.011	$.014	$.042	$.025	$.036
1972	26	20	46	$4.01	$3.14	$3.63	$.014	$.010	$.012	$.034	$.024	$.030
1973	29	25	54	$3.94	$2.98	$3.50	$.013	$.009	$.011	$.032	$.020	$.026
1974	28	17	45	$4.15	$3.55	$3.92	$.014	$.012	$.013	$.040	$.026	$.035
1975	18	13	31	$5.17	$3.39	$4.42	$.016	$.008	$.013	$.051	$.020	$.038
All vintages	239	158	397	$4.35	$3.55	$4.03	$.015	$.010	$.013	$.040	$.021	$.032

Source: Machlup, Leeson, and Associates.

commercial publishers and those of the university presses in the sample. It should be obvious that plant costs, a major component of total direct costs, are fixed in the sense that they do not increase with the number of copies printed of a book. Thus, it stands to reasons that for given plant costs per title, the titles with larger print-runs will have lower plant costs *per copy* than titles with smaller print-runs. Similarly, titles with more pages will have lower plant costs per page, and titles with more words will have lower plant costs per word.

We have already seen that the titles of commercial publishers in the sample have not only larger print-runs, but more pages per title, and more words per page than the titles of the university presses. This means that the disparity in terms of physical output between the two types of publishers is greater on a per-page basis than on a per-copy basis, and greater still on a per-1,000-word basis,[3] thus accounting for the progressively larger percentage differences in the standard costs. Incidentally, these three different results regarding the relative costs incurred by the two types of publishers illustrate rather well the importance of standardizing measures before attempting to make comparisons. The answer to a question such as *how much* higher the manufacturing cost of a book is at university presses than at commercial publishers will depend on which of the three standard measures one has in mind.

An explanation of why the three different standard measures result in somewhat different conclusions regarding relative costs of the two types of publishers does not explain fully why the university-press titles consistently exhibit higher direct costs than the commercially published titles. Granted that while some of the difference can be attributed to spreading fixed costs over a larger number of copies, pages, or words, this is only part of the story. Direct costs also contain variable costs, the cost of paper, printing, and binding, and these are incurred whenever an *additional* copy of a book is printed. Furthermore, we have already learned from Table

---

[3]A simple example will illustrate the point. If a university-press title has a print-run of 2,000 copies, has 250 pages of text, and has 350 words per page, and a commercially published title has a print-run of 3,000 copies, has 350 pages of text, and has 400 words per page, then, on a per-copy basis, the output of the commercially published title is 50 per cent higher than the output of the university-press title (3,000 copies compared with 2,000 copies); on a per-page basis, the output of the commercially published title is 110 per cent higher (1,050,000 pages compared with 500,000 pages); and on a per-1,000-word basis, 140 per cent higher (420,000 words compared with 175,000 words).

7.6.3 that these variable costs are all higher for the university-press titles: paper costs per signature per copy printed are higher by 30 per cent; printing costs per signature per copy printed are higher by 67 per cent; and binding costs per (hardbound) copy bound are higher by 23 per cent. It seems reasonable to speculate that part of the difference in direct cost per standard units for the two types of publishers might be a result of lower prices available to commercial firms because they provide larger volumes of business to their suppliers of printing services — more titles and more copies of each printed — than university presses.

MARK-UP FACTORS: THE MARGIN BETWEEN MANUFACTURING COST AND LIST PRICE

In addition to covering the direct costs of manufacturing, the publishers' sales revenues have to cover several categories of indirect expenses as well as the costs of distributing the books. Indirect expenses include operating expenses, such as editorial salaries, production, promotion, and selling expenses, and general and administrative expenses. In addition, provisions have to be made for unsalable inventory and noncollectible debts. There is an additional cost, which is not part of the publishers' direct or indirect costs, but which acts in the same direction. Publishers must offer an incentive to wholesalers and bookstores to induce them to carry and sell the books. The major incentive is usually provided by selling books to the distributors at some discount below list price. More will be said about discounts later on. Thus, in order to cover indirect expenses, to provide for discounts to distributors, and, in the case of commercial publishers, to earn profits as well, list price for each title has to be set at some multiple of direct manufacturing costs.

Direct costs and list price per copy, per page, and per 1,000 words of text are shown in Table 7.6.5 in constant 1977 dollars for the sample of 239 university-press titles and the sample of 158 commercially published titles. Also shown for each of the standard measures are the "mark-up" factors — the multiple by which direct manufacturing costs are multiplied to get an idea for an appropriate list price.

List Prices by Type of Publisher

Before going to the mark-up factors shown in Table 7.6.5, it might be helpful to look first at the average list prices of the titles involved. The prices as well as the costs appearing in the table have been deflated by an index of the prices of the value added component of Printing and Publishing

Industries ("Gross Product Originating" deflator), which provides a measure, presumably, of the price increases of a substantial portion of the goods and services purchased by publishers as inputs for their own productive processes. Hence, we may examine the average prices shown in Table 7.6.5 and subsequent tables with the following thoughts in mind: If the list prices expressed in constant 1977 dollars remained essentially *stable* over the years, one may conclude that the publishers increased the prices of their books in consonance with increases in the costs of the inputs they must purchase; if list prices in constant 1977 dollars *declined* over the years, the publishers raised the prices of their books less than the costs of the inputs they purchase; and if the constant-dollar list prices *increased* over the years, the publishers raised the prices of their books more than the costs of the inputs they purchase. These guidelines will help in determining whether, or to what extent, the publishers recognized the ongoing cost-and-price inflation over the period and took steps to keep pace with it.

Constant-dollar list prices of the average university-press book in the sample, per copy, per page, and per 1,000 words, seem neither to rise consistently nor to fall consistently, but fluctuate in value from one year to the next over the eight-year period. Their general level does not seem to change noticeably either up or down over the period and we may therefore conclude that for this small sample the prices of the publishers' final product maintained parity with the prices of their inputs. For the commercial publishers, list prices per copy follow essentially the same pattern, displaying no particular trend. Their list prices per page and per 1,000 words, however, show, between 1968 and 1974, a definite and strong upward movement and then a sharp drop in 1975. List price per page for the average book of commercial publishers increased, with only one interruption, from \$.039 in 1968 to \$.062 in 1974, a rise of nearly 60 per cent in constant-dollar values. List price per 1,000 words for the average book increased from \$.089 to \$.135 over the same period, a rise of more than 50 per cent. Thus, on a per-page and per-1,000-word basis, the commercial publishers raised their prices faster than the increases in the costs of their inputs. A comparison of average prices of the two types of publishers shows that, while the university-press books are less costly to the final purchasers *per copy*, they are more costly to buy than the books of commercial publishers on both a per-page and per-1,000-word basis. A copy of the typical university-press book costs \$15.62, and of the typical commercially published book \$17.14. However, per page the list price of the average university-press book is \$.055, some 12 per cent more than the \$.049 for the commercaily published books, and per 1,000 words \$.143, or 29 per cent more than the \$.111 for the for-profit publishers.

TABLE 7.6.5 Mark-Up Factors — Direct Cost and List Price per Copy, per Page, and per 1,000 Words in Constant 1977 Dollars, and the Multiplicative Factors (Mark-Up) by Which List Price Exceeds Direct Cost for 397 Titles (239 by University Presses, 158 by Commercial Publishers) by Vintage Years 1968 to 1975, and All Vintages Combined

		University-press titles								
		Per copy			Per page			Per 1,000 words		
Vintage	Number of titles	Direct cost per copy	List price per copy	Mark-up factor per copy	Direct cost per page	List price per page	Mark-up factor per page	Direct cost per 1,000 words	List price per 1,000 words	Mark-up factor per 1,000 words
1968	31	$4.67	$16.76	3.6	$.015	$.057	3.8	$.037	$.141	3.8
1969	35	$4.57	$16.26	3.5	$.016	$.060	3.8	$.043	$.163	3.8
1970	34	$5.35	$13.22	3.0	$.016	$.052	3.3	$.043	$.137	3.2
1971	38	$4.22	$14.44	3.4	$.016	$.054	3.4	$.042	$.143	3.4
1972	26	$4.01	$16.53	4.1	$.014	$.059	4.2	$.034	$.148	4.4
1973	29	$3.94	$16.19	4.1	$.013	$.055	4.2	$.032	$.133	4.2
1974	28	$4.15	$15.18	3.7	$.014	$.054	3.9	$.040	$.156	3.9
1975	18	$5.17	$17.85	3.5	$.016	$.050	3.2	$.051	$.139	2.7
All vintages	239	$4.35	$15.62	3.6	$.015	$.055	3.7	$.040	$.143	3.6

(continued)

TABLE 7.6.5, continued

Vintage	Commercially published titles									
		Per copy			Per page			Per 1,000 words		
	Number of titles	Direct cost per copy	List price per copy	Mark-up factor per copy	Direct cost per page	List price per page	Mark-up factor per page	Direct cost per 1,000 words	List price per 1,000 words	Mark-up factor per 1,000 words
1968	23	$3.26	$13.97	4.3	$.009	$.039	4.3	$.012	$.089	7.4
1969	24	$4.22	$18.02	4.3	$.011	$.047	4.3	$.022	$.095	4.3
1970	16	$3.81	$17.23	4.5	$.009	$.045	5.0	$.022	$.111	5.0
1971	20	$4.06	$18.34	4.5	$.011	$.049	4.5	$.025	$.110	4.4
1972	20	$3.14	$15.84	5.0	$.010	$.052	5.2	$.024	$.127	5.3
1973	25	$2.98	$17.66	5.9	$.009	$.054	6.0	$.020	$.126	6.3
1974	17	$3.55	$18.16	5.1	$.012	$.062	5.2	$.026	$.135	5.2
1975	13	$3.39	$19.01	5.6	$.008	$.043	5.4	$.020	$.098	4.9
All vintages	158	$3.55	$17.14	4.8	$.010	$.049	4.9	$.021	$.111	5.3

Source: Machlup, Leeson, and Associates.

Mark-Ups by Type of Publisher

Proceeding now to the topic of the relative mark-up of list prices above direct manufacturing costs, we see from Table 7.6.5 that, for all vintage years combined, the mark-up factors of the university-press titles were lower than the mark-up factors of the commercially published titles, and this is true for each of the three standard measures. Per copy, per page, and per 1,000 words, the not-for-profit publishers established a list price for the typical title that was, respectively, 3.6, 3.7, and 3.6 times direct manufacturing cost; the for-profit publishers established a list price that was, respectively, 4.8, 4.9, and 5.3 times direct manufacturing cost.

For individual vintage years, mark-up factors for the university presses were above 4.0 in only two years, 1972 and 1973. In contrast, mark-ups for commercial firms never fell below 4.0, and for the two vintage years, 1968 and 1973, were above 6.0 on a per-1,000-word basis. Even if we go behind the figures shown in Table 7.6.5 and calculate mark-up factors separately for hardbound titles and for paperbound titles, the same general picture emerges. For all vintage years combined, the 219 hardbound titles of university presses have mark-up factors per copy, per page, and per 1,000 words of 3.6, 3.7, and 3.7, respectively, while the 114 hardbound titles of commercial firms have mark-up factors of 4.8, 4.9, and 4.9, respectively. The 20 paperbound books of university presses have mark-up factors of 3.0, 2.8, and 2.8 for the three standard measures, while the 44 paperbound books of the commercial publishers have mark-up factors of 5.2, 5.3, and 5.4.

The obvious differences between the university presses and the commercial publishers in the values of mark-ups is not an unexpected finding for at least two reasons. First, unlike the commercial publishers, the university presses are not-for-profit organizations and are, by definition, not in business to earn profits. The commercial firms, on the other hand, are for-profit organizations and consequently must make an additional provision for profits when determining an appropriate mark-up. Secondly, university presses are, in many cases, not completely independent in a financial sense from their parent universities. As a result, part of their indirect expenses, such as office space, equipment, and mail services to name a few, may be defrayed with funds from the sponsoring institution. Even those university presses that are required by agreement with their universities to meet all of their expenses, often receive support from outside benefactors in the form of unrestricted funds or special subsidies that are used to defray some or all of the costs of publishing particular books.

Mark-Ups by Major Subject Areas

There are some interesting differences in direct costs, list prices, and mark-up factors among the three major subject areas — natural sciences, social sciences, and humanities. Table 7.6.6 contains for all vintage years combined the relevant figures on a per-copy basis for the two types of publishers.

With regard to direct cost per copy, the results displayed in the table suggest that among the three subject areas the university presses incur the highest costs per copy in the humanities, $4.70, and the lowest costs in the natural sciences, $3.85, while the commercial publishers incur the lowest costs per copy in the humanities, $2.35, and the highest in the natural sciences, $4.90, with direct costs per copy in the social sciences falling in between for both types of publishers.[4]

List prices vary accordingly. The university presses charge the highest prices for titles in the humanities, $16.08, and the lowest for titles in the natural sciences, $14.55, while the commercial firms charge the lowest prices in the humanities, $10.21, and the highest in the natural sciences, $25.02, with prices for titles in the social sciences falling in between for both types of publishers.

For the university-press titles the resulting mark-up factors for the natural sciences, social sciences, and humanities are 3.8, 3.8, and 3.4, respectively, and for the commercial publishers 5.1, 4.5, and 4.3, respectively.

The patterns of costs, prices, and mark-ups observed for the commercial publishers suggest something about how they may view the markets for books in the three subject areas. Apparently, they have found that they can charge top-dollar for the books they publish in the natural sciences and hence are able to apply the largest mark-ups to the direct costs of such titles. Indeed, applying as they do the highest mark-up, 5.1, to titles with the highest direct costs to begin with, $4.90, results in list prices far higher than for titles in the two other subject areas. If the publishers were unable to sell books in the natural sciences in sufficient quantities at these high prices, we would expect these titles to have the *lowest* mark-ups, thereby bringing list prices closer to the levels of titles falling under the other subject classifications. The commercial publishers in the sample seem to approach their

---

[4]This is just the reverse of what we observed earlier for plant costs. The university presses had their highest plant costs in the natural sciences and their lowest in the humanities, while the commercial publishers had their highest plant costs in the humanities and their lowest in the natural sciences. Apparently, the variable costs included in the total direct costs are responsible for the reversal.

TABLE 7.6.6 Mark-Up Factors by Major Subject Area — Direct Cost per Copy and List Price per Copy in Constant 1977 Dollars, and the Multiplicative Factors (Mark-Up) by Which List Price Exceeds Direct Cost, for 397 Titles (239 by University Presses, 158 by Commercial Publishers) by Major Subject Area for All Vintage Years, 1968-1975, Combined

	Natural sciences				Social sciences				Humanities			
	Number of titles	Direct cost per copy	List price per copy	Mark-up factor	Number of titles	Direct cost per copy	List price per copy	Mark-up factor	Number of titles	Direct cost per copy	List price per copy	Mark-up factor
All vintages												
University press	33	$3.85	$14.55	3.8	126	$4.14	$15.60	3.8	80	$4.70	$16.08	3.4
Commercial	66	$4.90	$25.02	5.1	59	$2.69	$12.19	4.5	33	$2.35	$10.21	4.3
All titles	99	$4.55	$21.53	4.7	185	$3.68	$14.51	3.9	113	$4.01	$14.37	3.6

Source: Machlup, Leeson, and Associates.

markets for humanities titles with less confidence, charging the lowest prices among the three subject areas. This, however, may be the result of the type of humanities books contained in the sample. If, for example, the sample contained a large proportion of very expensive art books, the results might be very different.

If these conjectures about the perceptions of the commercial publishers can be accepted as providing at least a partial explanation for the patterns observed in Table 7.6.6, then we might conclude that the university presses in the sample either publish their books for different audiences altogether or have, in general, very different experiences and perceptions than do commercial publishers regarding markets for books of the three subject areas.

DISCOUNTS BELOW LIST PRICE

A good portion of books sold do not pass directly from the publisher's warehouse to the final customer, but are sold first to intermediaries, or distributors, such as wholesalers and bookstores.[5] The intermediaries buy books from the publishers at a discount below list price and then re-sell them either at a smaller discount as, for example, when a wholesaler sells to a bookstore, or at no discount at all (full list price), as when a wholesaler sells to a final customer such as a library, or when a bookstore sells to an individual. Offering discounts to intermediaries as an incentive for carrying and selling books means that the publishers themselves receive for these copies less than the list price. The discounts may vary in size from just a few percentage points to 20 per cent, 40 per cent, and even higher, depending on the practices of the publisher, and frequently depending on the number of copies

---

[5]For example, according to data published in the 1975 edition of *Industry Statistics*, an annual publication of the Association of American Publishers prepared by John Dessauer, an industry statistician, a sample of 16 commercial firms that specialize in technical, scientific, business, and medical publications channeled some 50 per cent of total sales through intermediaries such as wholesalers and retail book stores. The remaining 50 per cent of sales was divided among the various categories of final purchasers — libraries and institutions, governments, industry, and individuals. A sample of 10 publishers of college textbooks channeled some 77 per cent of their sales through intermediaries, and according to the 1975 edition of *University Press Statistics*, also prepared by Mr. Dessauer, some 70 per cent of sales reported by 18 presses were channeled through intermediaries.

purchased, the type of book, its subject area and functional category, the intended audience, and so on. The same book is sometimes offered to different categories of customers at different discounts.

To obtain a measure of the size of the discounts offered by the two types of publishers in the cohort sample we can compare the average list price per copy of the titles with the average net (net of discounts) sales revenues actually received by the publishers per copy sold. Such a comparison results in a measure of an *effective* discount below list price, that is, a value that represents the average of the various discounts offered to different customers weighted by the number of copies sold to each. The discounts presented in Table 7.6.7 are effective discounts.

Before proceeding to the numerical data it is important to emphasize that the sample upon which the discussion of discounts is based is of a different composition than the uniform sample we have been observing all along in this chapter. Whereas the uniform sample contains 397 titles, 239 by university presses and 158 by commercial firms, the sample to which we will turn shortly contains 639 titles, 340 by university presses and 299 by commercial publishers. It was necessary to change the sample at this point because there were no data available from the publishers on sales revenue for several of the titles in the uniform sample of 397. That the new sample, nevertheless, is so much larger than the previous one is explained by the fact that values on only three variables were needed for a title to be included — list price, dollar sales in the first year of life, and number of copies sold in the first year of life. The last two magnitudes combined yield the sought-after value of sales revenue per copy. For the previous sample of only 397 titles, values had to be present for eight variables in order for a title to be included, and hence far fewer could qualify.[6]

Table 7.6.7 contains, again in constant 1977 dollars, average list price per copy, average net sales revenue per copy, and the resulting effective discount below list price, calculated for the sample of 639 book titles. The results by vintage year and by three major subject areas are shown for 340 university-press titles in the upper portion of the table and the results for analogous breakdowns are shown for 299 commercially published titles in the lower portion, with results for all vintage years combined for both types of publishers shown in the last row of the table.

---

[6]Of course, it would have been possible at the outset to have required in the selection of the uniform sample that data on sales revenue be available in order for a title to qualify. It was decided not to do so in order to avoid reducing the size of the uniform sample any further.

Since Table 7.6.7 contains average list prices by subject area for the two types of publishers, a statistic also shown in Table 7.6.6 but for the smaller uniform sample of 397 titles, we can compare the two sets of results to see what effect, if any, the increase in the sample size has on the averages obtained. In general, it seems correct to say that there are no great differences in the results for the two samples. For the university presses, books in the larger sample have only slightly higher list prices in the natural sciences, an average of $14.95 for the 44 titles in this sample compared with $14.55 for the 33 titles in the previous sample. Average list prices in the other two subject areas are somewhat lower for the larger sample, $14.15 (176 titles) compared with $15.60 (126 titles) for the previous sample in the social sciences and $14.38 (120 titles) compared with $16.08 (80 titles) in the humanities. For commercial publishers, the results for the two samples are not very different either. The average list price in the new, larger sample is, in the natural sciences, $25.84 (120 titles) compared with $25.02 (66 titles) in the previous sample; in the social sciences, $14.11 (126 titles) compared with $12.19 (59 titles) in the previous sample; and in the humanities, $11.09 (53 titles) compared with $10.21 (33 titles) in the previous sample. Thus, changing the size and composition of the sample has resulted in only minor changes in the calculated averages, a result that supports the claim made earlier in the chapter in the section on "An Optimistic Note on Sample Size" that, unlike the sales figures, values of list prices for related types of books are likely to exhibit relatively small variations within each category. Furthermore, since the new sample does not differ radically from the previous one, we can have greater confidence that the change in sample will not excessively impair the continuity and consistency of the analysis.

The results on average list price and net sales revenue per copy for titles of all subject areas and all vintage years combined are shown in the lower right-hand corner of Table 7.6.7. The average list price in constant 1977 dollars for all 639 titles equals $16.18 and the average net sales revenue equals $11.20. The difference between the two, that is, the effective discount, is $4.98, which is 30.7 per cent of list price. For both types of publishers and for all vintage years, titles in the natural sciences and humanities have similar effective discounts, 32.2 and 32.5 per cent of list price, respectively. Titles in the social sciences have a lower effective discount of only 28.7 per cent.

The 340 titles of the university presses for all vintage years combined have, in percentage terms, a slightly higher effective discount than do the 299 titles of commercial publishers: 32.4 per cent compared with 29.3 per cent. A possible explanation for the observed difference in effective discounts, though only a hunch, may be that university presses

TABLE 7.6.7 Average Discount below List Price by Major Subject Area — List Price per Copy and Net Sales Revenue per Copy in Constant 1977 Dollars, and the Resulting Percentage Discount below List Price for:
A. 340 Titles by University Presses by Major Subject Area and All Subject Areas, for Vintage Years 1968 to 1975, and All Vintage Years Combined
B. 299 Titles by Commercial Publishers by Major Subject Area and All Subject Areas, for Vintage Years 1968 to 1975, and All Vintage Years Combined
C. 639 Total Titles by Major Subject Area, All Vintages Combined

	Natural sciences				Social sciences				Humanities				All subject areas			
Vintage	Number of titles	List price per copy	Net sales revenue per copy	Average discount below list price per cent	Number of titles	List price per copy	Net sales revenue per copy	Average discount below list price per cent	Number of titles	List price per copy	Net sales revenue per copy	Average discount below list price per cent	Number of titles	List price per copy	Net sales revenue per copy	Average discount below list price per cent
A. University-Press Titles																
1968	5	$15.31	$12.52	18.2	24	$15.39	$11.96	22.3	14	$18.73	$12.72	32.1	43	$16.47	$12.27	25.5
1969	5	$15.10	$10.29	31.9	23	$14.03	$ 9.28	33.9	18	$15.67	$ 7.97	49.1	46	$14.79	$ 8.88	40.0
1970	5	$12.08	$ 8.47	29.9	26	$12.56	$ 8.54	32.0	15	$13.05	$ 8.45	35.2	46	$12.67	$ 8.50	32.9
1971	8	$17.90	$11.91	33.5	25	$13.81	$10.16	26.4	9	$11.82	$ 8.37	29.2	42	$14.17	$10.11	28.7
1972	5	$17.53	$12.44	29.0	20	$13.56	$ 8.76	35.4	16	$13.65	$ 9.51	30.3	41	$14.08	$ 9.50	32.5
1973	5	$14.73	$ 9.79	33.5	20	$14.22	$ 9.61	32.4	22	$15.77	$10.57	33.0	47	$15.00	$10.08	32.8
1974	6	$11.13	$7.40	33.5	21	$13.74	$8.98	34.6	16	$12.93	$ 8.04	37.8	43	$13.07	$ 8.41	35.7
1975	5	$14.85	$10.52	29.2	17	$16.56	$10.92	34.1	10	$10.73	$ 7.53	29.8	32	$14.47	$ 9.80	32.3
All vintages of uni-sity press titles	44	$14.95	$10.45	30.1	176	$14.15	$ 9.76	31.0	120	$14.38	$ 9.27	35.5	340	$14.33	$ 9.68	32.4

(continued)

TABLE 7.6.7, continued

Vintage	Number of titles	List price per copy	Net sales revenue per copy	Average discount below list price per cent	Number of titles	List price per copy	Net sales revenue per copy	Average discount below list price per cent	Number of titles	List price per copy	Net sales revenue per copy	Average discount below list price per cent	Number of titles	List price per copy	Net sales revenue per copy	Average discount below list price per cent
B. Commercially Published Titles																
1968	14	$24.24	$16.72	31.0	12	$15.73	$11.87	24.5	8	$12.87	$ 9.60	25.4	34	$18.56	$13.34	28.1
1969	19	$27.09	$18.73	30.9	13	$12.67	$10.07	20.5	10	$12.49	$10.49	16.0	42	$19.15	$14.09	26.4
1970	12	$25.63	$17.31	32.5	13	$14.49	$10.41	28.2	4	$ 9.51	$ 6.88	27.7	29	$18.41	$12.78	30.6
1971	19	$25.88	$19.85	23.3	22	$15.71	$11.73	25.3	4	$ 8.57	$ 7.84	8.5	45	$19.37	$14.82	23.5
1972	16	$23.36	$14.57	37.6	13	$18.17	$14.68	19.2	12	$10.74	$ 8.02	25.3	41	$18.02	$12.69	29.6
1973	17	$25.37	$16.35	35.6	17	$11.84	$ 8.69	26.6	5	$12.56	$ 8.50	32.3	39	$17.83	$12.00	32.7
1974	17	$23.74	$15.91	33.0	20	$11.97	$ 8.76	26.8	4	$11.33	$ 7.58	33.1	41	$16.79	$11.61	30.9
1975	6	$39.89	$22.36	43.9	16	$13.22	$ 8.95	32.3	6	$ 8.45	$ 6.69	20.8	28	$17.92	$11.34	36.7
All vintages of commercially published titles	120	$25.84	$17.42	32.6	126	$14.11	$10.51	25.5	53	$11.09	$ 8.49	23.4	299	$18.28	$12.93	29.3
C. All Vintages, University-Press and Commercially Published Titles																
All vintages	164	$22.92	$15.55	32.2	302	$14.13	$10.07	28.7	173	$13.37	$ 9.03	32.5	639	$16.18	$11.20	30.7

Source: Machlup, Leeson, and Associates.

sell a larger proportion of their books to libraries than do the commercial firms and thus channel a larger proportion of their sales through wholesalers of books who are usually offered the most favorable discounts.

Among university-press titles, those in the humanities have the highest percentage discounts of the three subject areas, with net sales revenues actually received per copy some 35.5 per cent below the average list price. Thus, even though the average list price of $14.38 for these 120 humanities titles is slightly higher than $14.15 for the 176 titles in the social sciences, the average revenue actually received per copy is lower for the humanities titles, $9.27 compared with $9.76 in the social sciences, because of the larger effective discounts in the humanities. The commercial publishers in the sample have the highest effective discount, 32.6 per cent below list price, for books in the natural sciences, the subject area with the highest list price among the three, $25.84 per copy. They have the lowest effective discount, 23.4 per cent below list price, for books in the humanities, the subject area with the lowest list price, $11.09 per copy. Books in the social sciences hold the middle position for both list prices and percentage discounts. By offering the highest discounts on books with the highest prices and the lowest discounts on books with the lowest prices the commercial publishers attain smaller differences among books of the three subject areas in terms of revenues actually received than they do in terms of list prices. Thus, for commercial publishers,

average list price in the natural sciences is:
 83 per cent higher than in the social sciences, and
 133 per cent higher than in the humanities;
however,

average net sales revenue in the natural sciences is only:
 66 per cent higher than in the social sciences, and
 105 per cent higher than in the humanities.

Over the years there does not seem to be any noticeable pattern in effective discounts and this is true for both types of publishers as well as for all three subject areas.

Discounts for the various functional categories, not shown in Table 7.6.7, are as follows: scholarly monographs, 35.2 per cent for 259 university-press titles and 28.7 per cent for 112 commercially published titles; professional-reference books, 29.8 per cent for 6 university-press titles and 31.5 per cent for 21 commercially published titles; college textbooks, 30.0 per cent for 28 university-press titles and 30.7 per cent for 113 commercially published titles; and general-interest books, 36.3 per cent for 35 university-press titles and 22.9 per cent for 30 commercially published titles.

MORE ON LIST PRICES

There is more to say about list prices in this look behind gross margins. We shall first see from the sample data the extent to which publishers raised the prices of titles over the years of their lives. We shall then compare the average list prices of titles in the cohort sample with average list prices of a much larger sample of titles in an effort to see the extent to which the cohort data can be considered representative of the population of books published in the United States.

Increases in the List Prices of Books over Their Lifetimes

Average list prices shown for each vintage year in Tables 7.6.6 and 7.6.7 are list prices that were established for the titles in the year of their publication. During inflationary periods, however, the price initially established will rarely remain unchanged by the publisher over a book's lifetime. This is illustrated very clearly by the figures presented in Table 7.6.8. Here the values are expressed in *current* dollar values, that is, unadjusted for price inflation, to show the increases in the nominal dollar prices that took place. In the left-hand portion of the table appear the average list prices in each year of life for a total of 383 university-press titles from the cohort sample, separated by year of publication. In the right-hand portion are the analogous figures for 312 commercially published titles. The number of titles in each cohort are shown below the average list prices. As a result of titles going out of print, the number of titles in the samples changes slightly in the later years of life for some cohorts. For example, there are 47 titles in the 1968 cohort of university-press titles, but one of them goes out of print in the eighth year of life. The average price shown, $12.66, refers to the remaining 46 titles in the group. In one instance, for the 1970 cohort of 55 titles, one title goes out of print in the fourth year of life and then is reprinted and returns to life again in the fifth year.

Reading the current-dollar values in Table 7.6.8 from top to bottom provides us with a glimpse of changes in the average list prices of books of successive cohorts, that is, of books published in different years. Reading the table from left to right provides a glimpse of changes in the average list price of the same groups of books in successive years of their lives. Thus, for example, the average list price in the first year of life for the 47 titles published in 1968 by university presses is $9.36. Reading across the row we see that eight years later, that is, in 1975, this same group of titles (minus one) had an average list price of $12.66, an increase of 35.3 per cent. On the other hand, the 34 new titles published in

TABLE 7.6.8 Average List Price per Title in Each Year of Life in Current (Undeflated) Dollars for 695 Titles (383 by University Presses, 312 by Commercial Publishers) by Vintage Years 1968 to 1975

Vintage	University-press titles								Per cent change, first year to last year
	Year of life								
	1st	2nd	3rd	4th	5th	6th	7th	8th	
1968	$ 9.36	$ 9.72	$ 9.92	$10.33	$10.60	$10.85	$11.91	$12.66	+35.3
Number of titles	47	47	47	47	47	47	47	46	
1969	$ 9.20	$ 9.22	$ 9.38	$ 9.58	$ 9.66	$10.66	$11.68	-	+27.0
Number of titles	51	51	51	51	51	51	50	-	
1970	$ 8.03	$ 8.14	$ 8.23	$ 8.57	$ 8.99	$ 9.62	-	-	+19.8
Number of titles	55	55	55	54	55	55	-	-	
1971	$ 9.76	$ 9.86	$10.04	$10.67	$11.26	-	-	-	+15.4
Number of titles	51	51	51	51	50	-	-	-	
1972	$ 9.96	$ 9.93	$10.50	$10.95	-	-	-	-	+9.9
Number of titles	47	47	47	46	-	-	-	-	
1973	$11.19	$11.27	$11.93	-	-	-	-	-	+6.6
Number of titles	50	50	50	-	-	-	-	-	
1974	$10.61	$10.75	-	-	-	-	-	-	+1.3
Number of titles	48	48	-	-	-	-	-	-	
1975	$12.98	-	-	-	-	-	-	-	-
Number of titles	34	-	-	-	-	-	-	-	
Per cent change 1968-1975	+38.7								

(continued)

TABLE 7.6.8, continued

	Commercially published titles								Per cent change, first year to last year
	Year of life								
	1st	2nd	3rd	4th	5th	6th	7th	8th	
1968	$10.27	$10.45	$11.23	$11.68	$11.75	$12.34	$12.74	$13.70	+33.4
Number of titles	42	42	42	42	42	42	42	40	
1969	$11.67	$12.16	$12.41	$12.47	$13.19	$14.00	$15.65	-	+34.1
Number of titles	42	42	42	42	42	42	42	-	
1970	$11.81	$11.93	$12.03	$13.24	$13.88	$15.25	-	-	+29.1
Number of titles	31	31	31	31	31	31	-	-	
1971	$13.48	$13.83	$14.31	$15.28	$17.14	-	-	-	+27.2
Number of titles	46	46	46	46	44	-	-	-	
1972	$12.65	$12.70	$13.14	$14.25	-	-	-	-	+12.6
Number of titles	41	41	41	40	-	-	-	-	
1973	$12.85	$12.77	$13.49	-	-	-	-	-	+5.0
Number of titles	40	40	39	-	-	-	-	-	
1974	$13.15	$13.42	-	-	-	-	-	-	+2.1
Number of titles	42	42	-	-	-	-	-	-	
1975	$16.17	-	-	-	-	-	-	-	-
Number of titles	28	-	-	-	-	-	-	-	
Per cent change 1968-1975	+57.4								

Source: Machlup, Leeson, and Associates.

1975 and shown in the bottom row of the table had, in their *first* year of life, an average list price of $12.98, 38.7 per cent above the average price of $9.36 for the 47 titles published in 1968.

For both types of publishers, the price increases over the lives of the same titles is slightly less than the price increases for successive cohorts of titles with one exception — the 1971 cohort of 46 titles of commercial publishers. Books in that cohort had their prices increased over the years from $13.48 in the first year of life (1971), to $17.14 in the fifth year of life (1975), or by 27.2 per cent. Over the same period, 1971-1975, the average list price of *new* titles rose from $13.48 to $16.17, an increase of only 22.5 per cent.

That publishers make such upward adjustments in the list prices of titles over their lives is perfectly sensible. The new prices charged today for books published years ago are, in effect, a reflection, not of original costs incurred years before, but of replacement costs — the cost of publishing the same title today. To sell at a list price that was set when the dollar was worth more paper, more labor, more of any good or service would be foolish, irresponsible, and surely uneconomical.

Table 7.6.8 shows a few interesting differences in list prices charged by the two types of publishers. In every case the average list prices of books of commercial publishers are higher than the prices of books of university presses. Moreover, the commercial firms were apt to raise the prices of the same titles over the years at a faster rate. In current dollars, average prices of titles published in 1971, for example, were raised over the subsequent four years, a period characterized by high rates of cost-and-price inflation in the economy as a whole, by 15.4 per cent by university presses and by 27.2 per cent by commercial publishers. This may help to explain the plight of university-press publishing in the early 1970's; university presses did not perceive that there was an inflation going on; in any case, they failed to act quickly enough to raise their prices to keep pace with it. Consequently, they charged, in real terms, less and less for their books as years went by.

A Comparison of the Cohort Sample with the Bowker Series

There are a total of 695 titles in the cohort sample for which list prices were obtained during the data-collection phase of the study. Average list prices for these titles, shown earlier in Table 7.6.8 in nominal dollar values, are shown in Table 7.6.9 in constant 1977 dollars, by vintage year and by major subject areas, separately for university presses and commercial publishers and then for both types of publishers combined.

There are somewhere between 30 and 40 thousand titles published in the United States each year, hence, by comparison the fewer than 100 titles per vintage year in the cohort sample constitute a rather small sample. In order to show that the average list prices of books in the cohort sample are of the same order of magnitude as the average list prices for much larger samples of books, Table 7.6.9 also presents the Bowker series of list prices for some 207,379 book titles.[7]

A few points about the derivation of the averages for the two sets of samples shown in Table 7.6.9 — the cohort sample and the Bowker series — ought to be mentioned before we look at the figures themselves. First, the cohort sample of 695 titles contains approximately 100 paperbacks. The Bowker series, on the other hand, contains "U.S. Hardcover Trade-Technical Books: Average Prices."[8] This heading may be misleading, however, since a footnote to the 1974 table remarks, "Not included are 'mass market paperbacks,'" and a footnote to the 1975 table remarks ". . . certain classes of books are known to be *under-reported* (some textbooks and many mass market paperbacks)." With regard to the first footnote, one wonders why it is necessary even to mention the exclusion of mass-market paperbacks in a table labeled "Hardcover Books," unless, of course, other types of paperbacks *are* included, so-called quality paperbacks, for example. Furthermore, why in the second instance are mass-market paperbacks said to be *under-reported*? Indeed, they should not be reported at all.

A second point worth noting is that prior to 1971 the Bowker averages were apparently calculated with each title being given equal weight in the average — as is the case in the cohort sample. After 1970, however, each *volume* was given equal weight, presumably meaning that the prices of individual volumes of books that have more than one volume under the same title are counted separately. If this is not confusing enough, the 1974 series of average list prices makes reference to the number of *books* in the sample, without saying whether it is titles or volumes.

With regard to classification by subject area the two samples are not strictly comparable either. For the cohort sample the sub-fields contained under each of the three major subject

---

[7]The Bowker list prices are taken from various editions of *The Bowker Annual of Library and Book Trade Information*.

[8]Actually, the headings of the tables in the *Bowker Annual* are not the same in every year. In 1974, for example, the title used is the one mentioned above in the text. In 1975 the title of the series reads "Average Price per Volume of Hardcover Books."

TABLE 7.6.9 Average List Price per Title in Constant 1977 Dollars by Major Subject Area for 397 Titles (239 by University Presses, 158 by Commercial Publishers), and for 207,379 Titles from the Bowker Series of List Prices, Vintage Years 1968-1975

	Average list price per title - cohort sample			
	University-press titles			
Vintage	Natural sciences	Social sciences	Humanities	All subject areas
1968	$15.31	$15.45	$17.25	$16.03
Number of titles	5	26	16	47
1969	$18.06	$14.30	$15.17	$15.10
Number of titles	6	24	21	51
1970	$10.70	$12.70	$12.29	$12.29
Number of titles	7	28	20	55
1971	$17.81	$14.19	$11.34	$14.29
Number of titles	11	28	12	51
1972	$18.77	$14.05	$12.84	$14.19
Number of titles	6	23	18	47
1973	$15.72	$14.18	$16.43	$15.41
Number of titles	6	21	23	50
1974	$11.13	$14.62	$12.39	$13.39
Number of titles	6	25	17	48
1975	$14.85	$16.19	$10.74	$14.38
Number of titles	5	19	10	34
All vintages	$15.46	$14.39	$13.89	$14.36
Combined number of titles	52	194	137	383

(continued)

TABLE 7.6.9, continued

Vintage	Average list price per title - cohort sample			
	Commercially published titles			
	Natural sciences	Social sciences	Humanities	All subject areas
1968	$23.77	$14.63	$12.66	$17.59
Number of titles	16	15	11	42
1969	$27.09	$12.67	$12.49	$19.16
Number of titles	19	13	10	42
1970	$25.01	$14.10	$ 9.51	$18.08
Number of titles	13	14	4	31
1971	$26.42	$15.71	$ 8.57	$19.74
Number of titles	20	22	4	46
1972	$23.35	$18.17	$10.74	$18.03
Number of titles	16	13	12	41
1973	$25.36	$11.87	$12.56	$17.69
Number of titles	17	18	5	40
1974	$23.74	$11.81	$11.33	$16.60
Number of titles	17	21	4	42
1975	$39.89	$13.23	$ 8.45	$17.92
Number of titles	6	16	6	28
All vintages	$25.78	$13.91	$11.15	$18.13
Combined number of titles	124	132	56	312

(continued)

TABLE 7.6.9, continued

Vintage	Natural sciences	Social sciences	Humanities	All subject areas
	Average list price per title - cohort sample			
	All titles combined			
1968	*$21.75*	*$15.14*	*$15.38*	*$16.77*
Number of titles	*21*	*41*	*27*	*89*
1969	*$24.92*	*$13.73*	*$14.30*	*$16.93*
Number of titles	*25*	*37*	*31*	*93*
1970	*$20.01*	*$13.16*	*$11.83*	*$14.37*
Number of titles	*20*	*42*	*24*	*86*
1971	*$23.36*	*$14.87*	*$10.65*	*$16.87*
Number of titles	*31*	*50*	*16*	*97*
1972	*$22.10*	*$15.53*	*$12.00*	*$15.97*
Number of titles	*22*	*36*	*30*	*88*
1973	*$22.84*	*$13.11*	*$15.74*	*$16.41*
Number of titles	*23*	*39*	*28*	*90*
1974	*$20.45*	*$13.34*	*$12.19*	*$14.89*
Number of titles	*23*	*46*	*21*	*90*
1975	*$28.51*	*$14.84*	*$ 9.88*	*$15.99*
Number of titles	*11*	*35*	*16*	*62*
All vintages	*$22.72*	*$14.20*	*$13.10*	*$16.05*
Combined number of titles	*176*	*326*	*193*	*695*

(continued)

TABLE 7.6.9, continued

Vintage	Bowker series of average list price per title for hardcover trade-technical books			
	Natural sciences	Social sciences	Humanities	All subject areas
1968	$20.93	$12.37	$12.74	$14.51
Number of titles	4,180	8,048	5,486	17,714
1969	$20.59	$14.33	$13.53	$15.38
Number of titles	3,696	8,778	5,364	17,838
1970	$23.88	$17.20	$16.07	$17.85
Number of titles	4,133	14,258	8,871	27,262
1971	$23.61	$20.43	$15.45	$19.41
Number of titles	4,960	15,562	9,314	29,836
1972	$22.50	$18.79	$15.99	$18.51
Number of titles	4,907	14,360	9,443	28,710
1973	$22.29	$16.18	$15.05	$16.80
Number of titles	4,828	14,365	9,975	29,168
1974	$24.23	$17.52	$14.21	$17.78
Number of titles	5,553	14,440	9,017	29,010
1975	$23.69	$17.81	$14.27	$17.94
Number of titles	5,625	13,916	8,300	27,841
All vintages	$22.84	$17.40	$14.85	$17.59
Combined number of titles	37,882	103,772	65,770	207,379

Sources: Machlup, Leeson, and Associates. <u>Bowker Annual of Library and Book Trade Information</u>, various editions.

headings — natural sciences, social sciences, and humanities — were shown in previous chapters. The Bowker series of list prices are reported in *The Bowker Annual of Library and Book Trade Information* by 23 sub-field classifications corresponding to various subject ranges of the Dewey Decimal System. Thus, it was necessary to reclassify each of these under one of the three major subject headings to obtain the figures shown in the table. The sub-fields of the Bowker classification falling under each of the three major headings used in this study are listed below.

Natural sciences, technology, and mathematics	*Social sciences*	*Humanities*
Agriculture	*Business*	*Art*
Medicine	*Education*	*Biography*
Science	*General works*	*Fiction*
Technology	*History*	*Language*
	Home economics	*Literature*
	Juveniles	*Music*
	Law	*Poetry, drama*
	Philosophy, psychology	*Religion*
	Sociology, economics	
	Sports, recreation	
	Travel	

This classification differs from that used for the cohort sample in a few important respects. Philosophy and psychology, sub-fields falling under different major subject areas in the cohort sample, are not separated in the Bowker series and so had to be assigned, as a pair, arbitrarily to either the social sciences or the humanities. We chose the social sciences. Also, the Bowker series contains many titles in a number of sub-fields that were of little interest to this study of "scholarly" books and which, as a consequence, are not well represented in the cohort sample. These include "Juveniles," "Sports, Recreation" and "Travel" under the social sciences, and "Fiction" under the humanities.

A final point regarding the two samples shown in Table 7.6.9 is that list prices in the cohort sample are shown separately for university presses and commercial publishers; no such breakdown is available for the titles in the Bowker series. The relative weight of university-press titles in the Bowker sample is not known. (Indeed, in some of the annual series from the *Bowker Annual* it is explicitly stated that university-press titles are excluded altogether; in others there is no mention of how such titles are treated.) Thus, there is no way of telling the extent to which the two samples differ on this count. It stands to reason that the cohort sample, in which

55 per cent of the titles are published by university presses, has a far smaller proportion of commercially published titles than does the Bowker sample. Hence, some of the differences observed in list prices for the two samples can be attributed to differences in their composition by type of publisher.

With all of these warnings in mind we may now look at the values presented in Table 7.6.9 for average list prices, expressed in constant 1977 dollars, for the cohort sample and the Bowker series.

Looking first at the results for all vintage years combined — shown in the last two rows of the table — we see that the average list price for all 695 books in the cohort sample is $16.05, slightly below, but still very close to, the $17.59 observed for the more than 207,000 titles in the Bowker series. We may note that the average price of $18.13 for the 312 books of commercial publishers in the cohort sample, is slightly *above* the Bowker average while the average price of $14.36 for the 383 books of university presses is *below* the Bowker average.

Relative prices of titles in the three major subject areas for all samples shown exhibit an extremely interesting regularity. Of the university-press titles and the commercially published titles in the cohort sample (and for both types of publishers combined) and of the titles in the Bowker series, books in the natural sciences have the highest prices, followed by books in the social sciences, with books in the humanities showing the lowest prices of the three categories. The largest differences in average list prices among the three subject areas is observed for books of commercial publishers in the cohort sample; the average title in the natural sciences costs $25.78 compared with $13.91 in the social sciences and $11.15 in the humanities. The smallest differences observed is for books of university presses; the average title in the natural sciences was offered for $15.46 compared with $14.39 in the social sciences and $13.89 in the humanities. These results bring to mind a point made earlier in the chapter after similar results were observed for a smaller sample — commercial firms have apparently learned that differing market conditions in the various subject areas allow the practice of price discrimination (in the economic, not legal, sense), meaning that revenues can be increased by charging higher prices in markets that are characterized by price-inelastic demand and lower prices in markets characterized by price-elastic demand. The experiences or perceptions of university presses have apparently been quite different, judging by the virtual uniformity of prices they charge for books in the different subject areas.

The differences in list prices among subject areas for the Bowker series are obvious. Though somewhat less pronounced than those observed for the commercial firms in the cohort sample, they are far more pronounced than those observed for the university presses.

Let us now consider price *changes* over the eight-year period shown. For all subject areas in the Bowker series, average list prices show a definite upward movement in the first four years, rising from $14.51 in 1968 to $19.41 in 1971. Since the prices in Table 7.6.9 are all expressed in constant 1977 dollars, the price increases observed are in "real" terms rather than in nominal terms, which indicates that the price increases outpaced inflation in the printing and publishing industries in general. After 1971, prices in the Bowker series fall somewhat for the first two years, first to $18.51 in 1972 and then to $16.80 in 1973, but rise in each of the next two years, to $17.78 in 1974 and $17.94 in 1975. The overall impression left by these trends is that the publishers increased prices in the late 1960's and very early 1970's, perhaps as a reaction to growing inflationary pressures in the economy in general, and then allowed prices to level off, in real terms, which implies that price increases for books just kept pace with the general price inflation in the output of the printing and publishing industries.

Changes in list prices for the commercial publishers in the cohort sample seem to parallel the changes for books in the Bowker series, with real prices rising somewhat in the late sixties and early seventies and then leveling off. Overall, the list prices for these publishers seem to have just kept pace with price inflation.

List prices of the university presses in the cohort sample show a different pattern over the period. Expressed in constant dollars, they actually fall in the early years of the series, from $16.03 in 1968 to $15.10 in 1969 to $12.29 in 1970. These drops in the real values of list prices imply that nominal prices were not increased fast enough by the university presses to keep up with the price inflation taking place in the prices of other goods produced by the printing and publishing industries, many of which are used as inputs to the production processes of publishers. After 1970 real list prices were increased slightly and then leveled off for the remainder of the period shown.

With regard to the three major subject categories, it seems that both university presses and commercial publishers were most reluctant to raise their prices in the humanities. For university presses, for example, prices for these titles fell from $17.25 in 1968 to $11.34 by 1971; they recovered a little in the two subsequent years. By 1975, however, the real price of the average title in the sample was down to $10.74, some 38 per cent below the $17.25 charged for the average humanities title in 1968. For the commercial publishers in the cohort sample, constant-dollar prices in the humanities went down from $12.66 in 1968 to $8.57 in 1971, made some recovery in the next two years, and then began falling again in 1974, ending the series at $8.45, the lowest average price of any of the eight years.

These developments are not visible in the Bowker series. There the average list prices of humanities titles did not decline, but were raised less rapidly than titles in the social sciences, but not noticeably faster than the prices of titles in the natural sciences.

THE PLIGHT OF THE UNIVERSITY PRESSES

With all the many comparisons made in this chapter, one may have lost sight of some of the strategic differences in costs and prices of the two types of publishers. It would not be unwarranted, therefore, though it is repetitive, to have a special section emphasizing the differences that can explain why loud complaints were heard in the early 1970's about the plight of scholarly publishing, at a time when commercial publishers seemed to be doing quite well.

First, we saw that direct manufacturing costs were higher for the books published by university presses than for those of commercial publishers, in part because university presses tend to publish more "short-run" books — books for which relatively few copies are printed. This was true in all eight years considered in the analysis; it was true no matter whether costs were measured on a per-copy, per-page, or per-1,000-word basis. In some years the differences were particularly large, for example, in 1975, when direct manufacturing costs for university presses were 53 per cent higher per copy, 100 per cent higher per page, and 155 per cent higher per 1,000 words than the costs of commercial publishers.

Secondly, we saw that for the university presses the "markups" — the multiplicative factor by which direct costs are multiplied to determine an appropriate list price — are consistently lower than for commercial publishers. Thus, the university presses are left with a smaller margin between direct costs and list prices, the margin needed to defray indirect expenses.[9] Furthermore, we saw some evidence that ef-

---

[9]An interesting sidelight to this story on the relative costs and mark-ups of the two types of publishers is that on a per-copy basis the university presses incur *higher* manufacturing costs than do the commercial firms, but apply a mark-up sufficiently small to establish list prices that are *lower* than those of the commercial firms. From the point of view of those who purchase and/or read the books, the lower prices charged by university presses are no doubt welcomed. However, since the titles of the commercial firms have, on average, more pages and more words per page, the buyer is actually paying more per page and per 1,000 words for the average university-press book.

fective discounts below list price are slightly higher for university presses than for commercial firms. This further reduces the relative margin between direct costs and list price for the not-for-profit publishers.

Thirdly, with regard to list prices per copy we saw that, on average, the university presses consistently charged less than the commercial firms. In addition, university presses tended to raise the prices of the same books over the years of their lives less than the commercial publishers.

Finally, with regard to the relative prices charged for books in the three subject areas, we saw that commercial publishers apparently took advantage of differences in demand conditions, charging comparatively high prices for books in the natural sciences and comparatively low prices for books in the humanities. In contrast, the university presses charged similar prices in all three areas.

We are left with the conclusion that on all four grounds the university presses are likely to end up with less satisfactory bottom lines on their income-and-expense statements than commercial publishing houses.

CHAPTER 7.7

BEHIND GROSS MARGINS: LIFETIME PATTERNS OF PHYSICAL SALES

The final questions to be considered in our look behind gross margins concern the distribution of physical sales ("unit sales," in the vernacular of the publishing industry) over a good portion of the lifetime of titles.

Specifically, we will use the cohort data to provide some tentative answers to the following questions:

> On average, how many copies of a title are likely to be sold over its lifetime? (Practical limitations prevent us here from observing sales over the entire lives of books. We will have to settle for a shorter, though significant, portion of the entire life — the first six years.)
>
> How are sales likely to be distributed over the years? That is, what per cent of sales for all years occur in the first and second years of life, the third year, the fourth, and so on?
>
> As has been the practice in this study, answers to these questions will be provided separately for titles of the two types of publishers, of the three major subject areas, and of the various functional categories.

SELECTING THE APPROPRIATE COHORTS

It was pointed out in Chapter 7.4 that in a study of cohorts of books one is confronted by a number of trade-offs between the span of years that can be observed for each cohort and the age of the most recent vintage of titles that would qualify for inclusion in the analysis. These trade-offs give rise to a variety of possible arrangements of the data on sales histories, with each providing a slightly different perspective on the question of patterns of sales over the lives of the titles.

Available Choices

Several possibilities for presenting the data were considered during the preparation of this chapter in an effort to determine which would be most suitable for a discussion of the patterns of physical sales that lie behind gross margins. Here are some of the arrangements that were considered:

1. One-year histories of sales for each of the 8 vintages, 1968-1975; the most recent vintage (relative to 1975) is 0 years old.
2. Two-year histories of sales for each of the 7 vintages, 1968-1974; the most recent vintage (relative to 1975) is 1 year old.
3. Three-year histories of sales for each of the 6 vintages, 1968-1973; the most recent vintage (relative to 1975) is 2 years old.
4. Four-year histories of sales for each of the 5 vintages, 1968-1972; the most recent vintage (relative to 1975) is 3 years old.
5. Five-year histories of sales for each of the 4 vintages, 1968-1971; the most recent vintage (relative to 1975) is 4 years old.
6. Six-year histories of sales for each of the 3 vintages, 1968-1970; the most recent vintage (relative to 1975) is 5 years old.
7. Seven-year histories of sales for each of the 2 vintages, 1968-1969; the most recent vintage (relative to 1975) is 6 years old.
8. Eight-year histories of sales for the 1 vintage, 1968; the most recent vintage (relative to 1975) is 7 years old.

Had we chosen the first arrangement, for example, we could have presented data for all eight vintage years, 1968 through 1975, but only on unit sales in the first year of life, not a very significant portion of the total lifetime of the average title in the cohort sample. Alternatively, we might have chosen the fourth arrangement and could have presented data for each of the five vintages, 1968 through 1972, displaying the pattern of unit sales over the first four years of life for the titles in each cohort. In fact, we prepared tables for all eight of the arrangements of data listed above, and went even further by preparing for each vintage additional breakdowns showing results by type of publisher, subject area, and functional category.

The Futility of Comparisons among Vintage Years

The exercise proved to be of great value in deciding how the data could best be organized and tabulated for the discussions in this chapter.

It became apparent from the many work tables made that little could be said with much confidence about the comparative performances of cohorts of titles of different vintage years. By dividing the entire cohort sample first into eight separate vintages and then by type of publisher, subject area, and functional category, the sample sizes became far too small to produce meaningful results. Here again, as was the case earlier with regard to net dollar sales in the calculations of gross margins, one or two titles with unusually large or small unit sales caused dramatic changes in the "average" calculated for the cohort to which they belong. Thus, we were forced to concede the futility of attempting to discover from such small samples whether there were any discernible trends in the patterns of lifetime sales of successive vintages of titles.

Reaching Back for Older Titles

A second observation made by studying the preliminary work tables was that a large majority of the titles in the cohort sample, both university press and commercial, had rather long life cycles, meaning that most books continued to sell for several years after the year of publication. We concluded that few valuable insights regarding patterns of "lifetime" sales could be gleaned from observing a mere one or two years of the total life history of a title. This meant that titles of more recent vintage would have to be ignored in the analysis; they are simply too young to tell us very much about the life of books.

The Need to Distinguish among Classes of Books

A third observation made from the work tables was that there exist obvious differences in patterns of physical sales over the lives of titles of different types of publishers, of different subject areas, and in different functional categories. It may be recalled that in the analyses of gross margins (in Chapter 7.5) and of direct manufacturing costs and list prices (in Chapter 7.6) important differences were also noted among these various classes of books. It therefore seems appropriate to provide, in the present chapter, analogous discussions on patterns of physical sales.

The Cohorts Chosen: A Combination of Vintage Years

Observations made on the preliminary work tables have thus provided the guidelines for selecting appropriate cohorts for the analyses in this chapter: (1) that no attempt be made to compare patterns of sales among titles of individual vintage years, (2) that the more recently published titles be omitted in an analysis of lifetime histories, and (3) that important differences in sales patterns exist among the categories of books distinguished in the earlier chapters.

The maximum number of years of life history that could be studied for any of the titles in the cohort sample is eight, but if this period of time were chosen as the observed life cycle only 94 titles, those published in 1968 (see Table 7.4.2), would qualify. (The eighth year of life for titles published in 1968 is 1975, the last year for which data are available.) A way of enlarging the sample would be to settle for a fewer number of years of history. If a seven-year life cycle were chosen, titles published in both 1968 and 1969 could be combined to form a single sample and observed; and if a six-year life cycle were chosen, titles published in 1968, 1969, and 1970 could be combined and observed. The size of the sample could be increased further by including titles published in 1971 but, again, only at the expense of an additional year of life history of all titles falling in the larger cohort. Since most of the titles continued selling even after six years of life — though only in relatively small quantities — it was decided not to reduce the available life histories to less than a six-year horizon. Thus, the cohorts selected for the analysis of life-cycle patterns of physical sales contain a total of 272 titles, each belonging to one of the three vintage years 1968, 1969, or 1970.[1]

In order to combine the data from these three vintage years into a single sample to form the collective 1968-1970 age group, unit sales had to be aligned, not according to the calendar year in which sales occurred, but according to sequential year. Thus, unit sales in the first year of life of books published in 1968 were combined with unit sales occurring in the first year of life of the books published in 1969 as well as with sales occurring in the first year of life of the books of the 1970 vintage. Sales in the subsequent years of life of books of the three vintage years were combined in an analogous fashion.

---

[1]According to Table 7.4.2, the cohort sample contains a total of 280 titles published in these three years. Eight of the titles, however, had no data available on unit sales and had to be omitted from the sample.

THE RESULTS: PHYSICAL SALES OF UNIVERSITY PRESSES AND COMMERCIAL PUBLISHERS

Of the 272 titles in the newly formed 1968-1970 age group, 152 were published by university presses and 120 by commercial publishers. Comparisons will be made of the patterns of unit sales of books over the first six years of life for these two types of publishers as well as for books of different subject areas and functional categories.

The results for each of these several samples of titles are presented in Tables 7.7.1 through 7.7.6 and are arranged in each table in the same manner. First, the number of titles in the sample is given. In the tables this number remains unchanged over the six-year period. In reality, it may be the case that some of the titles have gone out of print or are just poor sellers, registering zero sales sometime before the end of the six-year period. Such titles are still considered to be part of the age group, though selling zero copies per year. To exclude the nonsellers would be to overstate the values of number of copies sold of the average title in the age group. However, in an assessment of the sales performance of an age group, the number of books whose sales have fallen to zero is an interesting statistic in itself, and is shown for each sample presented.

The second item shown for each sample is the total number of copies sold for all titles combined in each year of life, and in the extreme right-hand column, for all six years combined. This is used to calculate the next two items on the tables, the percent of six-year sales occurring in each of these years and, for good measure, the cumulative per cent from year to year. The next item shown in the tables is average number of copies sold per title, calculated by dividing total number of copies sold in any year by the number of titles. Finally, the last line shows the number of copies with zero sales in any particular year.

With one exception, to be explained presently, none of the data on the tables are shown separately for the first and second year of life. The reason for combining the results for the first two years is that some titles are released for sale in the beginning of their year of publication and have several months in which to rack up sales, while other titles are released shortly before the end of their year of publication and have little opportunity to accumulate sales. Since the distribution of such titles is probably not uniform from one sample to the next, comparisons of sales in the first year would be misleading. Combining the first two years mitigates this problem to some extent. In order to show the degree of the possible obfuscation resulting from merging the first two years, we make an exception in the fifth line of each of the tables and let it exhibit separately for the two years the average number of copies sold per title.

By Type of Cover

Table 7.7.1 presents six-year sales histories of 152 university-press books published during the period 1968-1970, with results shown separately for hardbound and paperbound titles. In the first six years of life combined, physical sales of the 132 hardbound books totaled 270,800 copies or 2,052 copies sold per the average title. Physical sales of the 20 paperbound titles for all six years combined amounted to 71,200 copies or 2,560 copies sold per the average title, 73 per cent above the average for the hardbound titles. In each year of life shown, the average number of copies sold per title is lower for the hardbound titles. In the first year of life, the average hardbound book sold below 1,000 copies (to be exact, 963), while the average paperbound sold 1,280 copies. By the fifth year of life the hardbound books were selling at the rate of 107 copies per title, compared with 310 of the paperbacks. One of the factors contributing to the lower average sales of hardbound books is the number that have ceased selling altogether. By the sixth year of life, 20 out of 132 hardbound titles, a full 15 per cent of the sample, registered zero sales. Only one of the 20 paperbound titles, 5 per cent of that sample, had zero sales.

The distributions of total six-year sales among the individual years of life shown in the table also display different patterns for hardbound and paperbound books. Some 71.8 per cent of total sales occurred in the first two years of life for the hardbound titles compared with only 59.6 per cent for the paperbacks; the cumulative per cent of total sales occurring by the end of the third, fourth, and fifth years remains higher for the hardbound titles.

The results for the combined sample of hardbound and paperbound books are presented toward the bottom of Table 7.7.1. The results observed for all titles are in large part a consequence of the relative weights in the total of books of the two types of covers.

We ought to keep in mind, of course, that the samples upon which these observations are based are rather small, and thus may not be representative of the patterns of sales of university-press books in general.

The size of the sample of commercially published titles is even smaller than that of university presses. Table 7.7.2 presents the results for 92 hardbound, 26 paperbound and the entire sample of 118 titles of the commercial publishers. For these publishers too, the average number of copies sold per title of paperbound books is higher than the number of copies sold of the average hardbound book; for all six years combined the former titles sold, on average, 9,358 copies, 66 per cent more than the 5,637 copies sold of the average hardcover book. Notice, however, that the difference in the average number of copies sold per title for the two types of covers narrows con-

TABLE 7.7.1 Titles of University Presses — The Distribution of Number of Copies of Books Sold over the First Six Years of Life of Cohorts Containing 132 Hardbound Titles, 20 Paperbound Titles, and All 152 Titles Combined Published by University Presses during the Period 1968-1970, with Average Number of Copies Sold per Title and Number of Titles with Zero Sales in Each Period

	Year of life					
	1st and 2nd combined	3rd	4th	5th	6th	All 6 years combined
Hardbound						
Number of titles in cohort	132	132	132	132	132	132
Total number of copies sold	194,300	28,500	18,900	15,000	14,100	270,800
Per cent of six-year sales in each period	71.8	10.5	7.0	5.5	5.2	100.0
Cumulative per cent	71.8	82.3	89.3	94.8	100.0	-
Average number of copies sold per title	1st--963/ 2nd--510	216	143	114	107	2,052
Number of titles with zero sales	0	4	7	12	20	-
Paperbound						
Number of titles in cohort	20	20	20	20	20	20
Total number of copies sold	42,400	11,000	4,500	7,100	6,200	71,200
Per cent of six-year sales in each period	59.6	15.4	6.3	10.0	8.7	100.0
Cumulative per cent	59.6	75.0	81.3	91.3	100.0	-
Average number of copies sold per title	1st--1,280/ 2nd-- 840	550	225	355	310	3,560
Number of titles with zero sales	0	0	2	1	1	-
All titles						
Number of titles in cohort	152	152	152	152	152	152
Total number of copies sold	236,700	39,500	23,400	22,100	20,300	342,000
Per cent of six-year sales in each period	69.2	11.6	6.8	6.5	5.9	100.0
Cumulative per cent	69.2	80.8	87.6	94.1	100.0	-
Average number of copies sold per title	1st--1,004/ 2nd-- 553	260	154	145	134	2,250
Number of titles with zero sales	0	1	4	9	13	21

Source: Machlup, Leeson, and Associates.

siderably from the first year of life to the sixth. In the first year of life the average paperbound sold 2,323 copies, 64 per cent more than the average hardbound book at 1,416 copies. By the sixth year, the paperbounds were selling at the rate of 619 copies per title, only 20 per cent above the rate of 517 copies per title for hardbound books. However, with regard to the comparative distributions over the six-year period of total unit sales of hardcover and papercover books, the commercially published titles seem to display an ordering just the opposite of that observed for university presses, with sales of the paperbound books skewed more toward the earlier years than sales of hardbound books, though the difference between the two distributions is far less pronounced than the difference seen for university-press books.

The data tell nothing about the reasons behind the differences observed and there do not seem to be any obvious and compelling intuitive explanations to offer. The differences may reflect the actual comparative sales patterns of the two types of publishers or they may be a coincidence of sample selection.

Some interesting comparisons can be made of the various results observed for the two types of publishers. We see that the commercial firms sold over the six-year period a larger number of copies of the average title than the university presses: for hardbound books 5,637 copies, compared with 2,052, and for paperbound books 9,358 copies, compared with 3,560. The average for the hardbound titles of the commercial publishers was even above the average for the paperbound titles of the university presses.

We see also that the time-profile of total sales over the first six years after publication is markedly different for the two types of firms. For both hardbound and paperbound titles physical sales of the university-press books are concentrated more in the early years of life, implying that the likelihood of selling a title diminishes over the years more quickly for the university presses than for the commercial publishers in the sample.

The differences in physical sales observed here are consistent with, indeed, help account for, the differences in gross margins observed in Chapter 7.5 for cohorts of university-press and commercially published titles. To connect these findings with those of the previous chapter on costs and prices, we may formulate as a conclusion, expected from the outset but now confirmed by quantitative "evidence," that, in general, university presses spend more to produce books, charge lower prices to their customers, sell fewer copies, and earn less gross and net revenues than commercial publishers.

TABLE 7.7.2 Titles of Commercial Publishers — The Distribution of Number of Copies of Books Sold over the First Six Years of Life of Cohorts Containing 92 Hardbound Titles, 26 Paperbound Titles, and All 118 Titles Published by Commercial Publishers during the Period 1968-1970, with Average Number of Copies Sold per Title and Number of Titles with Zero Sales in Each Period

	Year of life					
	1st and 2nd combined	3rd	4th	5th	6th	All 6 years combined
Hardbound						
Number of titles in cohort	92	92	92	92	92	92
Total number of copies sold	257,500	91,700	64,700	57,100	47,600	518,600
Per cent of six-year sales in each period	49.6	17.7	12.5	11.0	9.2	100.0
Cumulative per cent	49.6	67.3	79.8	90.8	100.0	-
Average number of copies sold per title	1st--1,416/ 2nd--1,383	997	703	621	517	5,637
Number of titles with zero sales	0	2	4	4	6	-
Paperbound						
Number of titles in cohort	26	26	26	26	26	26
Total number of copies sold	129,400	42,500	34,100	21,200	16,100	243,300
Per cent of six-year sales in each period	53.2	17.5	14.0	8.7	6.6	100.0
Cumulative per cent	53.2	70.7	84.7	93.4	100.0	-
Average number of copies sold per title	1st--2,323/ 2nd--2,654	1,635	1,312	815	619	9,358
Number of titles with zero sales	0	0	1	1	2	-
All titles						
Number of titles in cohort	118	118	118	118	118	118
Total number of copies sold	386,900	134,200	98,800	78,300	63,700	761,900
Per cent of six-year sales in each period	50.8	17.6	13.0	10.3	8.3	100.0
Cumulative per cent	50.8	68.4	81.4	91.7	100.0	-
Average number of copies sold per title	1st--1,616/ 2nd--1,663	1,137	837	664	540	6,349
Number of titles with zero sales	0	0	2	5	8	10

Source: Machlup, Leeson, and Associates.

By Major Subject Areas

Table 7.7.3 contains the results on patterns of unit sales for books of university presses for each of the three major subject areas — natural sciences, social sciences, and humanities. Table 7.7.4 contains analogous figures for the commercially published titles.

With regard to the subject-area composition of physical sales of university-press books during the first six years of life, it appears that sales in the social sciences are somewhat more concentrated toward the earlier years than sales in the natural sciences or in the humanities. For the sample of books in the social sciences, some 71.8 per cent of all books sold over a six-year period were sold in the first two years of life. By contrast, the samples of books in the natural sciences and humanities sold, respectively, only 65.6 per cent and 66.8 per cent of total six-year sales in the first two years of life.

Among university-press books, those in the natural sciences registered the highest number of copies sold per the average title at 3,083 for all six years combined. Social sciences were next with 2,332, and humanities last with only 1,874. It is interesting to note that the sample of humanities titles has the lowest figure for average number of copies sold per title even though it has the highest proportion of paperbound titles, 9 out of 57 (16 per cent) compared with only 2 out of 18 (11 per cent) for the natural sciences, and 9 out of 77 (12 per cent) for the social sciences. We might have expected the higher proportion of the better selling paperbound titles to raise the average for that cohort above the averages for the other two subject areas. That this has not happened suggests that the humanities titles clearly sell less well than titles in the other two areas.

With regard to commercially published titles, the figures in Table 7.7.4 indicate that physical sales in the social sciences are less concentrated toward the early years of life than physical sales of the other two subject areas, an ordering just the opposite of that already seen for the university-press books. That the sales of books in the social sciences are distributed somewhat more evenly over the six-year period than sales in the other two subject areas is an unexpected result for at least one reason. There is a higher proportion of paperbound books in the sample titles of the social sciences — 17 out of 47 (36 per cent), compared with only 1 out of 47 (2 per cent) in the natural sciences and 8 out of 24 (33 per cent) in the humanities. We saw earlier that sales of paperbound books tend to be slightly more concentrated in the earlier

TABLE 7.7.3 Titles of University Presses by Major Subject Area — The Distribution of Number of Copies of Books Sold over the First Six Years of Life for 152 Titles of University Presses (18 in the Natural Sciences, 77 in the Social Sciences, and 57 in the Humanities) Published during the Period 1968-1970, with Average Number of Copies Sold per Title and Number of Titles with Zero Sales in Each Period

	Year of life					
	1st and 2nd combined	3rd	4th	5th	6th	All 6 years combined
Natural sciences						
Number of titles in cohort	18	18	18	18	18	18
Total number of copies sold	36,400	7,500	2,700	5,000	3,900	55,500
Per cent of six-year sales in each period	65.6	13.5	4.9	9.0	7.0	100.0
Cumulative per cent	65.6	79.1	84.0	93.0	100.0	-
Average number of copies sold per title	1st--1,322/ 2nd--700	417	150	278	217	3,083
Number of titles with zero sales	0	0	2	1	2	-
Social sciences						
Number of titles in cohort	77	77	77	77	77	77
Total number of copies sold	128,900	19,900	11,800	10,000	9,000	179,600
Per cent of six-year sales in each period	71.8	11.1	6.6	5.5	5.0	100.0
Cumulative per cent	71.8	82.9	89.5	95.0	100.0	-
Average number of copies sold per title	1st--1,078/ 2nd--596	258	153	130	117	2,332
Number of titles with zero sales	0	4	6	8	12	-
Humanities						
Number of titles in cohort	57	57	57	57	57	57
Total number of copies sold	71,300	12,100	8,900	7,100	7,400	106,800
Per cent of six-year sales in each period	66.8	11.3	8.3	6.7	6.9	100.0
Cumulative per cent	66.8	78.1	86.4	93.1	100.0	-
Average number of copies sold per title	1st--804/ 2nd--447	212	156	125	130	1,874
Number of titles with zero sales	0	0	1	4	7	-

Source: Machlup, Leeson, and Associates.

TABLE 7.7.4 Titles by Commercial Publishers by Major Subject Area — The Distribution of Number of Copies of Books Sold over the First Six Years of Life for 120 Titles of Commercial Publishers (48 in the Natural Sciences, 48 in the Social Sciences, and 24 in the Humanities) Published during the Period 1968-1970, with Average Number of Copies Sold per Title and Number of Titles with Zero Sales in Each Period (Excluding 2 Titles with Extreme Values)

	Year of life					
	1st and 2nd combined	3rd	4th	5th	6th	All 6 years combined
Natural sciences						
Number of titles in cohort	47	47	47	47	47	47
Total number of copies sold	82,800	13,600	11,600	10,000	9,600	127,600
Per cent of six-year sales in each period	64.9	10.7	9.1	7.8	7.5	100.0
Cumulative per cent	64.9	75.6	84.7	92.5	100.0	-
Average number of copies sold per title	1st--1,081/ 2nd--681	289	247	213	204	2,715
Number of titles with zero sales	0	0	0	1	3	-
Social sciences						
Number of titles in cohort	47	47	47	47	47	47
Total number of copies sold	245,800	98,800	72,300	59,700	47,100	523,700
Per cent of six-year sales in each period	46.9	18.9	13.8	11.4	9.0	100.0
Cumulative per cent	46.9	65.8	79.6	91.0	100.0	-
Average number of copies sold per title	1st--2,336/ 2nd--2,833	2,102	1,538	1,270	1,002	11,143
Number of titles with zero sales	0	2	3	0	2	-
Humanities						
Number of titles in cohort	24	24	24	24	24	24
Total number of copies sold	58,300	21,800	15,000	8,600	7,200	110,900
Per cent of six-year sales in each period	52.6	19.6	13.5	7.8	6.5	100.0
Cumulative per cent	52.6	72.2	85.7	93.5	100.0	-
Average number of copies sold per title	1st--1,254/ 2nd--1,226	908	625	358	300	4,621
Number of titles with zero sales	0	1	3	5	4	-

Source: Machlup, Leeson, and Associates.

years of life than hardcover books. Apparently, the influence toward greater concentration exerted on the distribution by the paperbound titles in the sample is out-weighed by a countervailing influence exerted by virtue of the titles being of a particular subject class. The superior "staying power" of books in the social sciences is also apparent from the patterns over the years in average number of copies sold per title. In the first year of life the average book in the social sciences sold 2,336 copies, 116 per cent more than the 1,081 copies sold per title in the natural sciences and 86 per cent more than the 1,254 copies in the humanities. By the sixth year of life books in the social sciences still sell at a comparatively healthy clip, 1,002 copies per title, now some 391 per cent above the 204 copies sold per title in the natural sciences and some 234 per cent above the 300 copies sold per title in the humanities.

An interesting comparison may be made between sales of university-press books in the natural sciences and sales of the commercially published books in the same subject area. With regard to profiles of physical sales over the first six years of life, books in the natural sciences of both types of publishers display very similar tendencies with approximately 65 per cent of physical sales in the first two years of life, 84 per cent in the first four years, and 93 per cent in the first five years. A most unexpected result, however, is that in the natural sciences the average number of copies sold per title is actually higher for university presses than for commercial firms — 3,083 as against 2,715 copies. This is an exceptional finding since in the other two subject areas average sales of commercially published titles are far higher than sales of university-press books. Can we think of an explanation for the exception? We may recall from Chapter 7.6 that the list prices charged by commercial firms for books in the natural sciences are far above the prices charged by university presses. To recall a few statistics, average list price in constant 1977 dollars for 120 titles published between 1968 and 1975 by commercial publishers was $25.84 compared with only $14.95 for 44 titles published over the same period for the university presses. The differences in prices may go a long way in explaining the differences observed in physical sales.

A few very rough calculations using these prices and rates of sale in combination will illustrate how much better off in terms of revenue the commercial firms are despite their lower sales per title. If, for the moment, we ignore discounts and make the counterfactual assumption that the list prices are the actual amount of revenue received by the publisher for each copy sold, then the university presses would have earned approximately $46,100 (in undiscounted, undeflated dollars) for their average title in the natural sciences (3,083 × $14.95), while the commercial publishers would have earned some $70,200 for their average title (2,715 × $25.84).

According to Table 7.7.4, the age group of commercially published books in the social sciences contains by far the best sellers of any of the three subject areas — 11,143 copies per the average title over six years of life compared with 4,621 copies in the humanities and the previously cited 2,715 copies in the natural sciences. These results may be explained, in part, by the larger proportion of paperbound titles (36 per cent) in the social sciences. This would not, however, constitute a completely satisfactory explanation of the differences because there is almost as large a proportion of paperbound titles (33 per cent) in the cohort of humanities books. It is probably safe to conclude that titles in the social sciences sell better in general.

By Functional Categories

The final comparisons to be made of patterns of physical sales pertain to differences among books of various functional categories. Results for the titles of university presses are presented in Table 7.7.5 and for the commercial publishers in Table 7.7.6.

Scholarly monographs are seen in Table 7.7.5 to constitute the bulk of the sample of university-press titles, with 123 out of 152, or 81 per cent of the total belonging to this category. The samples for the other categories are quite small by comparison — 4 professional-reference titles, 12 college texts, and 7 general-interest books. Such small samples undoubtedly will not provide very representative pictures of sales patterns. Fifteen of the 123 scholarly monographs, 12 per cent of the sample, were paperbound titles, while one of the 4 professional-reference titles, two of the 12 college textbooks, and one of the 7 general-interest titles were paperbacks.

Regarding average numbers of copies sold per title, there do not seem to be very large variations among books of the four categories over the first six years of life. The highest average is 2,992 copies for college texts, followed by 2,250 copies for professional-reference titles, 2,215 for scholarly monographs, and 2,100 copies for books of general interest.

Among the four functional categories, the four titles of professional-reference books exhibit the greatest concentration of sales in the first two years of life, with 82.2 per cent of total six-year sales occurring in that period. Scholarly monographs exhibit the least concentration of sales in the early years of life with 68.4 per cent occurring in the first two years.

In the sample of commercially published titles there were 54 scholarly monographs (including 13 paperbacks), 11 professional-reference books (no paperbacks), 40 college texts (including 9 paperbacks), 11 professional-reference books (no paperbacks), 40 college texts (including 9 paperbacks) and 5 general-interest titles (including 1 paperback). The general-interest titles had the largest average number of copies sold per title: 13,620 copies over the full six-year period. The lowest sellers were the scholarly monographs with an average of 4,702 copies. Even though this latter category had the lowest level of sales for any of the four functional categories of commercially published books, it was still above the level of any of the functional categories of the university-press titles.

The profile of sales over the first six years of life of the titles does not vary dramatically among the four categories of commercially published titles. The least concentrated sales were registered by college textbooks, not an unexpected result considering textbooks are expected, in general, to have longer active lives than other categories of books. This generalization does not hold for university presses; as shown in Table 7.7.5, it was scholarly monographs and not their textbooks that had the least bunching of sales in the earliest years.

TABLE 7.7.5 Titles by University Presses by Functional Categories — The Distribution of Number of Copies of Books Sold over the First Six Years of Life for 146 Titles of University Presses (123 Scholarly Monographs, 4 Professional-Reference Books, 12 College Texts, and 7 General Interest) Published during the Period 1968-1970, with Average Number of Copies per Title and Number of Titles with Zero Sales in Each Period

	Year of life		
	1st and 2nd combined	3rd	4th
Scholarly monograph			
Number of titles in cohort	123	123	123
Total number of copies sold	186,300	31,200	18,800
Per cent of six-years sales in each period	68.4	11.4	6.9
Cumulative per cent	68.4	79.8	86.7
Average number of copies sold per title	1st — 981/2nd — 533	254	153
Number of titles with zero sales	0	3	5
Professional-reference			
Number of titles in cohort	4	4	4
Total number of copies sold	7,400	500	200
Per cent of six-year sales in each period	82.2	5.6	2.2
Cumulative per cent	82.2	87.8	90.0
Average number of copies sold per title	1st — 1,375/2nd — 475	125	50
Number of titles with zero sales	0	0	0
College textbooks			
Number of titles in cohort	12	12	12
Total number of copies sold	26,500	4,600	1,900
Per cent of six-year sales in each period	73.8	12.8	5.3
Cumulative per cent	73.8	86.6	91.9
Average number of copies sold per title	1st — 2,028/2nd — 909	383	158
Number of titles with zero sales	0	1	3
General interest			
Number of titles in cohort	7	7	7
Total number of copies sold	10,300	1,300	1,700
Per cent of six-year sales in each period	70.1	8.8	11.6
Cumulative per cent	70.1	78.9	90.5
Average number of copies sold per title	1st — 957/2nd — 514	186	243
Number of titles with zero sales	0	0	0

(continued)

TABLE 7.7.5, continued

	Year of life		
	5th	6th	All 6 years combined
Scholarly monograph			
Number of titles in cohort	123	123	123
Total number of copies sold	18,700	17,500	272,500
Per cent of six-years sales in each period	6.9	6.4	100.0
Cumulative per cent	93.6	100.0	-
Average number of copies sold per title	152	142	2,215
Number of titles with zero sales	8	14	-
Professional-reference			
Number of titles in cohort	4	4	4
Total number of copies sold	300	600	9,000
Per cent of six-year sales in each period	3.3	6.7	100.0
Cumulative per cent	93.3	100.0	-
Average number of copies sold per title	75	150	2,250
Number of titles with zero sales	0	1	-
College textbooks			
Number of titles in cohort	12	12	12
Total number of copies sold	1,800	1,100	35,900
Per cent of six-year sales in each period	5.0	3.1	100.0
Cumulative per cent	96.9	100.0	-
Average number of copies sold per title	150	92	2,992
Number of titles with zero sales	3	4	-
General interest			
Number of titles in cohort	7	7	7
Total number of copies sold	800	600	14,700
Per cent of six-year sales in each period	5.4	4.1	100.0
Cumulative per cent	95.9	100.0	-
Average number of copies sold per title	114	86	2,100
Number of titles with zero sales	0	0	-

Source: Machlup, Leeson, and Associates.

TABLE 7.7.6 *Titles by Commercial Publishers by Functional Categories — The Distribution of Number of Copies of Books Sold over the First Six Years of Life for 110 Titles of Commercial Publishers (54 Scholarly Monographs, 11 Professional-Reference Books, 40 College Texts, and 5 General Interest) Published during the Period 1968-1970, with Average Number of Copies per Title and Number of Titles with Zero Sales in Each Period (Excluding Two Titles with Extreme Values)*

	Year of life		
	1st and 2nd combined	3rd	4th
Scholarly monograph			
Number of titles in cohort	54	54	54
Total number of copies sold	148,600	40,300	29,000
Per cent of six-year sales in each period	58.5	15.9	11.4
Cumulative per cent	58.5	74.4	85.8
Average number of copies sold per title	1st — 1,380/2nd — 1,372	746	537
Number of titles with zero sales	0	1	5
Professional-reference			
Number of titles in cohort	11	11	11
Total number of copies sold	36,700	9,800	8,700
Per cent of six-year sales in each period	50.7	13.5	12.0
Cumulative per cent	50.7	64.2	76.2
Average number of copies sold per title	1st — 2,045/2nd — 1,291	891	791
Number of titles with zero sales	0	0	0
College textbooks			
Number of titles in cohort	40	40	40
Total number of copies sold	146,000	60,600	46,600
Per cent of six-year sales in each period	45.8	19.0	14.6
Cumulative per cent	45.8	64.8	79.4
Average number of copies sold per title	1st — 1,650/2nd — 2,005	1,515	1,165
Number of titles with zero sales	0	1	0
General interest			
Number of titles in cohort	5	5	5
Total number of copies sold	32,200	11,100	7,600
Per cent of six-year sales in each period	47.3	16.3	11.2
Cumulative per cent	47.3	63.6	74.8
Average number of copies sold per title	1st — 3,220/2nd — 3,220	2,220	1,520
Number of titles with zero sales	0	0	0

(continued)

TABLE 7.7.6, continued

	Year of life		
	5th	6th	All 6 years combined
Scholarly monograph			
Number of titles in cohort	54	54	54
Total number of copies sold	22,400	13,600	253,900
Per cent of six-year sales in each period	8.8	5.4	100.0
Cumulative per cent	94.6	100.0	-
Average number of copies sold per title	415	252	4,702
Number of titles with zero sales	2	3	-
Professional-reference			
Number of titles in cohort	11	11	11
Total number of copies sold	9,100	8,100	72,400
Per cent of six-year sales in each period	12.6	11.2	100.0
Cumulative per cent	88.8	100.0	-
Average number of copies sold per title	827	736	6,582
Number of titles with zero sales	0	1	-
College textbooks			
Number of titles in cohort	40	40	40
Total number of copies sold	35,600	29,900	318,700
Per cent of six-year sales in each period	11.2	9.4	100.0
Cumulative per cent	90.6	100.0	-
Average number of copies sold per title	890	748	7,968
Number of titles with zero sales	1	2	-
General interest			
Number of titles in cohort	5	5	5
Total number of copies sold	7,300	9,900	68,100
Per cent of six-year sales in each period	10.7	14.5	100.0
Cumulative per cent	85.5	100.0	-
Average number of copies sold per title	1,460	1,980	13,620
Number of titles with zero sales	0	1	-

Source: Machlup, Leeson, and Associates.

APPENDIX 7.A

RATES OF INTEREST AND PRICE INDICES USED IN THE ANALYSIS

TABLE 7.A.1 Rates of Interest and Price Indices Used to Capitalize and Deflate, Respectively, the Flows of Costs and Revenues in the Calculations of Gross Margins for Cohorts of Titles

	Prime rate of interest charged by banks on short-term business loans (in per cent)	GNP implicit price deflator for printing & publishing industries (1977 = 100)
1961	4.50	50.74
1962	4.50	51.37
1963	4.50	49.33
1964	4.50	50.18
1965	4.54	51.37
1966	5.63	53.61
1967	5.61	55.30
1968	6.30	58.39
1969	7.96	60.91
1970	7.91	65.33
1971	5.72	68.28
1972	5.25	70.18
1973	8.03	72.63
1974	10.81	79.23
1975	7.86	90.25

Sources: Prime rate of interest from Annual Statistical Digest, Board of Governors of the Federal Reserve System, Washington, D.C., 1975 (Table 24) and Gross Product Originating Deflator for Printing and Publishing Industries (Standard Industrial Classification Code 27), U.S. Department of Commerce, Bureau of Economic Analysis, work files.

PART 8

JOURNAL PUBLISHING: COSTS AND GROSS MARGINS

CHAPTER 8.1

JOURNALS: SOLVING SOME MYSTERIES ON THE SUBJECT OF COSTS

A few of the tables presented in Chapter 3.5 on "The Cost of Journal Publishing" of Volume 2 of this study were seen to contain some unusual or enigmatic numerical results. These puzzles were pointed out to the reader in the discussions that accompanied the tables but owing to a shortage of time and money were left unsolved. We promised that if funds were made available we would return to the scene and open a full-scale investigation in an attempt to uncover what lay behind the observed results. This we have finally been able to do. The outcome of our investigation, recounted in the following pages, involves the following three topics:

(1) *A Jump in the Cost of Distribution* — In Tables 3.5.1 and 3.5.2 we found for the journals involved an unexplained jump in the cost of distribution between 1970 and 1971; as far as we could tell, no error of computation was involved.

(2) *A Curious Dip in Total Costs* — A number of changes were found in the levels of costs and in the ratio of certain cost elements to total manufacturing cost. For example, of a group of 13 commercially published journals, total cost of the lowest-cost journal showed a curious dip in 1974, falling from $13,800 to $7,800 and rising again to $19,900 in 1975.

(3) *The Ratio of Operating to Total Cost* — We found that the journals of commercial publishers showed the lowest ratios of operating to total cost. We want to try to determine whether this is merely a matter of different accounting techniques, or of real differences in the conditions under which commercial publishers, learned societies, and university presses operate.

Guidelines for the Investigations

Large quantities of numerical data of the type we have gathered for this research are likely to contain a number of unexpected or enigmatic values — a sudden jump in an otherwise stable time series, for example, or a consistent difference among types of publishers in the magnitudes of a given category of costs for which no theoretical explanation can be offered *a priori*.

An investigation might reveal (1) that the observed results are correct, that the data accurately reflect a genuine phenomenon which has taken place in the economic processes under study; or (2) that the observed results can be attributed to a sudden and unannounced change in the definitions used by the respondents involved; or (3) that the unusual results were caused by erroneous data. With regard to the third possibility, we can list a number of opportunities for making mistakes at any one of the several steps required to bring the data from their original sources — the individual responding firms — to their final arrangements on the statistical tables that we display throughout the pages of the study. Even if we make the counterfactual assumption that all of our respondents use comparable and unchanging definitions for any given variable, say "editorial costs," and that each uses the same method to compile their annual expenditures for such a category, we would still have to admit the possibility that errors are introduced by our own research staff, when transcribing the numbers from the respondents' records onto our worksheets, or when transferring the numbers from our worksheets to coding paper in preparation for keypunching, or when doing the keypunching, or when preparing the computer programs that process the data, and so on. While carefully-followed procedures of checking and rechecking can reduce to an acceptable level the number of clerical errors, they will usually fail to uncover all errors introduced by the processors of the data. This is a fact of life in empirical research.

We believe that, by and large, our data contain a tolerably small number of errors and inconsistencies. We were careful when combining the figures of different publishers to inquire about the definitions of the variables involved. Furthermore, the procedures used to check our work at each step in the compilation of the data were thorough and strict.

Thus, our purpose in this chapter is to seek answers to the following questions for each of the three "mysteries" listed above: Were the observed results, however unexpected, an accurate reflection of the real state of costs for the journals involved? Were they the result of some undocumented change in the definitions of the cost categories used by the participating publishers; or were they the product of some error made in the data somewhere along the line, an error that went undetected in our earlier research?

A JUMP IN THE COST OF DISTRIBUTION

The first mystery to unravel concerns a peculiar jump from 1970 to 1971 in the percentage share of total costs accounted for by distribution costs in a sample of journals published by learned societies.

In Chapter 3.5 on "The Cost of Journal Publishing," we divided the costs into two major categories — manufacturing cost and operating cost. The former refers to the cost of inputs that generate directly a material (physical, tangible) output, while the latter refers to payments for services which, however important or indispensable, do not produce tangible products. The components of manufacturing costs include (1) composition (typesetting) and ordinary graphics, (2) special graphics, (3) paper, and (4) printing and binding. Operating costs include (1) editorial, (2) promotion, (3) distribution, (4) postage, (5) general and administrative, and (6) all other. Because general-and-administrative expenses defy direct allocation to particular journals we decided to omit this category from the percentage distributions that were calculated for the various components of the cost of publishing.

The Mysterious Surge

In the last paragraph on page 149 of Volume 2, we stated:

> "The percentages computed for the [nine] components of cost are rather similar in Tables 3.5.1 and 3.5.2, as we should expect in view of the overlapping membership of the samples. A most conspicuous break may be noticed between 1970 and 1971, when the percentages for manufacturing costs seem to drop precipitously. Yet, this is merely a reflection of a sharp rise in operating expenses, by almost seven percentage points, and this rise is due entirely to a sudden increase in the cost of distribution. (We have made sure that no error of computation was involved, and we hope to be able, in a continued research effort, to do some detective work to find the reasons for the sudden jump in distribution cost.)"

Tables 8.1.1A and 8.1.1B contain reproductions of the relevant portions of Tables 3.5.1 and 3.5.2, highlighting the unusual surge in the cost of distribution between 1970 and 1971.

TABLE 8.1.1A A Reproduction of Portions of Table 3.5.1 of Volume 2 on "Journals" Showing an Unexpected Jump in the Cost of Distribution from 1970 to 1971

TABLE 3.5.1 Minimum, Maximum, Mean, and Median Cost (excluding General and Administrative) in Dollars, and Components of Manufacturing Costs and Operating Expenses as Percentages of Total Costs for 14 Journals Published by Learned Societies, 1966-1975

	1966	1967	1968	1969	
Total costs (in dollars) per journal					
Minimum		. . .		$ 22,300	
Maximum		. . .		$743,500	
Mean		. . .		$238,900	
Median		. . .		$100,000	
Costs (in per cent) by type				Per cent of total	Per cent of subtotal
Manufacturing costs		. . .			
Composition & ordinary graphics		. . .		37.8%	63.5%
Special graphics		. . .		3.1%	5.2%
Paper		. . .		8.3%	14.0%
Printing & binding		. . .		10.3%	17.3%
Total manufacturing costs		. . .		59.5%	100.0%
Operating expenses		. . .			
Editorial		. . .		32.2%	79.5%
Promotion		. . .		1.5%	3.7%
Distribution		. . .		1.1%	2.7%
Postage		. . .		2.9%	7.2%
All other		. . .		2.8%	6.9%
Total operating expenses		. . .		40.5%	100.0%
Total costs		. . .		100.0%	

(continued)

TABLE 8.1.1A continued

TABLE 3.5.1 Minimum, Maximum, Mean, and Median Cost (excluding General and Administrative) in Dollars, and Components of Manufacturing Costs and Operating Expenses as Percentages of Total Costs for 14 Journals Published by Learned Societies, 1966-1975

	1970		1971	
Total costs (in dollars) per journal				
Minimum	$ 27,000		$ 28,000	
Maximum	$810,800		$825,300	
Mean	$252,000		$263,200	
Median	$109,800		$131,200	
Costs (in per cent) by type	Per cent of total	Per cent of subtotal	Per cent of total	Per cent of subtotal
Manufacturing costs				
Composition & ordinary graphics	40.4%	68.0%	38.6%	72.8%
Special graphics	2.6%	4.3%	2.1%	4.0%
Paper	7.6%	12.7%	6.1%	11.5%
Printing & binding	8.9%	15.0%	6.2%	11.7%
Total manufacturing costs	59.5%	100.0%	53.0%	100.0%
Operating expenses				
Editorial	30.7%	75.8%	29.8%	63.4%
Promotion	3.7%	9.1%	3.6%	7.7%
Distribution	1.1%	2.7%	8.0%	17.0%
Postage	2.8%	6.9%	3.0%	6.4%
All other	2.2%	5.4%	2.6%	5.5%
Total operating expenses	40.5%	100.0%	47.0%	100.0%
Total costs	100.0%		100.0%	

(continued)

TABLE 8.1.1A continued

TABLE 3.5.1 Minimum, Maximum, Mean, and Median Cost (excluding General and Administrative) in Dollars, and Components of Manufacturing Costs and Operating Expenses as Percentages of Total Costs for 14 Journals Published by Learned Societies, 1966-1975

	1972		1973 . . .
Total costs (in dollars) per journal			
Minimum	$ 27,400		. . .
Maximum	$1,048,500		. . .
Mean	$ 294,900		. . .
Median	$ 130,300		. . .
Costs (in per cent) by type	Per cent of total	Per cent of subtotal	
Manufacturing costs			
Composition & ordinary graphics	39.3%	73.2%	. . .
Special graphics	2.4%	4.5%	. . .
Paper	6.0%	11.2%	. . .
Printing & binding	6.0%	11.2%	. . .
Total manufacturing costs	53.7%	100.0%	. . .
Operating expenses			
Editorial	30.0%	64.8%	. . .
Promotion	3.2%	6.9%	. . .
Distribution	7.7%	16.6%	. . .
Postage	3.2%	6.9%	. . .
All other	2.2%	4.8%	. . .
Total operating expenses	46.3%	100.0%	. . .
Total costs	100.0%		. . .

Source: Machlup, Leeson, and Associates, Information Through the Printed Word, Volume 2, "Journals," Table 3.5.1, pp. 145-146.

To quote once again from the narrative that accompanied the tables in that chapter:

> "According to Table 3.5.1 [reproduced here in Table 8.1.1A], the cost of distributing the journals was 2.7 per cent of operating expenses in 1970, but 17.0 per cent in 1971. The analogous figures in Table 3.5.2 [reproduced here in Table 8.1.1B] show the increase to be from 3.0 to 18.0 per cent. These increases of cost depressed all other cost percentages in 1971. For example, editorial expenses were down from 75.8 to 63.4 per cent in Table 3.5.1, and from 73.8 to 61.9 per cent in Table 3.5.2. The cost of promotion varied widely over the years relative to total operating expenses. We have not yet been able to look for the causes of these changes, but put this investigation on the agenda for continued research." p. 150.

Thus, we were at a loss for an explanation that would account for the unusual shift observed in the cost of distribution, and had neither the time nor the funds to conduct an investigation of the matter.

With the aid of a portion of the funds made available for our continued research, the reasons for the observed results have, at last, been uncovered.

In Search of Clues

The first task that had to be undertaken in the investigation was to find, from among the 140 journals for which we had obtained data on costs in various degrees of disaggregation, the two sub-samples, one of 14 journals, the other of 17 journals, for which costs are shown in Tables 3.5.1 and 3.5.2, respectively. This was not a trivial matter for two reasons. First, the identities of the individual journals contained in these samples were not known, even by us, when Chapter 3.5 was written. Hence, we could not simply return to our work files to find the names of the journals involved. We had intentionally left ourselves in the dark on such matters in order to reduce the possibility of revealing inadvertently the identities of the journals or publishers involved. To guard against such an occurrance, a tailor-made computer program was written in the earlier stages of our research to select anonymously all journals that qualified for each of the numerous analyses.

A second problem encountered in trying to reconstruct the samples was caused by a failure of our computer system. Shortly after we had finished work on the first three volumes, our data files were purged from their tapes. They had to be re-

TABLE 8.1.1B A Reproduction of Portions of Table 3.5.2 of Volume 2 on "Journals" Showing an Unexpected Jump in the Cost of Distribution from 1970 to 1971

TABLE 3.5.2 Minimum, Maximum, Mean, and Median Cost (excluding General and Administrative) in Dollars, and Components of Manufacturing Costs and Operating Expenses as Percentages of Total Costs for 17 Journals Published by Learned Societies, 1969-1975

	1969		1970	
Total costs (in dollars) per journal				
Minimum	$ 22,300		$ 27,000	
Maximum	$743,500		$810,800	
Mean	$225,700		$240,500	
Median	$ 98,800		$109,200	
Costs (in per cent) by type	Per cent of total	Per cent of subtotal	Per cent of total	Per cent of subtotal
Manufacturing costs				
Composition & ordinary graphics	35.2%	62.1%	37.8%	66.1%
Special graphics	3.1%	5.5%	2.7%	4.7%
Paper	8.2%	14.5%	7.6%	13.3%
Printing & binding	10.2%	18.0%	9.1%	15.9%
Total manufacturing costs	56.7%	100.0%	57.2%	100.0%
Operating expenses				
Editorial	33.1%	76.4%	31.6%	73.8%
Promotion	3.0%	6.9%	4.9%	11.4%
Distribution	1.3%	3.0%	1.3%	3.0%
Postage	2.8%	6.5%	2.7%	6.4%
All other	3.1%	7.2%	2.3%	5.4%
Total operating expenses	43.3%	100.0%	42.8%	100.0%
Total costs	100.0%		100.0%	

(continued)

TABLE 8.1.1B continued

TABLE 3.5.2 Minimum, Maximum, Mean, and Median Cost (excluding General and Administrative) in Dollars, and Components of Manufacturing Costs and Operating Expenses as Percentages of Total Costs for 17 Journals Published by Learned Societies, 1969-1975

	1971		1972 . . .	
Total costs (in dollars) per journal				
Minimum	$ 28,100		$ 27,400	
Maximum	$825,300		$1,048,500	
Mean	$253,400		$ 280,000	
Median	$130,900		$ 130,000	
Costs (in per cent) by type	Per cent of total	Per cent of subtotal	Per cent of total	Per cent of subtotal
Manufacturing costs				
Composition & ordinary graphics	36.2%	71.5%	37.1%	72.2%
Special graphics	2.2%	4.3%	2.4%	4.7%
Paper	6.0%	11.9%	5.8%	11.3%
Printing and binding	6.2%	12.3%	6.1%	11.9%
Total manufacturing costs	50.6%	100.0%	51.4%	100.0%
Operating expenses				
Editorial	30.6%	61.9%	30.6%	63.0%
Promotion	4.3%	8.7%	4.0%	8.2%
Distribution	8.9%	18.0%	8.6%	17.7%
Postage	2.8%	5.7%	3.0%	6.2%
All other	2.8%	5.7%	2.4%	4.9%
Total operating expenses	49.4%	100.0%	48.0%	100.0%
Total costs	100.0%		100.0%	

Source: Machlup, Leeson, and Associates, Information Through the Printed Word, Volume 2, "Journals," Table 3.5.2, p. 148.

entered from the original punched cards before we could proceed with the investigation. When the data were restored to computer tapes, we used our tailor-made program to select again the journals belonging to the two samples in question. From among all 140 journals with data on costs (a subset of the 171 journals on our computer files altogether) we sought those that could fulfill two requirements: they had to have data on costs separated into the nine items shown on Tables 3.5.1 and 3.5.2, and they had to have these data for all of the years shown on the table — 1966 through 1975 in the case of Table 3.5.1, and 1969 through 1975 in the case of Table 3.5.2. We adjusted the program slightly to obtain this time the code numbers of the journals that qualified for the samples.

It might be inconsistent with our desire to maintain the anonymity of the contributing publishers with regard to data on particular journals if we were to reveal the number of learned societies represented in each of the samples under investigation. We shall remain silent on this point. It is important to note, however, that the journals of one publisher in particular weigh rather heavily in the samples.

A Blind Alley

In Chapter 3.5 we warned that an analysis based solely on the relative distribution of total costs among the various components may be deceptive. It is conceivable, for example, that the jump in the relative weight of Distribution Costs was caused, at least in part, by a *decrease* in dollar values of some or all of the other costs listed, rather than to an *increase* in the dollar value of the cost of distribution. In order to see if this was in fact what had happened, we derived the absolute dollar values of each of the categories of costs shown in the tables. For the sample of 14 journals of Table 3.5.1, the distribution costs were as follows:

. . .	1969	1970	1971	1972	. . .
	$40,372	$44,617	$214,550	$228,031	

and for the 17 journals of Table 3.5.2:

. . .	1969	1970	1971	1972	. . .
	$51,195	$56,914	$297,703	$309,010	

Clearly, in 1971 there was a dramatic jump in the cost of distributing the journals; the possibility that the abrupt change might have been caused by a drop in the costs of other categories was thus eliminated. There was indeed a precipitous increase in the recorded cost of distribution, absolute as well as relative. But why?

Back on the Track

We took the investigation onto the next step. By observing distribution costs separately for each of the publishers involved, we would be able to see whether the jump in 1971 had been experienced by all — in which case we might tentatively conclude that there had been some change in the cost of distributing journals affecting several firms — or whether it had been experienced by only one of the publishers — a result that would lead one to suspect that the jump was merely an idiosyncracy of that particular firm. We shall not show the figures, but can report that the observed jump in the costs of distribution was traced to a single publisher. Furthermore, the jump was not confined to a single journal, but was seen for each and every one of the journals published by the learned society in question.

We began to search for reasons that might account for the reported increases and one possibility seemed worthy of consideration: that the increase in the total cost of distribution for this publisher resulted from an increase in the circulation of their journals, that is, in the number of subscriptions by libraries or by individual subscribers. If additional copies of the journals had been distributed, it would make sense to expect the cost of distribution to rise, although the large size of the increase in costs could only have been caused by a tremendous increase in circulation, an improbable development over a period of just one year. At any rate, a look at the circulation of these journals for the period 1969-1972 excluded this possibility: increases in subscriptions were definitely not responsible for the jump in the total cost of distribution in 1971. As a matter of fact, circulation for the journals as a group declined over the period, from 133,670 in 1969 to 114,460 in 1972, (or from 129,640 in 1970 to 120,370 in 1971) for the sample of 14, and from 172,850 in 1969 to 157,380 in 1972 (or from 176,600 in 1970 to 166,062 in 1971) for the sample of 17 journals.

The Solution

We had by this time reached a point in the investigation where the information readily available to us — the material in our own work files and data bank — could provide no further clues about what was behind the surge in Distribution Costs. We therefore had no choice but to go back to the publisher to ask for help in finding an explanation. We could only hope that detailed records of activities occurring more than eight years ago were still available somewhere in the files of the firm.

We were fortunate. The publisher was able to provide the explanation. To quote directly from the letter sent by one of their officials, "The difference [in distribution costs shown for 1970 and 1971] stems from a change in our accounting system which allowed better allocation of indirect costs. Specifically, 'Distribution Costs' encompassed only mailing costs through 1970. Beginning with 1971 'Subscription Fulfillment' was allocated to each journal and included in the 'Distribution Costs' category." (The words in brackets were added by us.)

This, finally, cleared up the mystery. Before 1971, there were several overhead, or indirect expenses, incurred by the publisher that were not allocated to individual journals and hence not shown on our questionnaires or entered on our computer files; the cost of subscription fulfillment was among them. Beginning in 1971, the publisher allocated these costs to individual journals. This is consistent with the data that appear on our questionnaires. They show, not only an increase in costs under "Distribution" beginning in 1971, but an entirely new category for each of the journals as well: "General and Administrative." Recall that we deliberately excluded General and Administrative costs from the tables presented in the text because of the arbitrary manner in which publishers assign costs to this category. Had this publisher decided to lump all of the newly allocated costs under General and Administrative beginning in 1971, instead of assigning some portion to Distribution, no surge in distribution costs would have shown up on our tables. Of course, the change in the accounting procedures was not only reasonable but in conformance with best accounting practice: whenever expenses can be allocated without excessive difficulties, such allocation ought to be made; it improves the information derived from the accounting system. We had commented on this point in Volume 2 on page 143.

The Moral

This exercise has demonstrated that statistical measurements of components of operating expenses are apt to be unreliable. Our unsuppressed pessimism regarding this problem cast a dim shadow in Chapter 3.5 when we wrote: "Our comments on the various elements of operating expenses add up to a sense of resignation regarding the possibility of obtaining consistent and comparable data for operating expenses. In our tabulations, we shall not suppress any information obtained from the publishers' records or reports (except the figures for general and administrative expenses), but in our analysis we shall discount the economic significance of these data." (Volume 2, p. 142.)

A CURIOUS DIP IN TOTAL COSTS

As we proceeded with the analysis of the "Cost of Journal Publishing" in Chapter 3.5 of Volume 2, we discovered a few more curious results that seemed to warrant further investigation. For a sample of commercially published journals we noticed (1) that total cost of the lowest-cost journal in a group of thirteen commercially published journals (displayed in Table 3.5.5 of Volume 2) showed a curious dip in 1974, falling from $13,800 to $7,800 and rising again to $19,900 in 1975; and (2) for the same sample the relative weights of manufacturing costs and operating expenses fluctuated widely from year to year. To get to the bottom of these anomalies, we had to follow a procedure similar to that described in the preceding sections. Since we have explained already in some detail our *modus operandi*, we can forego a step-by-step recounting of the investigation and get right to the results.

The Dip

In our investigation of the strange dip in total cost shown for a commercially published journal in Table 3.5.5, we had to rely completely on information contained in our own files. The publisher of the journal in question was not prepared to provide any additional help. As a consequence, we were forced to draw upon circumstantial clues and thus had to speculate about what had gone wrong.

Our investigation of the figures led ultimately to a discovery that the dramatic dip and subsequent surge in costs was *not* an accurate reflection of the true costs of the journal in question. When the problems had been found and corrected, total costs for the three years 1973, 1974, and 1975 became far less volatile than the uncorrected figures. What were the misdemeanors of the originally-published figures? Have we been able to apprehend the transgressors and rehabilitate them?

Digging Behind the Values

The difference between the two sets of costs was confined to a single category or, more accurately, a single conglomeration of various categories (promotion, distribution, postage, all other) under operating expenses. None of the values of manufacturing costs (composition and ordinary graphics, special graphics, and paper, printing and binding) were found to be in error, nor was there any apparent problem with the editorial costs.

We were dealing in this case with the costs of a single journal. This made our job somewhat easier. We did not, as in the preceding assignment, have to reconstruct an entire sample in order to find from among the numerous possible combinations of journals the one that produced values of costs identical with those displayed in our table. The commercially published journal whose total costs were shown in Table 3.5.5 was quickly identified.

Next we had to separate the total costs of this journal into the four principal components. It became evident that the fluctuation had its origin in one of the components of the category containing four items of cost (promotion, distribution, postage, all other). However, all we knew was the lump-sum values for this composite. This was not enough. We had to try to further separate these values into *their* component parts. We were surprised, indeed, we were baffled by what we found.

As we proceeded to break down the operating costs that were, up to this point, shown only as a single lump sum, we derived separate figures for six categories; (1) the costs of promotion, (2) distribution, (3) postage, (4) cost of reprints, and two categories unfamiliar to us — (5) postage recovered, and (6) "recovered funds." We could not obtain from the publisher any clarification on the meaning of these last two terms. That these categories had negative entries indicated that both were sources of revenue for the journal, rather than costs.

Speculations on the Causes

If either of these is a type of subsidy from an outside source rather than, say, the recovery of funds spent incorrectly or unnecessarily in earlier years, then they should not have been included in operating costs at all. In our original presentations in Chapter 3.5 of Volume 2 we followed for all journals the convention of excluding subsidies, whether they were listed by the publishers as positive entries on the "revenue" side of the ledger or as negative entries on the "costs" side. Assuming these values are subsidies, we must concede an error on our part. Without the publisher's help, however, there is no way of knowing for sure. Let us put this question aside and proceed on the assumption that the figures in question do not represent subsidies.

Of the six categories of operating costs listed above, only one, recovered funds, was found to be responsible for the pronounced dip in operating expenses, and by extension, for the dip in total cost for the journal as shown in Table 3.5.5 of

Volume 2. The other five categories of cost were found to be correct as originally specified. We had misinterpreted the values of recovered funds for 1973 and 1975 when transcribing the data from the questionnaire onto our coding sheets. The errors were then carried through to the table.

Thus we had found that the erratic values of a single cost category, whose definition was not familiar to us, was creating all of the trouble. We should have detected and corrected this problem in our earlier work but had failed to do so.

What Does It Mean?

A few additional comments are in order. We discovered a few unusual values for some of the other categories of operating expenses of this journal during the course of the investigation just described. For example, editorial costs were found to be $100 in 1973 and zero in the two subsequent years. These values may well be incorrect; or perhaps they reflect only a fraction of total editorial costs; or perhaps they are correct in the sense that editorial services are donated by professional members of the disciplines served by the journals; or perhaps these costs are defrayed in part by a professional society. These are all possible explanations but none suggest how we are supposed to combine such arbitrary values with those of other publishers and come up with anything resembling sensible results.

We also discovered that the journal under investigation had only zero values shown for distribution costs. This raises a similar question. Apparently, this publisher chose not to allocate distribution costs to individual journals, or at least not to this particular journal, yet some other publishers may do some type of allocation. How is one to make sense out of results derived aggregating figures of such diverse character?

REMAINING CURIOSITIES

We have not yet discussed the third mystery listed at the beginning of this chapter — the differences among commercial publishers, learned societies, and university presses in the ratios of operating to total cost. Specifically, we found in our analyses on the "Cost of Journal Publishing" in Chapter 3.5 that the journals of commercial publishers showed the lowest ratios of operating to total cost and asked: "Is it merely a matter of different accounting techniques, or does it reflect real differences in the conditions under which the three types of publishers operate, or differences in operating practices they have adopted?" p. 171.

One of the most significant results flowing from the two investigations recounted in this chapter is the realization that our hunch about operating expenses, expressed in Chapter 3.5 of Volume 2, was correct: because of the variety of accounting techniques and formulas used by publishers for allocating overhead or "joint" costs, it is virtually impossible to obtain consistent and comparable data on operating expenses. Surely, we must discount the economic significance of findings based on incomparable data.

We are unable, therefore, to provide any definitive answers that would account for the differences in the ratios of operating to total costs among publishers. We are inclined to believe that the differences observed in our statistical tables primarily reflect differences in accounting techniques among the publishers. This is not to say that important differences do not, in fact, exist among broad classes of publishers; but our data on operating expenses are not up to the task of bringing the differences to light. We place much greater confidence in our analyses of "Gross Margins Above Specified Costs," in Chater 3.6 of Volume 2 and in our discussions on "Journals: Gross Margins Above Specified Costs — Over Time And By Field" in this volume. Gross margins are gross revenues minus direct manufacturing costs — composition, paper, printing, and binding — and are therefore contributions to operating expenses and net revenue. The interested reader is referred to these discussions.

CHAPTER 8.2

JOURNALS: GROSS MARGINS ABOVE SPECIFIED COSTS — OVER TIME AND BY FIELD

The analyses of gross margins presented in Chapter 3.6 of Volume 2 were based entirely on a sample of 47 journals with data from 1970 to 1975. Additional samples that span longer periods of time were available to us but had to be ignored — time and funds had run out.

In this chapter we shall complete our presentation on gross margins, first by analyzing a sample of 35 journals with data from 1966 to 1974; then by presenting discussions on gross margins by field, a second objective left unattained in the earlier volume; and finally, by studying the effects on gross margin of revenues from page charges by authors and from the sale of advertising space.

Calculating Gross Margins

The definition of gross margin of a journal used in this analysis is the arithmetic difference between gross revenue and manufacturing cost. Gross revenue consists of the total revenues publishers receive from all sources for producing and distributing their journals, including payments from authors, sponsors, benefactors, advertisers, buyers of back issues and reprints and, of course, subscribers. Manufacturing cost consists of the expenses considered as inevitable in the production of the journal that are clearly allocable to the particular issues produced during a year — the costs of composition, graphics, paper, printing, and binding. Thus,

(1)		Gross Revenue (from all sources)
(2)	minus	Manufacturing Cost (for composition, graphics, paper, printing, binding)
(3)	equals	Gross Margin (contribution toward operating and overhead expenses and, possibly, Net Revenue)

We focus on gross margin defined in this matter to avoid the questionable practice of allocating expenses to individual journals that are really not allocable. Such expenses include general and administrative costs, payments for the performance of various editorial functions and payments for some promotional activities. Apportionment of nonallocable expenses is too arbitrary and too inconsistent to be used in analysis.

GROSS MARGINS OVER TIME

The original sample of 47 journals contained 17 published by learned societies, 8 by university presses and 22 by commercial publishers. The period covered was 1970-1975. Analyzing a sample for a longer time period meant having to settle for fewer journals: as the period of coverage increased, the number of publishers able to supply the necessary data decreased. For example, if we wanted to cover the ten-year period 1966-1975, we would have had a sample of only 20 journals with data sufficient to calculate gross margins. We discovered, however, that by dropping just one year, 1975, the size of the sample would increase by 15 journals. This was due to the timing of data collection: a few of the respondents had provided their data during 1975, before figures for that year were available. In view of the advantages of a larger sample, we chose to analyze the gross margins of this group of 35 (containing 28 journals published by learned societies, 2 by university presses and 5 by commercial publishers) and to compare the results with the original group of 47.

The Original Group of Forty-Seven

Data on gross revenue, manufacturing costs, and gross margins were presented in Chapter 6.3 in terms of averages — per journal and per page — for the sample of 47 journals as a whole and separately for each of the three types of publishers. Principal among the observations made in that chapter were:

(1) Gross revenue per journal measured in current dollars for all 47 journals combined rose from \$97,230 in 1970 to \$134,900 in 1975, an increase by 38.8 per cent. Gross margin as a per cent of gross revenue, however, did not vary inordinately over the period, only between a high of 55.6 per cent in 1972 and a low of 50.9 per cent in 1974.

(2) A comparison among the three types of publishers of average gross revenues per journal in 1975 revealed that they amounted to \$380,250

for learned societies, $243,160 for commercial publishers, and only $37,830 for university presses. The same ordering prevailed also with regard to manufacturing cost and gross margin.

(3) With regard to gross margin per journal as a per cent of gross revenue, the commercial publishers achieved top rank in five out of the six years, with the learned societies in second place, and the university presses invariably in last place.

(4) Gross margin per page followed a different order. In 1975 gross margin per page was $88.10 for learned societies, $78.50 for commercial publishers, and $30.10 for university presses. These rankings held for every year except 1970, when the gross margin per page of journals of commercial publishers slightly exceeded that of learned societies.

A New Sample of Thirty-Five

Tables 8.2.1 and 8.2.2 contain for learned societies and commercial publishers, respectively, average number of pages per journal, average gross margin per journal, average gross margin per page, and gross margin as a per cent of gross revenue. (We decided not to display the results for the university presses because the sample for the longer time period contained only five journals.) Both tables contain results for the original groups of journals and for the newly formed groups covering the longer period. As an aid in comparing the two time series we have included in the tables two columns of percentage changes, one pertaining to both samples showing changes over the period 1970-1974 and the other pertaining to only the longer time series showing changes over the period 1966-1974. A second feature of these tables should be noted. Unlike the tables presented in Volume 2, we have chosen here to omit the values of gross revenue and manufacturing cost, the minuend and subtrahend from which gross margins are derived. This decision was prompted in large part by our wish to save space, but also because both gross revenue and manufacturing costs can easily be calculated from the information contained in the tables. For example, in Table 8.2.1, average gross margin per journal for the group of 17 is, in 1970, $142,330. We know also from the table that this value is 50.9 per cent of gross revenue. Hence, dividing gross margin by the decimal fraction .509, produces the value of gross revenue,

TABLE 8.2.1 Journals of Learned Societies —
Average Number of Pages Per Year, Gross Revenue Per Journal, and Gross Revenue Per Page for Journals of Learned Societies (17 Journals, 1970-1975 and 28 Journals, 1966-1974)

Learned societies	1966	1967	1968	1969
17 Journals, 1970-1975				
Number of pages (average per journal)				
Gross margin (average per journal)				→
Gross margin per page (average per journal)				→
Gross margin as a per cent of gross revenue				
28 Journals, 1966-1974				
Number of pages (average per journal)	2,416	2,566	2,699	2,674
Gross margin (average per journal)	$80,220	$98,310	*	$120,750
Gross margin per page (average per journal)	$33.20	$38.30	*	$45.10
Gross margin as a per cent of gross revenue	41.4	45.8	*	47.7

*Note: Complete data not available.

(continued)

TABLE 8.2.1, continued

Learned societies	1970	1971	1972	1973
17 Journals, 1970-1975				
Number of pages (average per journal)	2,295	2,204	2,389	2,263
Gross margin (average per journal)	$142,330	$156,900	$197,110	$181,600
Gross margin per page (average per journal)	$62.00	$71.20	$82.50	$80.20
Gross margin as a per cent of gross revenue	50.9	53.7	56.2	54.7
28 Journals, 1966-1974				
Number of Pages (average per journal)	2,724	2,661	2,775	2,712
Gross margin (average per journal)	$129,790	$142,580	$159,980	$161,160
Gross margin per page (average per journal)	$47.60	$53.60	$58.10	$59.40
Gross margin as a per cent of gross revenue	47.1	50.1	50.7	51.3

(continued)

TABLE 8.2.1, continued

Learned societies	1974	1975	Per cent change 1966-1974	Per cent change 1970-1974
17 Journals, 1970-1975				
Number of pages (average per journal)	2,180	2,191	-	-5.0%
Gross margin (average per journal)	$158,630	$193,030	-	+11.5%
Gross margin per page (average per journal)	$72.80	$88.10	-	+17.4%
Gross margin as a per cent of gross revenue	48.4	50.8	-	-4.9%
28 Journals, 1966-1974				
Number of pages (average per journal)	2,539	-	+5.1%	-6.8%
Gross margin (average per journal)	$152,020	-	+89.5%	+17.1%
Gross margin per page (average per journal)	$59.90	-	+80.4%	+25.8%
Gross margin as a per cent of gross revenue	47.1	-	+13.8%	0.0%

Source: Machlup, Leeson, and Associates. Results for the Sample of 17 Journals from Tables 3.6.1 and 3.6.2 of Volume 2 of Information Through the Printed Word, pp. 176 & 178.

approximately $279,630. Since manufacturing cost is the difference between gross revenue and gross margin, its value can easily be calculated directly from the results just obtained. In this example manufacturing cost equals $137,300.[1]

Overlapping Samples

The samples presented in Volume 2 and those discussed here have some journals in common. It will be helpful to keep this in mind when comparing the results. The number of journals in the 1970-1975 time series only, the number in both time series, and the number in the 1966-1974 time series only are given in the table below. For the sake of consistency in our references to the total sample sizes containing 47 and 35 journals, respectively, we include university presses here, even though their gross margins will not be discussed.

	Number of Journals in the 1970-1975 Time Series Only	Number of Journals in Both Time Series	Number of Journals in the 1966-1974 Time Series Only
Learned Societies	6	11	17
University Presses	6	2	0
Commercial Publishers	17	5	0
All Publishers	29	18	17

Resulting Total Sample Sizes: 47 (29 + 18) and 35 (18 + 17)

Thus, the group of 47 contains 29 journals that are not in the group of 35, and the group of 35 contains 17 journals that are not in the group of 47. Note that only in the case of learned societies are there journals in the longer time series that do not also fall in the shorter time series.

---

[1]Because of rounding, the values of gross revenue and manufacturing cost calculated here differ slightly from the actual values shown in Table 3.6.1 of Volume 2.

Gross Margins per Journal and per Page, by Type of Publisher

It would not be very informative to display and discuss the gross margins of the sample of 35 journals combined, that is, with the journals of all publishers lumped together. We prepared a table containing these aggregate figures, but the 28 journals of learned societies were found to dominate the results so completely that looking at the combined figures was not much different from looking at the learned societies in isolation. We shall therefore proceed immediately to the discussion of gross margins of learned societies and commercial publishers.

Table 8.2.1 contains the results for the journals of learned societies and Table 8.2.2 for commercial publishers. The sample size of five for the latter type of publisher for the longer time period, 1966-1974, is also rather small. We offer the figures and the accompanying discussions as examples only, in the nature of case studies, certainly unfit to serve as the basis for even the most tenuous generalizations.

Before turning to the main objective of this section, that of presenting gross margins for time periods longer than were made available in Volume 2, we shall consider the secondary objective, that of comparing for both types of publishers the results observed for the pairs of samples that span different, though overlapping, time periods. Thus, we raise the question: Do the pairs of samples of different size and composition shown for the two types of publishers produce roughly similar results? A finding that the latter of the two possibilities holds, while far from establishing the inferential power of the data, would at least bolster our confidence in the didactic value of the small samples with which we are working.

If we compare the results for learned societies for the years that overlap in Table 8.2.1, we see that journals in the sample of 17 that belong to the shorter series have, on average, fewer pages (per journal) and larger gross margins (per journal, per page, and as a per cent of gross revenue) than journals belonging to the sample of 28. Still, the order of magnitude of the values for the two groups is roughly similar. Even the directions of change, positive or negative, from one year to the next display a measure of consistency, except that in 1973 all three measures of gross margin fell from the previous year for the group of 17 and rose for the group of 28, and in 1974 gross margins per page moved in different directions. As shown in the last column of the table, the two samples also exhibited similarities in the per cent changes that occurred from the first to the last year of the overlapping period, 1970-1974. The number of pages fell for both groups, by 5.0 per cent for the sample of 17 and by 6.8 per cent for the sample of 28; gross margins per journal and per page rose for both samples; and gross margin as a per cent of gross revenue varied least among all variables, dropping by 4.9 per cent for the group of 17 and remaining unchanged for the group of 28.

That the two samples in Table 8.2.1 display similar characteristics is not a wholely unexpected outcome since they do have eleven journals in common. Thus, in the case of learned societies, changing the composition of the samples to obtain a longer series did not alter radically the values and trends observed for the statistics we seek to analyze.

The samples of journals published by commercial publishers are displayed in Table 8.2.2. As we noted earlier, the sample size is very small for the 1966-1974 time series, only five journals. The sample of 22 and the sample of five display some similar values over the period they have in common, particularly with regard to average number of pages. In 1970 the group of 22 averages 1,478 pages while the group of five has 1,492 pages, on average; the former grew by 18.6 per cent, the latter by 21.4 per cent over the common period. Gross margins per journal and per page are similar, particularly in 1972, 1973, and 1974, while gross margin as a per cent of gross revenue is consistently higher in each year for the sample of 22.

Having concluded that the pairs of samples shown for both types of publishers are similar, we may now turn to the longer time series covering the period 1966-1974. Comparing Tables 8.2.1 and 8.2.2 we notice that, as in the case of the six-year samples, the average number of pages per journal of learned societies was consistently higher than for the commercial publishers. Yet, Table 8.2.2 shows for commercial publishers a steady increase in pages: the average number of pages in these five journals increased from 1,230 in 1966 to 1,812 in 1974, that is, by 47.2 per cent. For the learned societies, average number of pages per journal increased much less, from 2,416 in 1966 to 2,539 in 1974, although this latter figure is considerably below the peak of 2,775 pages reached in 1972. The sudden reduction in number of pages published in 1974, compared with the preceding five or six years, may reflect an economy drive by the publishing societies; alternatively it may possibly be traced to the appearance of new competing journals in the same or related fields of knowledge, drawing away a portion of the supply of publishable manuscripts.

With regard to average gross margins per journal, the learned societies show for each year larger figures than the commercial publishers, though the differences tended to diminish in the more recent years. In 1966, average gross margin was $80,220 for the 28 journals of the societies, 114 per cent above the $37,450 figure observed for the 5 journals of the commercial firms. By 1974, however, the difference was only 35 per cent, $152,020 for the learned societies and $112,720 for the commercial publishers — the percentage increase over

TABLE 8.2.2 Journals of Commercial Publishers — Average Number of Pages Per Year, Gross Revenue Per Journal, and Gross Revenue Per Page for Journals of Commercial Publishers (22 Journals, 1970-1975 and 5 Journals, 1966-1974)

Commercial publishers	1966	1967	1968	1969
22 Journals, 1970-1975				
Number of pages (average per journal)				
Gross margin (average per journal)				→
Gross margin per page (average per journal)				→
Gross margin as a per cent of gross revenue				
5 Journals, 1966-1974				
Number of pages (average per journal)	1,230	1,348	1,357	1,454
Gross margin (average per journal)	$37,450	$33,660	$38,970	$47,170
Gross margin per page (average per journal)	$30.40	$25.00	$28.70	$32.40
Gross margin as a per cent of gross revenue	41.3	34.9	36.0	35.9

(continued)

TABLE 8.2.2, continued

Commercial publishers	1970	1971	1972	1973
22 Journals, 1970-1975				
Number of pages (average per journal)	1,478	1,634	1,651	1,741
Gross margin (average per journal)	$95,220	$92,820	$99,280	$100,470
Gross margin per page (average per journal)	$64.40	$56.80	$60.10	$57.70
Gross margin as a per cent of gross revenue	59.3	54.6	56.2	53.7
5 Journals, 1966-1974				
Number of pages (average per journal)	1,492	1,528	1,566	1,619
Gross margin (average per journal)	$69,700	$76,190	$91,800	$100,690
Gross margin per page (average per journal)	$46.70	$49.90	$58.60	$62.20
Gross margin as a per cent of gross revenue	43.0	44.5	48.8	48.9

(continued)

TABLE 8.2.2, continued

Commercial publishers	*1974*	*1975*	*Per cent change 1966-1974*	*Per cent change 1970-1974*
22 Journals, 1970-1975				
Number of pages (average per journal)	*1,753*	*1,705*	-	*+18.6%*
Gross margin (average per journal)	*$117,750*	*$133,800*	-	*+23.7%*
Gross margin per page (average per journal)	*$67.20*	*$78.50*	-	*+4.3%*
Gross margin as a per cent of gross revenue	*54.8*	*55.0*	-	*-7.8%*
5 Journals, 1966-1974				
Number of pages (average per journal)	*1,812*	-	*+47.3%*	*+21.4%*
Gross margin (average per journal)	*$112,720*	-	*+201.0%*	*+61.7%*
Gross margin per page (average per journal)	*$62.20*	-	*+104.6%*	*+33.2%*
Gross margin as a per cent of gross revenue	*46.9*	-	*+13.6%*	*+9.1%*

Source: Machlup, Leeson, and Associates. Results for the Sample of 22 Journals from Tables 3.6.1 and 3.6.2 of Volume 2 of Information Through the Printed Word, pp. 176 & 178.

the period was far higher for the for-profit publishers, 201.0 per cent, compared with 89.5 per cent for the not-for-profit societies.

The differences in gross margins between the two types of publishers is largely removed when gross margins are calculated on a per-page basis. This is, of course, a consequence of larger number of pages contained in the society journals. In 1966 gross margin per page for the average journal was $33.20 for learned societies and $30.40 for the commercial firms; in the last three years of the series the ordering was reversed, with values for the commercial firms above those of societies. In 1974, for example, the figure for societies was $59.90 and for commercial firms $62.20. We notice that the commercial firms had lost some ground in 1967 and 1968, when their gross margins per page, $25.00 and $28.70, respectively, fell below the 1966 level of $30.40. They had a steady recovery after that, registering a 104.6 per cent increase over the entire period. The increase for the journals of learned societies was, by comparison, 80.4 per cent.

Relative gross margins, that is, the dollar values taken as a per cent of gross revenues, are also similar for the two types of publishers, although the percentages for the commercial firms are consistently below those of the learned societies. We may recall that for the samples spanning the shorter time series, also shown on these tables, relative gross margins were higher for the commercial firms in four out of the six years. For both time-series the percentage changes from the first year to the last are virtually identical for the two types of publishers.

Real Values of Gross Margins: Adjustments for Price Inflation

Before concluding our discussion on the behavior of gross margins over time, we ought to consider one additional topic: the "real" values of the figures involved, that is, gross margins adjusted for changes in the purchasing power of the dollar. Observations on purely financial, or "nominal," dollar values over a period characterized by economy-wide inflation in the prices of goods and services is apt to be misleading. After all, the quantity of services or physical products acquired by a journal publisher for one dollar of his gross margin (or net income, for that matter) in 1966 was, owing to the subsequent cost inflation, greater than the quantity he was able to purchase for a dollar in 1974. The magnitudes shown in Tables 8.2.1 and 8.2.2 are all expressed in nominal dollars and thus do not reflect the real purchasing power available to the publishers.

In order to convert the various nominal values to real values we have to select an appropriate price deflator. The choice is not a trivial matter. Numerous price deflators, or price indices, are available for converting current dollars of various years into constant dollars of a chosen base year; the adjusted figures obtained by using different deflators might convey somewhat different meanings.[2]

We have chosen for our purposes the "Implicit Gross Product Originating Deflator for Printing and Publishing Industries" compiled by the Department of Commerce. This deflator reflects the price increases of a large proportion of the goods and services regularly purchased by journal publishers as inputs for their production processes.

The gross margins shown as current values in Tables 8.2.1 and 8.2.2 are presented in Table 8.2.3 in terms of "constant" 1977 dollars. The price-index numbers used to deflate the nominal dollars are shown in the bottom row of the table. The per cent changes shown in the two columns at the far right of the table can be given the following interpretion: percentages equal or close to zero indicate that gross margins have just kept pace with price inflation in the goods and services purchased by journal publishers; negative percentages indicate that gross margins have lagged behind price inflation, so that the real value of gross margins has fallen; and positive values indicate that gross margins have grown at a faster rate than the rate of price inflation, so that the real value of gross margins has increased.

According to the figures presented in Table 8.2.3, gross margins measured in constant 1977 dollars showed gains over the 1966-1974 period both for learned societies and for commercial publishers. Over the shorter period, 1970-1974, the results were mixed, with some of the samples posting gains and others showing losses.

Considering first the samples spanning the longer time period, we see that average gross margin per journal for the 28 journals of learned societies increased in real terms from $149,640 in 1966 to $191,870 in 1974, or by 28.2 per cent. Real gross margins for the learned societies reached their peak in 1972 at $227,960, then declined in the two subsequent years. Over a portion of the 1966-1974 period, from 1970 to 1974, the real value of gross margins per journal fell by 3.4 per cent, from $198,670 to $191,870. Real gross margin per page for the learned societies increased from 1966 to 1974 from $61.90 to $75.60, or by 22.1 per cent, a slightly lower rate than per journal. Again, the peak was reached in 1972 with a gross margin of $82.80 per page (in 1977 dollars).

For the sample of five journals of commercial publishers, gains in real value of gross margins, both per journal and per

---

[2]Price indices are also discussed in Chapter 5 of Part 7 of this volume in the cohort analysis of gross margins in book publishing.

TABLE 8.2.3 Gross Margins of Learned Societies and Commercial Publishers in Constant 1977 Dollars

	1966	1967	1968	1969	1970	1971
Learned societies						
17 Journals, 1970-1975						
Gross margin (average per journal)					$217,860	$229,790
Gross margin per page (average per journal)					$94.90	$104.30
28 Journals, 1966-1974						
Gross margin (average per journal)	$149,640	$177,780	*	$198,240	$198,670	$208,820
Gross margin per page (average per journal)	$61.90	$69.30	*	$74.00	$72.90	$78.50
Commercial publishers						
22 Journals 1970-1975						
Gross margin (average per journal)					$145,750	$135,940
Gross margin per page (average per journal)					$98.60	$83.20
5 Journals 1966-1974						
Gross margin (average per journal)	$ 69,860	$ 60,870	$66,740	$ 77,440	$106,690	$111,580
Gross margin per page (average per journal)	$56.70	$45.20	$49.20	$53.20	$71.50	$73.10
Gross product originating deflator for printing and publishing industries (1977 = 100.00)	53.61	55.30	58.39	60.91	65.33	68.28

*Note: Complete data not available.

(continued)

TABLE 8.2.3, continued

	1972	1973	1974	1975	Per cent change 1966-1974	Per cent change 1970-1974
Learned societies						
17 Journals, 1970-1975						
Gross margin (average per journal)	$280,860	$250,030	$200,220	$213,880	-	-8.1%
Gross margin per page (average per journal)	$117.60	$110.40	$91.90	$97.60	-	-3.2%
28 Journals, 1966-1974						
Gross margin (average per journal)	$227,960	$221,890	$191,870	-	+28.2%	-3.4%
Gross margin per page (average per journal)	$82.80	$81.80	$75.60	-	+22.1%	+3.7%
Commercial publishers						
22 Journals 1970-1975						
Gross margin (average per journal)	$141,460	$138,330	$148,620	$148,250	-	+2.0%
Gross margin per page (average per journal)	$85.60	$79.40	$84.80	$87.00	-	-14.0%
5 Journals 1966-1974						
Gross margin (average per journal)	$130,810	$138,630	$142,270	-	+103.7%	+33.3%
Gross margin per page (average per journal)	$83.50	$85.60	$78.50	-	+38.4%	+10.0%
Gross product orignating deflator for printing and publishing industries (1977 = 100.00)	70.18	72.63	79.23	90.25		

Sources: Machlup, Leeson, and Associates, Tables 8.2.1 & 8.2.2, and U.S. Department of Commerce, Bureau of Economic Analysis, work files.

page, were above those registered by the sample containing 28 journals of learned societies. Gross margin per journal increased from $69,860 in 1966 to $142,270 in 1974, or by 103.7 per cent, while gross margin per page increased from $56.70 to $78.50, or by 38.4 per cent. Gains in gross margin over the 1970-74 period for this small sample of five journals were 33.3 per cent on a per-journal basis and 10.0 per cent on a per-page basis.

For the samples that span the shorter period, we see that for the years in which the pairs of time series overlap, changes in the real values of gross margin were less encouraging. Gross margin in constant 1977 dollars declined over the period for the 17 journals of learned societies, by 8.1 per cent on a per-journal basis and by 3.2 per cent on a per-page basis. Although the commercial firms made a slight gain in real gross margin per journal, by 2.0 per cent for 22 of their journals, they lost in real gross margin per page, as this figure declined from $98.60 in 1970 to $84.80 in 1974, or by 14.0 per cent.

These figures show that even the seemingly healthy gains in gross margins measured in current dollars turned out to be much smaller, and in some cases real losses, when expressed in terms of dollars of equivalent purchasing power. For the learned societies in particular, the accelerating inflation characterizing the early-to-mid 1970's, in combination with poorer performances in current-dollar gross margins over that period, actually led to a fall in real terms.

GROSS MARGINS BY FIELD

We put the following question to our computer. "How many journals are there on your memory tapes with data sufficient to calculate gross margins for the three consecutive years 1972, 1973, and 1974?" The answer came back, "Eighty-six." It was for this sample that we decided to calculate gross margins by field. We had asked also for the number of journals available for the single year 1974. There were a few more; 93. It seemed worthwhile, however, to sacrifice these additional seven journals in order to triple the years of coverage. Observations on gross margins for a single year would provide us with no means of checking whether our results were unusual, or atypical, owing perhaps to a sudden change in the demand for journals, or in their costs. On the other hand, were we to try to obtain an even longer time series of four consecutive years by adding one additional year to the three chosen, that is, by adding either 1971 or 1975, the sizes of the sample would have been reduced substantially, to 60 journals if the 1971-1974 series had been chosen, and to 55 journals in the 1972-1975 series.

The Sample of 86

The sample of 86 contains journals belonging to 15 fields. The classification scheme that we designed for use throughout our research and continue to use in Table 8.2.4 contains a total of 32 fields, 17 of which are not represented in our sample. In some of the fields no scholarly journals are published, for example in classes Nos. 27-30. That several academic disciplines, served by numerous learned journals, show zeros in the tabulation, for example, Nos. 5 and 10, is a consequence of the procedures used in collecting our data. We wanted data on gross revenues and manufacturing costs from some of the smaller learned societies and university presses located throughout the United States. This ambition explains why we had difficulties in including adequate numbers of journals in humanistic disciplines. Attempts to expand our coverage of small publishers by sending questionnaires through the mail met with only very limited success, especially by comparison with our preferred technique, that of arranging for members of our own staff to visit the publishers and collect the data first hand.

The distributions of the 86 journals among the fields of our classification scheme and by type of publisher are given in Table 8.2.4.

Thus, a majority of the journals in our sample belong to physical, medical, and technological fields and most, 48 of the 86, are published by learned societies. A disproportionately high number of journals, 38, fall under the heading "Physical Sciences," and 32 of these are published by learned societies. In some fields the samples are quite small, as few as a single journal, but we decided to record their gross margins anyway. Even though we display data for individual journals we are not in danger of breaching our pledge of confidentiality. It would be virtually impossible to identify any of these journals from the information shown here.

Before turning to the discussion of gross margins by field we present in Table 8.2.5 (in current dollars, not adjusted for price inflation) the results for all 86 journals combined. Thus, for the sample as a whole, gross revenues for the years 1972-1974 were $181,710, $184,590, and $196,170, respectively, with manufacturing costs of $85,480, $87,110, and $98,068 in the three years; hence, the average gross margins per journal were $96,230, $97,480, and $98,110. When in 1974 the average number of pages per journal for the sample fell and gross margins per journal rose, gross margin per page posted an increase, from $60.00 in 1972 and $60.80 in 1973, to $62.90 in 1974. Finally, the relative gross margin, that is, its ratio to gross revenues, declined slightly over the period, going from 53.0 per cent to 52.8 per cent and then to 50.0 per cent by 1974.

TABLE 8.2.4 Distribution of 86 Journals by Field and Type of Publisher

Field	Learned soci-eties	Univer-sity presses	Commer-cial pub-lishers	All pub-lishers
1. Life sciences (excluding medical science, biomedical technology, nursing)	1	0	4	5
2. Physical sciences	32	0	6	38
3. Environmental science and environmental technology	1	0	0	1
4. Mathematics and mathematical logic	0	1	1	2
5. Statistics	0	0	0	0
6. Engineering (excluding environmental technology)	10	0	0	10
7. Medical sciences	1	2	9	12
8. Other applied sciences and science tool subjects (including computer science, agriculture, military science, naval science)	1	0	1	2
9. Psychology	0	0	1	1
10. Economics	0	0	0	0
11. Business administration	0	0	0	0
12. Political science and government	0	2	0	2
13. Law	0	0	0	0
14. Philosophy and religion	1	1	0	2
15. History and archaeology	0	1	0	1
16. Geography	0	0	0	0
17. Anthropology, sociology, and urban studies	0	1	1	2
18. Physical education	0	0	0	0
19. Occupational education	0	0	0	0
20. Education (n.e.c.)	1	1	2	4
21 Home economics	0	0	0	0
22. Language and linguistics	0	2	0	2
23. English composition, communication, speech, etc.	0	0	0	0
24. Literature, English, foreign, comparative	0	2	0	2
25. Music	0	0	0	0
26. Art and art history	0	0	0	0
27. Fiction	0	0	0	0
28. General, adult	0	0	0	0
29. General, juvenile	0	0	0	0
30. Games and sports	0	0	0	0
31. Other	0	0	0	0
32. Interdisciplinary	0	0	0	0
Total	48	13	25	86

Source: Machlup, Leeson, and Associates.

Of course, these figures combine journals serving 15 different fields of knowledge and published by three different types of publishers. We shall now look at gross margins separately for the subsamples of journals in the various fields, and hope thereby to gain an idea of the diversity of performances that have contributed to the aggregate figures just discussed.

TABLE 8.2.5 Gross Revenue, Manufacturing Cost, Gross Margin per Journal and per Page, and Gross Margin as a Per Cent of Gross Revenue for 86 Journals (48 by Learned Societies, 13 by University Presses, and 25 by Commercial Publishers), 1972-1974

All Fields Combined-86 Journals (Values Expressed as Averages Per Journal)			
	1972	*1973*	*1974*
Gross revenue	*$181,710*	*$184,590*	*$196,170*
Manufacturing cost	*$ 85,480*	*$ 87,110*	*$ 98,060*
Gross margin	*$ 96,230*	*$ 97,480*	*$ 98,110*
Number of pages	*1,604*	*1,602*	*1,560*
Gross margin per page	*$60.00*	*$60.80*	*$62.90*
Gross margin as a per cent of gross revenue	*53.0*	*52.8*	*50.0*

Number Published by:		
	Learned societies	*48*
	University presses	*13*
	Commercial publishers	*25*

Source: Machlup, Leeson, and Associates.

The Results by Field

Table 8.2.6 presents, for each of the 15 fields, gross revenues, manufacturing cost, gross margin, number of pages, gross margin per page, and gross margin as a per cent of gross revenue, all expressed as averages per journal. When we rank

TABLE 8.2.6 Gross Revenues by Field — Gross Revenue, Manufacturing Cost, Gross Margin per Journal and per Page, and Gross Margin as a Per Cent of Gross Revenue for 86 Journals Separated into 15 Fields of Knowledge, 1972-1974

	1972	1973	1974
Life sciences — 5 journals (Values expressed as averages per journal)			
Gross revenue	$243,260	$266,530	$287,670
Manufacturing cost	$119,630	$140,010	$165,820
Gross margin	$123,630	$126,520	$121,850
Number of pages	2,251	2,475	2,754
Gross margin per page	$54.90	$51.10	$44.20
Gross margin as a per cent of gross revenue	50.8	47.5	42.3
Number of journals published by: Learned societies		1	
University presses		0	
Commercial publishers		4	
Physical sciences — 38 journals (Values expressed as averages per journal)			
Gross revenue	$261,370	$259,940	$273,400
Manufacturing cost	$126,740	$124,940	$137,930
Gross margin	$134,630	$135,000	$135,470
Number of pages	2,449	2,435	2,271
Gross margin per page	$55.00	$55.40	$59.70
Gross margin as a per cent of gross revenue	51.5	51.9	49.6
Number of journals published by: Learned societies		32	
University presses		0	
Commercial publishers		6	
Environmental sciences — 1 journal (Values expressed as averages per journal)			
Gross revenue	$472,760	$433,120	$408,000
Manufacturing cost	$106,140	$101,860	$127,720
Gross margin	$366,620	$331,260	$280,280
Number of pages	1,172	1,200	1,162
Gross margin per page	$312.80	$276.00	$241.20
Gross margin as a per cent of gross revenue	77.5	76.5	68.7
Number of journals published by: Learned societies		1	
University presses		0	
Commercial publishers		0	

(continued)

TABLE 8.2.6, continued

	1972	1973	1974
Mathematics — 2 journals (Values expressed as averages per journal)			
Gross revenue	$39,070	$45,820	$53,170
Manufacturing cost	$23,360	$25,950	$25,570
Gross margin	$15,710	$19,870	$27,600
Number of pages	1,042	897	729
Gross margin per page	$15.10	$22.20	$37.80
Gross margin as a per cent of gross revenue	40.2	43.4	51.9
Number of journals published by: Learned societies		0	
University presses		1	
Commercial publishers		1	
Engineering — 10 journals (Values expressed as averages per journal)			
Gross revenue	$98,090	$105,900	$114,140
Manufacturing cost	$44,920	$ 45,570	$ 54,210
Gross margin	$53,170	$ 60,330	$ 59,930
Number of pages	751	759	835
Gross margin per page	$70.80	$79.50	$71.80
Gross margin as a per cent of gross revenue	54.2	57.0	52.5
Number of journals published by: Learned societies		10	
University presses		0	
Commercial publishers		0	
Medical sciences — 12 journals (Values expressed as averages per journal)			
Gross revenue	$190,270	$203,640	$223,070
Manufacturing cost	$ 87,360	$ 95,170	$109,360
Gross margin	$102,910	$108,470	$113,710
Number of pages	1,179	1,132	1,206
Gross margin per page	$87.30	$95.80	$94.30
Gross margin as a per cent of gross revenue	54.1	53.3	51.0
Number of journals published by: Learned societies		1	
University presses		2	
Commercial publishers		9	

(continued)

TABLE 8.2.6, continued

	1972	1973	1974
Applied sciences — 2 journals (Values expressed as averages per journal)			
Gross revenue	$31,720	$29,150	$33,270
Manufacturing cost	$10,470	$11,160	$11,780
Gross margin	$21,250	$17,990	$21,490
Number of pages	323	323	306
Gross margin per page	$65.80	$55.70	$70.20
Gross margin as a per cent of gross revenue	67.0	61.7	64.6
Number of journals published by: Learned societies		1	
University presses		0	
Commercial publishers		1	
Psychology — 1 journal (Values expressed as averages per journal)			
Gross revenue	$15,700	$22,800	$24,300
Manufacturing cost	$ 7,700	$12,600	$15,400
Gross margin	$ 8,000	$10,200	$ 8,900
Number of pages	394	587	591
Gross margin per page	$20.30	$17.30	$15.30
Gross margin as a per cent of gross revenue	51.0	44.7	36.6
Number of journals published by: Learned societies		0	
University presses		0	
Commercial publishers		1	
Political science — 2 journals (Values expressed as averages per journal)			
Gross revenue	$42,960	$40,300	$40,460
Manufacturing cost	$20,240	$24,730	$26,510
Gross margin	$22,720	$15,570	$13,950
Number of pages	649	656	645
Gross margin per page	$35.00	$23.70	$21.60
Gross margin as a per cent of gross revenue	52.9	38.6	34.5
Number of journals published by: Learned societies		0	
University presses		2	
Commercial publishers		0	

(continued)

TABLE 8.2.6, continued

	1972	1973	1974
Philosophy/religion — 2 journals (Values expressed as averages per journal)			
Gross revenue	$31,840	$34,940	$33,110
Manufacturing cost	$12,730	$11,750	$11,490
Gross margin	$19,110	$23,190	$21,620
Number of pages	390	429	443
Gross margin per page	$49.00	$54.00	$48.80
Gross margin as a per cent of gross revenue	60.0	66.4	65.3
Number of journals published by: Learned societies		1	
University presses		1	
Commercial publishers		0	
History/archaeology — 1 journal (Values expressed as averages per journal)			
Gross revenue	$25,950	$30,110	$31,050
Manufacturing cost	$14,900	$12,990	$13,970
Gross margin	$11,050	$17,120	$17,080
Number of pages	368	452	342
Gross margin per page	$30.00	$37.90	$50.00
Gross margin as a per cent of gross revenue	42.6	56.9	55.0
Number of journals published by: Learned societies		0	
University presses		1	
Commercial publishers		0	
Anthropology, sociology, urban studies — 2 journals (Values expressed as averages per journal)			
Gross revenue	$47,480	$45,810	$53,670
Manufacturing cost	$24,400	$24,470	$29,130
Gross margin	$23,080	$21,340	$24,540
Number of pages	588	589	571
Gross margin per page	$39.20	$36.30	$43.00
Gross margin as a per cent of gross revenue	48.6	46.6	45.7
Number of journals published by: Learned societies		0	
University presses		1	
Commercial publishers		1	

(continued)

TABLE 8.2.6, continued

	1972	1973	1974
Education — 4 journals (Values expressed as averages per journal)			
Gross revenue	$57,470	$48,790	$61,090
Manufacturing cost	$18,440	$18,520	$23,430
Gross margin	$39,030	$30,270	$37,660
Number of pages	507	479	520
Gross margin per page	$77.00	$63.20	$72.40
Gross margin as a per cent of gross revenue	67.9	62.0	61.6
Number of journals published by: Learned societies		1	
University presses		1	
Commercial publishers		2	
Language/linguistics — 2 journals (Values expressed as averages per journal)			
Gross revenue	$15,340	$17,800	$18,650
Manufacturing cost	$11,100	$ 8,300	$ 8,890
Gross margin	$ 4,230	$ 9,500	$ 9,760
Number of pages	484	363	388
Gross margin per page	$8.70	$26.10	$25.20
Gross margin as a per cent of gross revenue	27.6	53.4	52.3
Number of journals published by: Learned societies		0	
University presses		2	
Commercial publishers		0	
English literature — 2 journals (Values expressed as averages per journal)			
Gross revenue	$26,620	$26,580	$26,450
Manufacturing cost	$16,190	$15,880	$15,370
Gross margin	$10,430	$10,700	$11,080
Number of pages	522	502	454
Gross margin per page	$20.00	$21.30	$24.40
Gross margin as a per cent of gross revenue	39.2	40.3	41.9
Number of journals published by: Learned societies		0	
University presses		2	
Commercial publishers		0	

Source: Machlup, Leeson, and Associates.

the 15 fields from largest to smallest average gross margins per journal in 1972, we obtain the order shown in Table 8.2.7.

TABLE 8.2.7 Ranking of Journals in 15 Fields on the Basis of Average Gross Margin per Journal in 1972

		Number of journals	Average gross margin per journal in 1972
1.	Environmental Science	1	$366,620
2.	Physical Science	38	$134,630
3.	Life Sciences	5	$123,630
4.	Medical Sciences	12	$102,910
5.	Engineering	10	$ 53,170
6.	Education	4	$ 39,030
7.	Anthropology, Sociology, and Urban Studies	2	$ 23,080
8.	Political Science	2	$ 22,720
9.	Other Applied Sciences	2	$ 21,250
10.	Philosophy and Religion	2	$ 19,110
11.	Mathematics	2	$ 15,710
12.	History and Archaeology	1	$ 11,050
13.	English Literature	2	$ 10,430
14.	Psychology	1	$ 8,000
15.	Language and Linguistics	2	$ 4,230

Source: Machlup, Leeson, and Associates.

It is apparent that in 1972 the journals in the sample belonging to fields of the natural sciences, medical sciences, and technology hold a clear edge over the journals in the social sciences and humanities. Furthermore, if we were to rank the fields in this manner for 1973 and 1974 the positions of the first six fields would remain unchanged. There would, however, be some shuffling of places over the three-year period among the subject areas holding intermediate positions. For example, mathematics moves up to the seventh position by 1974 and political science falls to twelfth place. The three lowest-ranked fields, English literature, psychology, and language and linguistics, change places among themselves over the period, but remain as a group "in the cellar."

Rankings based on gross margins per page (shown only in Table 8.2.6) are somewhat different, owing, primarily, to the diversity in average number of pages published per year among the journals of various fields. Still, six of the seven fields that rank highest on this criterion are in natural or medical sciences, or technological areas. These positions are maintained intact over the three-year period. The five fields of lowest rank in 1972 are history and archaeology, psychology, English literature, mathematics, and language and linguistics. This latter ranking is slightly upset in the subsequent years, but four of these five lowest-ranking fields remain among the bottom five. The field of history and archaeology moves up to seventh place by 1975, while political science, formerly in tenth place moves down to fourteenth.

We have thus far ranked the fields only on the basis of absolute dollar values — average gross margin per journal and per page — without taking account of the ratios of gross margins to gross revenue by field. It would be informative to do so, because the absolute value of gross margin alone tells nothing about the magnitude of revenues earned or of costs incurred by the journals. These ought to be considered. If, for example, a journal has an absolute gross margin of $45,000 and accomplishes this with gross revenues of, say, only $85,000 we should rate its economic performance above a journal with the same absolute gross margin, but with gross revenues of, say, $500,000. In the first case, gross margin as a per cent of gross revenue, or the relative gross margin, is a substantial 53 per cent, but in the second case it is only a meager 9 per cent. Thus, the latter of the two journals had to pull in almost six times the revenue of the former in order to produce an absolute dollar gross margin of equivalent size. It is in this sense that we can say the former journal "out-performed" the latter.

Before proceeding, we ought to consider for a moment a situation converse to the one just described, where two journals have equal relative gross margins but different dollar gross margins. In this situation, the journal with the higher gross margin in terms of dollars would be considered the healthier of the two by virtue of its capacity to defray a larger proportion of the publisher's operating and overhead expenses and thereby contribute more toward net income or, in the case of for-profit firms, net profits before taxes. We shall return to this point shortly.

When we rank the 15 fields according to their performance as measured by gross margin as a per cent of gross revenue in 1972, we obtain the order shown in Table 8.2.8.

TABLE 8.2.8 Ranking of Journals in 15 Fields on the Basis of Gross Margin as a Per Cent of Gross Revenue in 1972

		Number of journals	Gross margin as a per cent of gross revenue in 1972
1.	Environmental Science	1	77.5
2.	Education	4	67.9
3.	Other Applied Sciences	2	67.0
4.	Philosophy and Religion	2	60.0
5.	Engineering	10	54.2
6.	Medical Sciences	12	54.2
7.	Political Science	2	52.9
8.	Physical Science	38	51.5
9.	Psychology	1	51.0
10.	Life Sciences	5	50.8
11.	Anthropology, Sociology, and Urban Studies	2	48.6
12.	History and Archaeology	1	42.6
13.	Mathematics	2	40.2
14.	English Literature	2	39.2
15.	Language and Linguistics	2	27.6

Source: Machlup, Leeson, and Associates.

The single journal in environmental sciences retains its first-place position, with a relative gross margin of 77.5 per cent of gross revenues. Language and linguistics is again in last place, having a gross margin equal to only 27.6 per cent of gross revenue. Many of the other fields have moved to higher or lower positions compared with their rankings on the basis of dollar-value gross margin. For instance, life sciences fell from third to tenth place and physical sciences from second to eighth. On the other hand, psychology moved up from fourteenth place to ninth and education advanced from sixth place into second.

In attempting to judge the relative performance of journals in the various fields on the basis of their rankings by gross margins as a per cent of gross revenue, we should consider two points. First, there are, in many cases, small differences in relative gross margins of journals in different fields. For example, from engineering, which occupies fifth position, to anthropology and sociology, which occupies the eleventh position, the size of relative gross margin varies only slightly, from 54.2 per cent to 48.6 per cent. Such slight differences among fields leads to a considerable amount of shifting in the ranks in the subsequent two years. Secondly, we may refer back to the comment regarding the performances of journals with equivalent or nearly equivalent relative gross margins. In such cases, the dollar values of gross margins should take some weight in the assessment. To cite one example, the ten journals in the field of engineering rank fifth with a relative gross margin of 54.2 per cent, while the twelve medical journals rank a close sixth with a value of 54.1 per cent. Their absolute average gross margins, however, are $53,170 and $102,910, respectively. Hence, the contribution to operating expenses and overhead of the latter sample of journals is nearly twice the contribution of the former. On this criterion, the medical journals have handily out-performed the engineering journals. The table contains a number of other examples of this sort.

Accounting for the Wide Variations

What factors, aside from the small sample sizes with which we are dealing, may account for the wide differences in gross margins that are observed among several fields?

The economic performances of gross margins in the various fields seem to be correlated with the type of publisher producing the journals. Results on gross margin by type of publisher presented in an earlier section of this chapter and in Chapter 3.4 of Volume 2, showed that, in general, journals of learned societies had the highest gross margins, followed by commercial publishers, with university presses invariably in last place. In the sample of 86 just discussed, journals in fields of the natural sciences, medical sciences and technology that showed comparatively healthy gross margins were published, for the most part, by learned societies and commercial firms, whereas journals in fields of the social sciences and humanities that showed poorer performances were published, by and large, by university presses. From Table 8.2.6, we find that of the 71 journals counted among the six highest-ranking fields in Table 8.2.7, 46 were published by learned societies and 21 by commercial firms, while only four were published by university presses. On the other hand, of the 15 journals in the nine fields of lowest rank, only two were by learned societies, three by commercial publishers, but ten by university presses. In the interest of scholarship, university presses are prepared to publish journals in fields that promise comparatively little in the way of financial success.

That we observe a relationship between gross margins and the type of publishers producing the journals, however, does not account fully for the differences in performances among fields. To shed light on this question we present in the next section a closer look at the size and composition of revenues.

THE EFFECTS OF PAGE CHARGES AND ADVERTISING ON GROSS MARGINS

In Volume 2 we had a chapter on gross revenues from journal publishing. There we discussed the main sources of revenue, chiefly in their relation to total gross revenue and subscription prices. The following discussion extends those analyses: by examining the relation between the main sources of revenue and the sizes of gross margins.

Needless to say, the capacity to earn revenues is the chief determinant of the financial success of the journal. Revenues from subscriptions provide the bulk of total revenue for most journals, but many rely also on alternative sources. Some not-for-profit publishers levy page charges for the articles they publish, though this practice has developed primarily in fields of the natural sciences and engineering in which a relatively large number of researchers and authors are affiliated with financially strong corporations or perform their research under grants from governmental agencies and foundations.

A third source of revenue for journal publishers is derived from selling advertising space, though success in earning significant amounts of revenue from this source is determined by the circulation, or more importantly, by the number of readers of the journal. Advertisers are not likely to pay much for space in a journal that reaches only a few hundred readers.

Other, sometimes considerable, sources of revenue include sales of reprints and sales of back issues; less significant have been revenues from the sales of microfilm, mailing lists, permission fees for the reproduction of articles and notes, and cash subsidies and gifts.

We may shed some light on the role played by these various sources of revenue in determining the size of gross margins if we separate the sample of 86 journals into four groups: (1) those with revenue from page charges and advertising, (2) those with revenue from page charges but not from advertising, (3) those without revenue from page charges but with revenue from advertising, and (4) those with revenue from neither page charges nor advertising. We would expect a high proportion of journals in fields showing relatively healthy gross margins to fall under one of the first three categories mentioned above and fields with poorer performances to fall under the fourth.[3]

We present results on gross margins for journals that fall into each of these four categories of revenue separately for learned societies, university presses, and commercial publishers in Tables 8.2.9, 8.2.10, and 8.2.11, respectively.

We should note, however, that only learned societies levy page charges; hence categories (1) and (2), which draw on this source of revenue, include no journals of university presses or commercial publishers, whereas categories (3) and (4) include all three types of publishers. To be more specific, Table 8.2.9A presents data for 10 journals of learned societies obtaining revenues from both page charges and advertising; Table 8.2.9B presents data for 15 journals of learned societies obtaining revenue from page charges but not from advertising; Table 8.2.9C presents data for 5 journals of learned societies obtaining revenues from advertising but not from page charges; and Table 8.2.9D presents data for 18 journals of learned societies obtaining revenues from neither page charges nor advertising. With regard to university presses, Table 8.2.10 presents data for 12 journals obtaining revenue from advertising but not from page charges (the single university-press journal with revenues from neither page charges nor advertising is not shown on any table). Finally, with regard to commercial publishers, Table 8.2.11A presents data for 9 journals obtaining revenue from advertising but not from page charges and Table 8.2.11B presents data for 16 journals obtaining revenues from neither page charges nor advertising.

The fact that page charges are levied only by learned societies is not merely an accident of sample selection. As a

---

[3]Some readers may raise the question of the part played by manufacturing cost in explaining the comparative performances of gross margins by field. We might consider that most of the journals in our sample that belong to the natural sciences and technology are precisely those that show the largest gross margins, and are published by professional societies or commercial firms producing more than one journal and, in some instances, more than ten. In addition, the journals that ranked highest tend, on average, to contain more pages per year. Thus, we might expect these journals to reap the advantages of large-scale production. The data displayed in Table 8.2.6, however, cannot be used to test this hypothesis directly. The required analyses are rather involved and cannot be given adequate consideration here. We shall therefore only suggest the possibility of economies of scale as a factor contributing to the relative performances of journals of different fields, and leave a more thorough discussion of the concepts involved to another chapter.

TABLE 8.2.9 Learned Societies — Gross Revenues by Source of Funds, Manufacturing Costs, and Gross Margins per Journal, per Page, and As a Per Cent of Gross Revenue for Journals with Revenues: A. from Both Page Charges and Advertising; B. from Page Charges but not from Advertising; C. from Advertising but not from Page Charges; and D. from neither page Charges nor Advertising, 1972-1974

	A. 10 Journals of learned societies with revenues from page charges and advertising						B. 15 Journals of learned societies with revenues from page charges but not from advertising					
	1972		1973		1974		1972		1973		1974	
		Per cent of total revenue		Per cent of total revenue		Per cent of total revenue		Per cent of total revenue		Per cent of total revenue		Per cent of total revenue
Average number of pages per journal	3,333		3,182		3,046		1,683		1,733		1,652	
Average revenue from:												
Subscriptions	$223,530	56.3	$217,890	56.5	$223,030	59.2	$111,150	55.6	$110,610	54.2	$135,250	61.2
Page charges	$102,990	25.9	$ 92,020	23.9	$ 85,560	22.7	$ 69,010	34.6	$ 70,770	34.7	$ 68,280	30.9
Advertising	$ 12,780	3.2	$ 12,990	3.4	$ 11,570	3.1	0	0.0	0	0.0	0	0.0
All other	$ 57,910	14.6	$ 62,220	16.2	$ 56,520	15.0	$ 19,620	9.8	$ 22,570	11.1	$ 17,500	7.9
Total gross revenue (average per journal)	$397,210	100.0	$385,120	100.0	$376,680	100.0	$199,780	100.0	$203,950	100.0	$221,030	100.0
Manufacturing cost (average per journal)	$207,440		$206,600		$227,120		$ 91,390		$ 88,360		$ 92,630	
Gross margin (average per journal)	$189,770		$178,520		$149,560		$108,390		$115,590		$128,400	
Gross margin per page (average per journal)	$56.90		$56.10		$49.10		$64.40		$66.70		$77.70	
Gross margin as a per cent of gross revenue	47.8		46.4		39.7		54.3		56.7		58.1	
Number of subscribers (average per journal)	6,290		6,200		6,290		5,780		5,660		5,720	
Average price of an annual subscription	$35.50		$35.10		$35.50		$19.20		$19.50		$23.60	

	A. Field	Number of journals	B. Field	Number of journals
Fields included in the sample	Life sciences	1	Physical sciences	8
	Physical sciences	7	Engineering	7
	Medical sciences	1		
	Other applied sciences	1		
	Total	10	Total	15

(continued)

TABLE 8.2.9, continued

	C. 5 Journals of learned societies without revenues from page charges but with revenue from advertising						D. 18 Journals of learned societies with revenues from neither page charges nor advertising					
	1972		1973		1974		1972		1973		1974	
		Per cent of total revenue		Per cent of total revenue		Per cent of total revenue		Per cent of total revenue		Per cent of total revenue		Per cent of total revenue
Average number of pages per journal	1,579		1,548		1,564		1,260		1,186		1,120	
Average revenue from:												
Subscriptions	$161,080	36.5	$158,380	36.1	$168,530	37.8	$62,620	85.3	$63,230	83.6	$82,190	86.8
Page charges	0	0.0	0	0.0	0	0.0	0	0.0	0	0.0	0	0.0
Advertising	$259,330	58.7	$250,830	57.2	$252.120	56.6	0	0.0	0	0.0	0	0.0
All other	$ 21,210	4.8	$ 29,450	6.7	$ 25,170	5.6	$10,790	14.7	$12,360	16.4	$12,550	13.2
Total gross revenue (average per journal)	$441,620	100.0	$438,660	100.0	$445,820	100.0	$73,410	100.0	$75,590	100.0	$94,740	100.0
Manufacturing cost (average per journal)	$115,420		$113,060		$148,160		$55,700		$56,560		$70,680	
Gross margin (average per journal)	$326,200		$325,600		$297,660		$17,710		$19,030		$24,060	
Gross margin per page (average per journal)	$206.60		$210.30		$190.30		$14.10		$16.00		$21.50	
Gross margin as a per cent of gross revenue	73.9		74.2		66.8		24.1		25.2		25.4	
Number of subscribers (average per journal)	25,950		$25,340		$25,790		$2,130		$2,260		$2,210	
Average price of an annual subscription	$6.20		$6.30		$6.50		$29.40		$28.00		$37.20	
					Number of journals						Number of journals	
Fields included in the sample	Physical sciences				3		Physical sciences				14	
	Environmental sciences				1		Engineering				3	
	Philosophy and religion				1		Education				1	
			Total		5				Total		18	

Source: Machlup, Leeson, and Associates.

matter of policy, foundations and other agencies of the federal government that provide funds for research permit authors to pay page charges to not-for-profit organizations, such as learned societies, with money provided by the grants and contracts, but prohibit such payments to for-profit commercial publishers.[4] That none of the university presses in the sample have revenue from page charges may be a consequence of the journals that happen to fall in our sample, but is more likely a reflection of their own practices of precluding such payments by authors.

Only one university-press journal qualified for the fourth category — journals with revenues from neither page charges nor advertising — so we decided not to include this journal from the analysis.

For each subsample of journals in the tables that follow, we divide total revenues into four components — from subscriptions, from page charges, from advertising, and from all other sources. This last category includes revenue from the sale of reprints, the sale of back issues and microfilm and revenues from permission fees. It does not include cash subsidies or gifts.

In addition to the contributive shares of revenue from the four sources, Tables 8.2.9 through 8.2.11 present several other characteristics pertinent to an evaluation of comparative performances. These include, in terms of averages per journal, number of pages, manufacturing costs, gross margins per journal and per page, gross margin as a per cent of gross revenue, number of subscribers (circulation), and average price of an annual subscription. This latter figure represents the weighted average of differential subscription rates charged to different categories of subscribers, such as individuals, students, and institutions, and is calculated by dividing subscription revenue by the number of subscribers. Also shown on the tables is the number of journals by field belonging to each subsample.

---

[4]An interesting side-note on the policies of government foundations on the question of page charges has relevance for our analysis of gross margins by field. The National Science Foundation, a major supporter of research in the natural sciences and technology, provides funds through their research grants with which authors may pay page charges for the articles they publish. This is not the case with the National Endowment for the Humanities, a major supporter of research in humanistic fields. The Endowment prohibits payment of page charges to all types of publishers with funds provided through their grants.

Learned Societies

Looking first at the learned societies, we see from Table 8.2.9 that of the four samples shown, the five journals of Panel C, with revenues from advertising but not from page charges, have the largest total gross revenues and the highest gross margins, whether measured per journal, per page, or as a per cent of gross revenue. In 1972, for example, these journals collected, on average, $441,620 in total revenue, with 58.7 per cent of this amount accounted for by revenues from advertising. The resulting gross margins for that year were $326,200 per journal and $206.60 per page; relative gross margin was 73.9 per cent of gross revenue. That these five journals turned in such high performances on all counts can be attributed in large part to their capacity for earning advertising revenues, and this was undoubtedly made possible by their unusually large circulation — 25,950 subscribers for the average journal in the sample — more than four times the number of the ten journals of Panel A with 6,290 subscribers in 1972, the second-highest of the four averages. Furthermore, the large relative share of advertising revenue in the sample of five made it possible for their publishers to charge much lower subscription prices, only $6.20 for the year in question, compared with $19.20 for the 15 journals with revenues from page charges but not from advertising in Panel B, $29.40 for the 18 journals with revenues from neither page charges nor advertising in Panel D, and $35.50 for the ten journals with revenues from both page charges and advertising in Panel A.

The journals ranking second on the basis of total gross revenue are those that collect revenues from both page charges and advertising. These are shown in Panel A. Gross revenues were $397,210 in 1972, but declined to $385,120 in 1973 and to $376,680 in 1974, largely as a result of the diminishing contributions made by page charges, in terms of dollars as well as percentages of total revenue. The latter measure fell from 25.9 per cent of the total in 1972 to 22.7 per cent by 1974. Advertising revenues made almost insignificant contribution to total revenue for these journals, around 3 per cent of the total in each year. This is probably explained by the relatively small number of subscribers for the average journal in this category. Even the miscellaneous item, containing all other sources of revenue, yielded more than advertising did — 14.6 per cent in 1972, 16.2 per cent in 1973, and 15.0 per cent in 1974.

In addition to ranking second in terms of gross revenue, the ten journals of Panel A also had the second-highest gross margins per journal, though the figure declined over the three years from $189,770 in 1972 to $149,560 by 1974. In terms of gross margin per page, on the other hand, the ten journals of Panel A were surpassed in each year by the 15 journals of Panel B, those with revenues from page charges but not from advertising. This is a direct consequence of the difference in number of pages published. The average journal in the sample of ten in Panel A had approximately twice the number of pages as the average journal in the sample of 15 in Panel B. Relative gross margins are also lower for the sample of ten in Panel A than for the sample of 15 in Panel B.

Because of these mixed results for these two samples it would be difficult to rate their overall performance and designate which has earned second place and which has earned third place behind the five journals of Panel C. Even if we were to judge the two samples on the basis of the differences in subscription prices, \$35.50 in 1972 for the ten journals of Panel A compared with only \$19.20 for the 15 journals of Panel B, we would want to make an adjustment for differences in the number of pages actually purchased for these prices. An adjustment would show that a subscriber paid only \$10.70 per 1,000 pages for the average journal in the latter sample, a reversal of the relative prices of the annual subscriptions.

The fourth sample of journals of learned societies in Table 8.2.9 contains the 18 that have revenues from neither page charges nor advertising. The results displayed in Panel D show that on all counts these are the poorest performers. Average total revenues are far below those of any of the other three samples: \$73,410 in 1972, \$75,590 in 1973, and \$94,740 in 1974. Naturally, these journals rely heavily on subscriptions for their revenue, with approximately 85 per cent of total revenue derived from this source. Gross margins per journal were comparatively small, ranging from \$17,710 in 1972 to \$24,060 in 1974 and gross margin per page ranged from a low \$14.10 to \$21.50, still very small by comparison with the other samples. Relative gross margins range from 24.1 per cent of gross revenue in 1972 to 25.4 per cent in 1974, by far the worst showing on the table. To emphasize the contrasts in performances we may compare these 18 journals in 1974, their best year on all counts, with the five journals of Panel C for the same year; the differences are striking. Average gross revenues for the five is 4.7 times higher, gross margin per journal is 12.4 times higher, gross margin per page is 8.9 times higher and relative gross margin is 2.6 times higher than for journals in the sample of 18. Furthermore, these 18 journals with revenues from neither page charges nor advertising have fewer subscribers and fewer pages per year than journals in any of the other three samples. That there are relatively few subscribers helps explain why these journals have no revenue from advertising; the purchasers of advertising space would be reluctant to place their ads in a journal that reaches so few readers. Finally, the journals in this sample of 18 are the most expensive on the basis of subscription price per 1,000 pages. In 1972, for example, the price of 1,000 pages was approximately \$23.30, nearly six times the price of \$3.90 for 1,000 pages of the five journals in Panel C.

By way of a summary of these results on the effects of revenues from page charges and advertising on gross margins of the journals of learned societies, we might emphasize some of the points already discussed and add a few additional comments.

On the basis of all measures presented, journals with revenues from advertising but not from page charges registered by far the best economic performances. Journals with revenues from neither page charges nor advertising showed for all of our measures the poorest performances. Between these extremes were the journals of the two remaining categories, those with revenues from both page charges and advertising, and those with revenues from page charges but not from advertising.

The four samples of journals provide a good deal of support for our *a priori* judgment that journals with larger circulations would be more likely than smaller ones to obtain substantial revenues from advertising.

We might speculate that the five journals in Panel C that turned in the best economic performances among all four groups are less specialized and written in less technical language than journals of the other groups. Such attributes would make these journals of interest to a wider audience and would account for their relatively large circulations.

Our observations on the samples of journals in Panels A and B suggest that page charges make a significant contribution to the publishers' gross margins, accounting for between one-quarter and one-third of gross revenues. Without revenue from page charges, for example, the 15 journals of Panel B would have had in 1972 total gross revenue of $130,700 instead of $199,780; gross margin per journal would be only $39,380 instead of $108,390, gross margin per page only $23.40 instead of $64.40, and relative gross margin only 30.0 per cent of gross revenue instead of 54.3 per cent. These are large differences, though we note that even without revenues from page charges, the journals of Panels A and B would have performed at least as well as, and in most cases better than, the 18 journals of Panel D that had revenues from neither page charges nor advertising. Finally, there seems to be no particular correspondence between the fields in which the journals are classified and the combinations of the various sources of revenue available to them. We note, for example, that all four samples contain a large proportion of journals that belong to the same field — physical sciences.

University Presses

Results for the twelve journals of university presses that have revenue from advertising but not from page charges are presented in Table 8.2.10. These journals are smaller in terms of number of pages published than any of the samples of journals of learned societies. Indeed, the average university-

TABLE 8.2.10 University Presses — Gross Revenues by Source of Funds, Manufacturing Costs, and Gross Margins per Journal, per Page, and as a Per Cent of Gross Revenue for 12 Journals with Revenue from Advertising but not from Page Charges, 1972-1974

	1972		1973		1974	
		Per cent of total revenue		Per cent of total revenue		Per cent of total revenue
Average number of pages per journal	540		528		516	
Average revenue from:						
Subscriptions	$32,450	79.6	$33,880	84.3	$34,040	83.5
Page charges	0	0.0	0	0.0	0	0.0
Advertising	$ 2,330	5.7	$ 2,030	5.0	$ 2,350	5.8
All other	$ 5,970	14.7	$ 4,300	10.7	$ 4,390	10.7
Total gross revenue (average per journal)	$40,750	100.0	$40,210	100.0	$40,780	100.0
Manufacturing cost (average per journal)	$22,090		$21,930		$23,060	
Gross margin (average per journal)	$18,660		$18,280		$17,720	
Gross margin per page (average per journal)	$34.60		$34.60		$34.30	
Gross margin as a per cent of gross revenue	45.8		45.5		43.5	
Circulation (average per journal)	4,910		4,970		4,840	
Average price of an annual subscription	$6.60		$6.80		$7.00	

Fields included in the sample		Number of journals
	Medical sciences	2
	Political science	2
	Philosophy and religion	1
	History and archaeology	1
	Anthropology/sociology	1
	Education	1
	Language and linguistics	2
	Literature	2
	Total	12

Source: Machlup, Leeson, and Associates

press journal had less than 550 pages in any of the three years, or less than half the number of pages of even the smallest journals of learned societies, those in Panel D of Table 8.2.9.

The journals of university presses also have smaller total revenues than any of the samples containing journals of learned societies. Revenues amount to about $45,500 in each of the three years shown with only 5 to 6 per cent of this total accounted for by revenue from advertising. Owing to smaller manufacturing cost, the gross margins of the average university-press journal of $18,660 in 1972, $18,280 in 1973, and $17,720 in 1974 are on a par with the worst-performing journals of learned societies, again, the 18 journals of Panel D in Table 8.2.9. Because the university presses publish fewer pages in their journals, gross margins per page, approximately $34.00 in each of the three years, are substantially above the analogous figures for the worst-performing journals of learned societies, but still far below the figures for the other three samples of Table 8.2.9. Relative gross margins of the university-press journals, 45.8 per cent of gross revenue in 1972, 45.5 per cent in 1973, and 43.5 per cent in 1974, are similar in value to the ten journals of learned societies in Panel A of Table 8.2.9, those that collect revenues from both page charges and advertising.

A remarkable feature of these university-press journals is their low price. In spite of their comparatively weak economic performances relative to the learned societies, they manage to charge a price per journal, an average of $6.60 to $7.00 over the three-year period, far below all but the most economically successful journals of the societies. On a per-1,000-page basis the university-press journals lose some of their advantage, but are still far lower than the price per 1,000 words of the most expensive society journals — the 18 of Panel D — and on the same order of magnitude as the prices of the society journals of Panels A and B.

With regard to the fields included in the sample of university-press journals, we see from the list of fields in Table 8.2.10 that only a small proportion, two of the twelve, are in the natural sciences, but that the remaining ten belong to fields of the social sciences and, for the most part, to fields of the humanities.

Commercial Publishers

The journals of commercial publishers fall under two categories: a sample of nine with revenue from advertising but, of course, with no revenue from page charges, shown in Panel A of Table 8.2.11; and a sample of six with revenues from neither page charges nor advertising, shown in Panel B of Table 8.2.11. Total gross revenues for these journals that sell advertising space are among the highest of any of the samples we have studied thus

TABLE 8.2.11 Commercial Publishers — Gross Revenues by Source of Funds, Manufacturing Costs, and Gross Revenues per Journal, per Page, and as a Per Cent of Gross Revenue for Journals with Revenues: A. from Advertising but not from Page Charges; and B. from neither Page Charges Nor Advertising

	A. 9 Journals of commercial publishers without revenue from Page Charges but with Revenue from Advertising					
	1972		1973		1974	
		Per cent of total revenue		Per cent of total revenue		Per cent of total revenue
Average number of pages per journal	1,470		1,508		1,662	
Average revenue from:						
Subscriptions	$106,950	43.3	$124,360	46.1	$132,050	44.0
Page charges	0	0.0	0	0.0	0	0.0
Advertising	$100,000	40.5	$102,750	38.1	$116,870	38.9
All other	$ 39,910	16.2	$ 42,640	15.8	$ 51,320	17.1
Total gross revenue (average per journal)	$246,860	100.0	$269,750	100.0	$300,240	100.0
Manufacturing cost (average per journal)	$117,440		$131,020		$153,100	
Gross margin (average per journal)	$129,420		$138,730		$147,140	
Gross margin per page (average per journal)	$88.00		$92.00		$88.50	
Gross margin as a per cent of gross revenue	52.4		51.4		49.0	
Circulation (average per journal)	6,730		7,480		8,090	
Average price of an annual subscription	$15.90		$16.60		$16.30	

Fields included in the sample		Number of journals
	Life sciences	3
	Medical sciences	6
	Total	9

(continued)

TABLE 8.2.11, continued

B. 16 Journals of Commercial Publishers with Revenue from Neither Page Charges Nor Advertising

	1972		1973		1974	
		Per cent of total revenue		Per cent of total revenue		Per cent of total revenue
Average number of pages per journal	1,530		1,640		1,580	
Average revenue from:						
Subscriptions	$106,800	90.7	$114,860	93.1	$132,890	91.8
Page charges	0	0.0	0	0.0	0	0.0
Advertising	0	0.0	0	0.0	0	0.0
All other	$ 10,910	9.3	$ 8,450	6.9	$ 11,830	8.2
Total gross revenue (average per journal)	$117,710	100.0	$123,310	100.0	$144,720	100.0
Manufacturing cost (average per journal)	$ 48,620		$ 54,420		$ 57,760	
Gross margin (average per journal)	$ 69,090		$ 68,890		$ 86,960	
Gross margin per page (average per journal)	$45.20		$42.00		$55.00	
Gross margin as a per cent of gross revenue	58.7		55.9		60.1	
Circulation (average per journal)	1,930		1,940		2,060	
Average price of an annual subscription	$55.00		$59.20		$64.50	

Fields included in the sample		Number of journals
	Life sciences	1
	Physical sciences	6
	Mathematics	1
	Medical sciences	3
	Other applied sciences	1
	Psychology	1
	Education	2
	Anthropology/sociology	1
	Total	16

Source: Machlup, Leeson, and Associates.

far — $246,860 in 1972, $269,750 in 1973, and $300,240 in 1974 — higher than all but two groups of the journals of learned societies — those with revenues from both page charges and advertising and those with revenues from advertising alone. The contributive shares of advertising revenues in total revenues are substantial for these commercial publishers, accounting for 40.5 per cent of the total revenue in 1972, 38.1 per cent in 1973, and 38.9 per cent in 1974.

Average gross margins for the commercially published journals increased from $129,420 in 1972 to $147,140 by 1974, placing them, again, in third place behind the two samples of journals of learned societies mentioned above. We should add one qualification to this ranking; in 1974 there was a near tie between the gross margin of the journals of commercial publishers and the gross margin of the ten journals of learned societies with revenues from page charges and advertising. The figures are $147,140 and $149,560, respectively. It is interesting to note that the nine commercially published journals managed, without the benefit of revenues from page charges, to produce gross margins of the same order of magnitude as the society journals with revenues from both page charges and advertising (in Table 8.2.9A), and of an even higher order of magnitude than the society journals with revenues from page charges alone (in Table 8.2.9B). Furthermore, gross margins per page are higher for the commercially published journals — $88.00, $92.00, and $88.50 for the three years in question — than for either of these two samples of learned societies. This is especially noteworthy with regard to the journals of learned societies that have revenues from page charges but not from advertising, because the average number of pages in these journals is roughly equivalent to the number of pages in the commercially published journals. A comparison among these three samples of *relative* gross margins reveals few substantial differences.

Having noted some of the differences and similarities among the three samples (8.2.9A, 8.2.9B, 8.2.11A) with respect to revenues and gross margins, we might conclude this portion of the discussion by comparing subscription prices charged to the buyers. Here too, the journals of commercial firms compare favorably with their not-for-profit counterparts. The average prices of an annual subscription for the nine journals of commercial firms are $15.90 in 1972, $16.60 in 1973, and $16.30 in 1974, which is much below the prices of both samples of journals of the societies, particularly the sample containing journals with revenues from both page charges and advertising, for which prices were $35.50, $35.10, and $35.50 in the same three years.

There is little difference in price among the three samples, however, when calculated on a per-1,000-page basis. For example, in 1972 the nine commercially published journals were priced at $10.80 per 1,000 pages, the ten journals of learned societies with revenue from both page charges and advertising were priced at $10.70 and the 15 journals of learned societies with revenues from page charges alone were priced at $11.40 per 1,000 pages.

Focusing now on the two samples of commercially published journals in Table 8.2.11, we see several important differences between those that sell advertising space and those that do not. To note first the few similarities, we see that average number of pages per journal and gross margin as a per cent of gross revenue are of comparable magnitudes for the two samples. The relative gross margins are somewhat higher for the journals in Panel B (those that have no revenues from advertising); this can be attributed in large part to their comparatively low manufacturing costs, which, in turn, may be a result of not having to compose (typeset) and print any advertising pages.

A third similarity can be seen between the *dollar* values of average revenue from subscriptions: in 1972 the nine journals with revenue from advertising collected an average of $106,950 in subscription revenue; the 16 journals with no revenue from advertising collected $106,800 in the same year. There are close similarities in subscription revenue in the two subsequent years as well. The relative contributions that these similar dollar amounts make to total revenue, however, are hardly comparable. Subscription revenue accounts for between 43 per cent and 46 per cent of total revenue for the journals with advertising but between 90 per cent and 93 per cent of total revenue for the journals without advertising.

With regard to total gross revenue, gross margin per journal, and gross margin per page for the two samples we can make a general statement without reciting the long list of individual dollar amounts involved: for all three of these measures, the dollar amounts for the journals with no advertising revenue are approximately one half of the corresponding amounts recorded for the journals that do obtain revenue from the sale of advertising space.

With regard to circulation, the journals with no advertising revenues have relatively small numbers of subscribers, as we have expected: 1,930 in 1972, 1,940 in 1973, and 2,060 subscribers in 1974. The journals that do carry advertising have circulations nearly four times as large as these figures.

The average price of an annual subscription is three to four times higher for the journals with no advertising, amounting to $55.00 in 1972, $59.20 in 1973, and $64.50 in 1974. These journals also have the highest price per 1,000 pages of any journals considered in our analysis. In 1972, for example, the price was $35.90 for 1,000 pages, and in 1974, $40.80. By comparison, the 18 journals of learned societies with revenues from neither page charges nor advertising (Table 8.2.9D) had smaller gross revenues and smaller gross margins per journal and per page than this sample of 16 commercially published journals, yet charged less — only $23.30 per 1,000 pages in 1972 and $33.20 in 1974.

Concluding Remarks

In the interest of clarity, we ought to emphasize a few of the major observations made in the preceding sections.

Journals of learned societies and commercial publishers that derive revenue from advertising have, in general, healthier gross margins and lower subscription prices than journals that do not.

Journals with revenues from neither page charges nor advertising have, for learned societies and commercial publishers, smaller gross margins, fewer subscribers, and higher subscription prices than journals with revenue from either of these two sources.

For journals of learned societies, revenues from page charges make significant contributions to the economic performances of the journals.

Before we conclude the discussions of gross margins, we may return briefly to the question of whether the wide variations in gross margin among fields discussed in an earlier section of this chapter can be attributed, at least in part, to differences in the sources of revenue available to the journals. If sources of revenue have a strong influence in determining the performance observed in different fields, then we would expect a high proportion of the journals in the fields with healthy gross margins, principally those in the natural sciences and technology, to be among the samples of journals that derive revenues from advertising or from both advertising and page charges; and, conversely, a high proportion of the journals in fields with less healthy gross margins, principally those in the humanities, to belong to the samples with revenues from neither page charges nor advertising.

The data we presented in Tables 8.2.9 through 8.2.11 do not provide full support for these expectations, largely because the journals in the humanistic fields with the poorest financial performances are published by university presses, and most of them do draw revenue from advertising (though the contributive shares of advertising revenue for these journals are very small, only around 5 or 6 per cent). On the other hand, some journals in fields of the natural sciences and technology (see Table 8.2.11B) have moderately healthy gross margins, yet collect revenues from neither page charges nor advertising. Hence, one has to look beyond the sources of revenue in order to account for differences in gross margins among fields.

CHAPTER 8.3

JOURNALS: STATISTICAL EXPENSE FUNCTIONS

*ARTHUR ROSENZWEIG**

In this chapter we present statistical analyses of the determinants of publishers' expenditures on the manufacture of their journals, that is, expenditures on composition and on paper, printing, and binding. We use the term "expense" function rather than "cost" function to describe the model used in our statistical tests in order to allude to the fact that, as a rule, journal publishers do not themselves compose or print or bind the journals, but purchase these services from outside vendors. We shall elaborate on this point in a subsequent section.

The primary purpose of the analysis is to determine if manufacturing expenses bear any systematic relation to the *quantities* of composition, paper, printing, and binding purchased from the vendors of these goods and services. A distinctive feature of the method is a separation of manufacturing expenses into their pre-run component (composition) and their run-off component (paper, printing, and binding). The significance of this separation rests on the assumption that because the two separate steps in the manufacturing process are different by nature, economies may characterize one but not the other; if they are lumped together, a clear picture of the relationship between expenses and quantities purchased could not be obtained.

We shall see that publishers may often secure lower prices when they purchase in larger quantities. This source of economies in publishing reflects the nature of the manufacturing process and is *independent* of both the overall scale of the manufacturer's operations and of the scale of the publisher's own organization. Hence, the cost reductions are not "economies of scale" according to the accepted definition in economic theory. Rather they are attributable to indivisibilities in the use of resources in the manufacturing process. Our analysis will suggest, for example, that the set-up costs incurred

---

*The formulations and analyses presented in this chapter were prepared by Arthur Rosenzweig, an adjunct member of our research staff.

for any printing run is one type of indivisibility, in that roughly the same lump-sum cost is incurred regardless of size of print run, and this leads to considerably higher manufacturing costs for journals with shorter runs. These and related issues will be explored in greater detail when we turn to the formulation of our expense functions.

Stages in the Production of Journals

The process by which a journal is produced comprises a sequence of stages. Manuscript selection, technical editing, copy editing, composition, printing, binding, and mailing are all technically independent steps in the publication of a journal. Each step can be carried out at a different moment in time, at a different location, or, in fact, by a different firm. The production decisions of the publisher include not only the determination of the quantities of final output to be produced — i.e., how many pages, articles, copies, issues — but also the time schedule for the performance of the steps and the locations at which they are to be performed. None of these are once-and-for-all decisions, although some of them are revised more frequently than others.

Decisions regarding the quantities of final output are, perhaps, revised most frequently. The frequency of the issue tends to remain fixed from year to year but has occasionally been changed by some journals. The number of copies of an issue may vary little among issues in a given year because circulation is established on the basis of annual subscriptions, but circulation can vary significantly from one year to the next. The number of pages and articles per issue can vary from issue to issue and from year to year.

The time schedule for the performance of steps may also change. Publication lags — the period of time between the submission of a manuscript and its acceptance (or rejection) for publication, and the period of time between the acceptance of the manuscript and its publication — have tended to grow in the recent past.

The locations of some of these steps have changed. For some journals, the selection of manuscripts, the technical editing of articles, and the copy editing take place at different parts of the country depending on the institutional affiliations and places of residence of editors and referees. Much more important is the fact that currently, few publishers, if any, manufacture their own journals. Instead, they purchase the services of compositors, printers and binders. Even the servicing of subscriptions is farmed out: subscription agents keep subscription lists, and printers or binders (they are often the same firm) are responsible for mailing the issue.

Implications for an Analysis of Costs

These characteristics of the publication process must be kept in mind in any serious attempt at empirical analysis of the costs of publishing journals. Typically, analysis of cost data of publishers has focused on the relationship between the total annual cost of publication and the annual output of the journal. For example, statistical cost functions have been estimated relating annual expenses attributed to the publication of a journal to the annual numbers of pages and copies produced. Other statistical cost functions have explained variations in the yearly expenses incurred by a publisher for all of his journals to more aggregate indexes of annual output. While some of the pitfalls inherent in these experiments have been duly recognized — such as the problem of dealing with accounting expenses that have been arbitrarily allocated — others relating to the characteristics mentioned above have not.

An example relates to the fact that the manufacturing of the journal is not done by the publisher but is done under contract with independent establishments. Hence, at the manufacturing stage, the publisher is not a producer but a purchaser of goods and services. Statistical cost functions relating annual cost to annual output are based in theory on the production function of the firm. According to the theory, when prices paid for resources used in production are given, the relation between cost and output reflects a dual relationship between output and the quantities of resources used to produce it. Thus, for example, one may investigate returns to scale or returns to variable proportions directly in terms of the behavior of cost as a function of output. The production function of the publisher, however, does not include the manufacturing of the journal, whereas manufacturing expenses — money paid to compositors, printers, and binders — are a significant portion of total cost. Therefore, variations in total cost reflect charges incurred under contracts with manufacturing firms which may or may not be completely accounted for by variations in the final output of the publisher. In this case if, for example, we observe that publishers' costs per unit of output are lower when output is greater, we may ask whether this reflects the presence of economies in the publishers' operations or the presence of economies in the manufacturers' operations that are passed through to the publishers, or whether it reflects some other factor such as the structure of the market for the goods and services produced by compositors, printers, or binders. A statistically estimated relation between published output and the total expenses incurred by the publisher in producing that output will not be revealing in this respect.

Empirical Tests Undertaken

The discussion of the last paragraph supplies the motivation for the empirical analysis undertaken in subsequent sections. We wish to know whether the manufacturing expenses of publishers for their journals bear any systematic relation to the quantities of goods and services purchased from the manufacturers and for which these expenses were incurred. We shall investigate this question by considering separately expenditures for composition, on the one hand, and expenditures for printing and binding, on the other, and estimating a series of statistical equations for each of these components of total manufacturing expenses. The estimated equations, which we shall refer to as "expense functions" since they are not cost functions in the traditional sense, will be based on data for 35 journals for six years from 1969 through 1974. These expense functions will serve to isolate the relation between expenditures and quantities purchased from other factors that influence expenditures, such as inflationary charges in costs and technological progress, although we may be able to gain some insight on the latter as well.

The two cases will be considered in turn. For purposes of exposition, we begin with expenditures for printing and binding. In each case, before proceeding to the statistical analysis, we shall offer a characterization of the production processes and purchasing decisions involved. The characterization will serve to motivate the formulation of the expense functions to be estimated.

EXPENSE FUNCTIONS: PRINTING AND BINDING

In printing, the elementary operation is producing the individual print-run. This involves, first, setting up the press with plates, paper, and ink, and making appropriate adjustments for such things as the speed of operation and the force with which the printing medium will meet the paper. During the running of the press, paper is fed through the press and impressions are made. At the end of the operation there is the clean-up which readies the press for the set-up of the next run. Some techniques link the printing with some or all of the subsequent finishing and binding activities.

Measuring Output

If we take as our measure of output of the print run the number of impressions made, we may approximate this by multiplying the number of pages to be printed by the number of copies to be printed. We shall refer to this product — pages times copies — as the number of impressions.

Commercial printers who accept work on a contract basis (as distinguished from, say, printers of newspapers who print nothing else) are typically called upon to do a variety of jobs during any given period of time. Each job may be differentiated from the next according to the number of impressions it requires. Printers' costs per period are determined not only by the number of jobs but also by the sizes of these jobs in terms of numbers of impressions.

In any given period of time, printers will also incur certain fixed costs — i.e., costs that do not vary with either the number of jobs or the sizes of jobs during this period. Printers will want to earn enough revenue to cover both the fixed and variable components of total cost. From the point of view of expenses incurred by publishers, however, only the variable costs of printing are relevant since, as we shall see, prices charged by printers will vary from job to job during the period according to the way in which costs vary from job to job with the number of impressions.

Costs are likely to vary less than proportionally with the number of impressions over a considerable range of impressions. For one thing, jobs of different sizes call for different printing techniques — i.e., different types of presses are most efficient over different ranges of impressions — and the presses used to print larger jobs are absolutely more cost-efficient than those used to print smaller jobs. A commercial printer will typically own several types of presses.

Moreover, the costs of operating a given press will vary less than proportionally with the number of impressions printed over a wide range of impressions. The fact that the quantities of resources devoted to setting up and cleaning up the press do not vary significantly with the number of impressions is the crucial factor here. Another important factor, closely related to the first, may be that the total time required for a run varies less than proportionally with the number of impressions. We mention this explicitly because "run time" is a variable that printers often use when figuring the costs of a job.

Thus, there are two reasons why journals with proportionally larger printing runs are not likely to cost proportionally more to print than journals with shorter print-runs. Both have to do with indivisibilities of resources used in printing: first, set-up and clean-up costs are not significantly lower for shorter runs; second, the greater efficiency of equipment used for larger runs is not available for smaller runs. Both imply that the unit costs — cost per impression — of printing journals with larger printing runs should be lower than for "short-run journals," to use an expression common in the trade,[1]

[1]The terms "short-run book" or "short-run journals" usually refer to the small number of copies produced. The "short run" here should not be confused with the "short run" of economic theory defined as a period of time during which the quantities of some resources — such as plant and equipment — cannot be increased.

at least this should be so for a considerable range of impressions. The question now arises whether these cost reductions are passed on to the publishers in the form of lower prices per impression for larger-run jobs.

The Hypothesis Tested

All this does not mean that printers operate under conditions of "increasing returns." That is, during any given period of time, total cost will be an increasing function of the number of jobs, and one can reasonably expect the marginal-cost-of-jobs function to be increasing as well.[2] However, it seems plausible that printers will charge proportionally less for proportionally larger jobs, at least over some range. This is the hypothesis we shall test here. Stated another way, while the price per impression may be the same for jobs of the same size, it may be substantially higher for very small jobs and decreasing with the size of the job up to some point.

The primary objective of publishers in contracting with printers is to have the issues of their journals printed at the lowest possible expense to themselves. There should be no serious obstacle to attaining this objective. The number of printing establishments is large, even within a given geographic locality, so that prices for jobs of different sizes are likely to be competitive and therefore standardized. Publishers choose the efficient technique for the size (in terms of impressions) of the issue by choosing a printer who owns that technique. As the size of the issues of his journals changes from year to year, a publisher may change the technique used by contracting with a different printer.

We may reasonably expect, therefore, that the observed expenditure per impression for a journal of a given number of impressions per issue represents the minimum attainable. Furthermore, from the previous discussion, we should expect to observe lower costs per impression for journals with greater numbers of impressions per issue, at least over a considerable range of impressions. Hence, we posit an empirical expense function in which the total expenditure for the printing of the issue increases at first less than proportionally with the number of impressions to be printed, until some relatively large number of impressions is reached beyond which the function increases at a more than proportional rate. Our expense function thus resembles the total variable cost function of traditional economic theory, whose average function is U-shaped.

---

[2]That is, each additional job of uniform size is more costly to undertake than the one preceding it.

Specifying the Functional Form

A simple functional form that exhibits the above properties is one in which the cost to the publisher of printing the issue is a cubic function of the number of impressions in the issue. Thus,

$$\text{Expense of Printing} = a_1(pc) + a_2(pc)^2 + a_3(pc)^3,$$

where expense of printing the issue is expressed in dollars, p is the number of pages in the issue, c is the number of copies, and pc is the product of pages times copies, representing the number of impressions. The values of the coefficients a_2 and a_3 indicate the ranges over which expenditure per impression is increasing or decreasing. If, for example, a_2 is negative while a_3 is positive, expenditure per issue will be decreasing until the number of impressions attains a value of $-(a_2/2a_3)$, after which expenditure per issue will be increasing.

The argument we have made to motivate the above expense function for printing can be carried over to the subsequent finishing and binding activities. These activities, when they are not directly linked to the printing process through the use of integrated equipment, may be characterized in exactly the same manner as the printing activities, at least with regard to the relation between variations in cost and variations in output. As before, the size of the job generally determines the choice of technique, with some techniques being substantially more efficient for jobs with larger numbers of pages and copies. Again there are set-up costs and clean-up costs which do not vary significantly among jobs using the same equipment. Hence, what we have said about the relation between expenditures for printing and the number of impressions in the issue applies also to expenditures for printing and binding combined, and the combined expense function takes the same functional form; i.e.,

$$\text{Expense of Printing and Binding} = a_1(pc) + a_2(pc)^2 + a_3(pc)^3.$$

Since we have data for the combined expense and not for its components, it is the combined expense function we shall use in our statistical experiments. First, however, it will be necessary to make certain modifications to the variables of the function dictated by the nature of the available data.

Modifications

Our statistical analysis utilizes a sample of 35 journals for which we have data on annual expenditures for printing and binding, and on the annual number of pages, annual circulation and number of issues in each year from 1969 through 1974. The 35 journals in the sample are published by five publishers: two society publishers, one commercial publisher, and two university presses.

The combined expense function described in the previous section is formulated as a relation between the printing and binding expense of a single issue and the number of impressions — pages times copies — in the issue. Since our data are in terms of *annual* totals, we shall have to modify the variables in the expense function accordingly.

First, we shall have to assume that the number of pages does not vary significantly among the issues of a journal in any year, so that the annual number of pages divided by the number of issues published per year will provide a close approximation of the number of pages in any of the issues of the same year. Secondly, we shall take the annual circulation of the journal to represent the number of copies of each of the issues produced during the same year. The number of copies produced generally exceeds circulation, so that this variable will be an underestimate. We can now represent the number of impressions in each issue of the same year as the product of the number of pages per issue as derived above and the annual circulation of the journal. Hence, the calculated number of impressions will be the same for each of the issues of a journal in any given year.

Finally, we shall calculate average expenditures for printing and binding per issue by dividing the annual expenditures by the number of issues per year. It will be convenient to use this as the dependent variable. By spreading annual expenditures over issues, we are also averaging out any variations in prices charged by printers and binders during the year that are due to factors other than changes in the number of impressions per issue, including such factors as changes in wages paid or changes in the prices of paper and other materials used in printing and binding.

Keeping in mind the modifications made in the combined expense function of the previous section, and using upper-case letters to distinguish the modified variables from their counterparts in the original version, we may write the final form of the equation to be estimated as follows:

$$EPB/I = a_1(PC/I) + a_2(PC/I)^2 + a_3(PC/I)^3 + e,$$

where

EPB = annual expenditure for printing and binding, in thousands of current dollars,

I = number of issues per year

PC = annual number of impressions, the product of annual number of pages (P) and annual circulation (C), in millions, and

e = stochastic disturbance term, assumed to be normally distributed with zero mean

The coefficients of this equation will be estimated using six different sets of cross-sectional data on journals, one set for each of the six years for which we have data. Thus we will have six estimated equations altogether for the same cross-section of 35 journals but each estimate will pertain to a different year. We do this rather than pool the observations for all years primarily for two reasons. First, it will provide us with six sets of results with which to judge the appropriateness of our functional specification. Secondly, our expenditures data are in current dollars and these may vary from year to year because of factors not accounted for in our equation. These factors include changes in the relative prices of resources acquired and used by printers and binders, changes in the overall rate of inflation of these prices, and changes in the extent to which price changes are transmitted by printers and binders to the publishers who purchase their services. Although there exist time series of cost indices for some of the resources used in printing and binding, these indices are not specific enough for us to have confidence in their relevance to the expenditures we are explaining. Moreover, even if we had very specific information on actual changes in prices, we have no convincing theory that would allow us to postulate their expected influence on the variables and parameters of our equations. We can however expect our estimated parameters to change from year to year at least partially in response to these factors, and shall later make some attempt to gauge their effect.

We now turn to the results of our experiment, obtained by ordinary least-squares regression.

Results of the Regression for Printing and Binding

Table 8.3.1 presents the estimated values of the coefficients of the expense functions for printing and binding. The first column contains the year, hence, each row in the table gives the results of estimation for a particular year. The second column shows the number of observations, the same for each year. The third, fourth and fifth columns contain the three independent variables that enter into the expense function. The numerical value of the estimated coefficient of each variable in the equation for a given year appears in the column assigned to that variable. Below the value of each coefficient appears in parentheses, the value of the t-statistic for the hypothesis that the coefficient is equal to zero. A single or double asterisk denotes whether this hypothesis can be rejected at the .001 or .01 level of significance, respectively.

The results provide surprisingly favorable evidence of the appropriateness of the type of expense function we have hypothesized. The signs of the coefficients in the equation for each year indicate that the expense of printing and binding the

TABLE 8.3.1 Results of the Regressions for the Expense of Printing and Binding Journals, 1969-1974

Year	*Number of observations (journals)*	*Estimated coefficients (t-values in parentheses)*		
		$(\frac{PC}{I})$	$(\frac{PC}{I})^2$	$(\frac{PC}{I})^3$
1969	*35*	*+3.38*	*-0.52*	*+0.03*
		*(12.78)**	*(6.06)**	*(4.78)**
1970	*35*	*+3.24*	*-0.50*	*+0.03*
		*(12.42)**	*(5.57)**	*(4.25)**
1971	*35*	*+3.22*	*-0.59*	*+0.04*
		*(7.91)**	*(3.72)**	*(2.91)***
1972	*35*	*+3.23*	*-0.54*	*+0.03*
		*(9.86)**	*(4.75)**	*(3.77)**
1973	*35*	*+3.77*	*-0.69*	*+0.04*
		*(10.06)**	*(5.10)**	*(4.07)**
1974	*35*	*+4.66*	*-0.79*	*+0.05*
		*(13.75)**	*(6.65)**	*(5.48)**

*Note: * denotes significance at the .001 level; ** denotes significance at the .01 level.*

Source: Machlup, Leeson, and Associates (with Arthur Rosenzweig).

issue rises at first less than proportionally with increases in the number of impressions per issue, but eventually begins to rise more than proportionally with increases in the latter quantity. These signs do not change at all among equations for different years. The levels of significance of the coefficients (from the t test) are favorably low for all coefficients in all years. The t-values are all significant at the .001 level with the exception of one which is significant at the .01 level.

Graphical Illustration

The function we have estimated seems to be stable also in the sense that the values of the coefficients do not seem to change very much from one year to the next. But this conclusion may be misleading. It would be difficult to tell whether the function changes from year to year merely by looking at the table. To assist us in comparing the estimated equations for different years, we shall provide a graphical illustration. Rather than graph the expense functions directly, however, we shall graph the average-expense functions which can easily be derived from the total-expense functions specified in a previous section. The equations for the average-expense function express printing-and-binding expenditure per impression, rather than expenditure per issue, as a function of the number of impressions per issue. A graphical representation of the average functions will be more convenient for comparative purposes.

We derive the average-expense function from the equation for the total-expense function as follows. The total-expense function is

$$EPB/I = a_1(PC/I) + a_2(PC/I)^2 + a_3(PC/I)^3.$$

Dividing both sides of the equation by (PC/I), impressions per issue, yields

$$EPB/PC = a_1 + a_2(PC/I) + a_3(PC/I)^2.$$

This expresses expenditure per impression (EPB/PC) as a function of the number of impressions per issue (PC/I). Since the estimates of a_2 and a_3 derived above are, respectively, negative and positive, expenditure per impression will be decreasing, at a minimum, or increasing with the number of impressions per issue as the latter is, respectively, less than, equal to, or greater than the quantity $-(a_2/2a_3)$.

Graphs of the estimated average expense functions for the six years are presented in Figure 8.3.1. The vertical axis measures expenditure per impression in current dollars per thousand impressions. The horizontal axis measures the number of impressions per issue in millions of impressions. The endpoints of the graph for each year are determined by that year's minimum and maximum numbers of impressions per issue among journals in the sample. Thus, for example, the graph for 1974 extends over a domain from the 1974 sample minimum of 0.08 million impressions per issue to the sample maximum of 10.32 million impressions.

We note first that the six curves are strikingly similar in shape. Each shows expenditure per impression falling over a considerable range of impressions per issue, but eventually attaining a minimum, and finally increasing. The curves for the first five years, 1969-1973, are positioned fairly close to each other, while the curve for 1974 seems to be significantly above the others.

Figure 8.3.1 can be interpreted with the help of Table 8.3.2. As before, the first column lists the years and the

Figure 8.3.1 Graphical Representation of
Estimated Average Expense Functions for Six Years

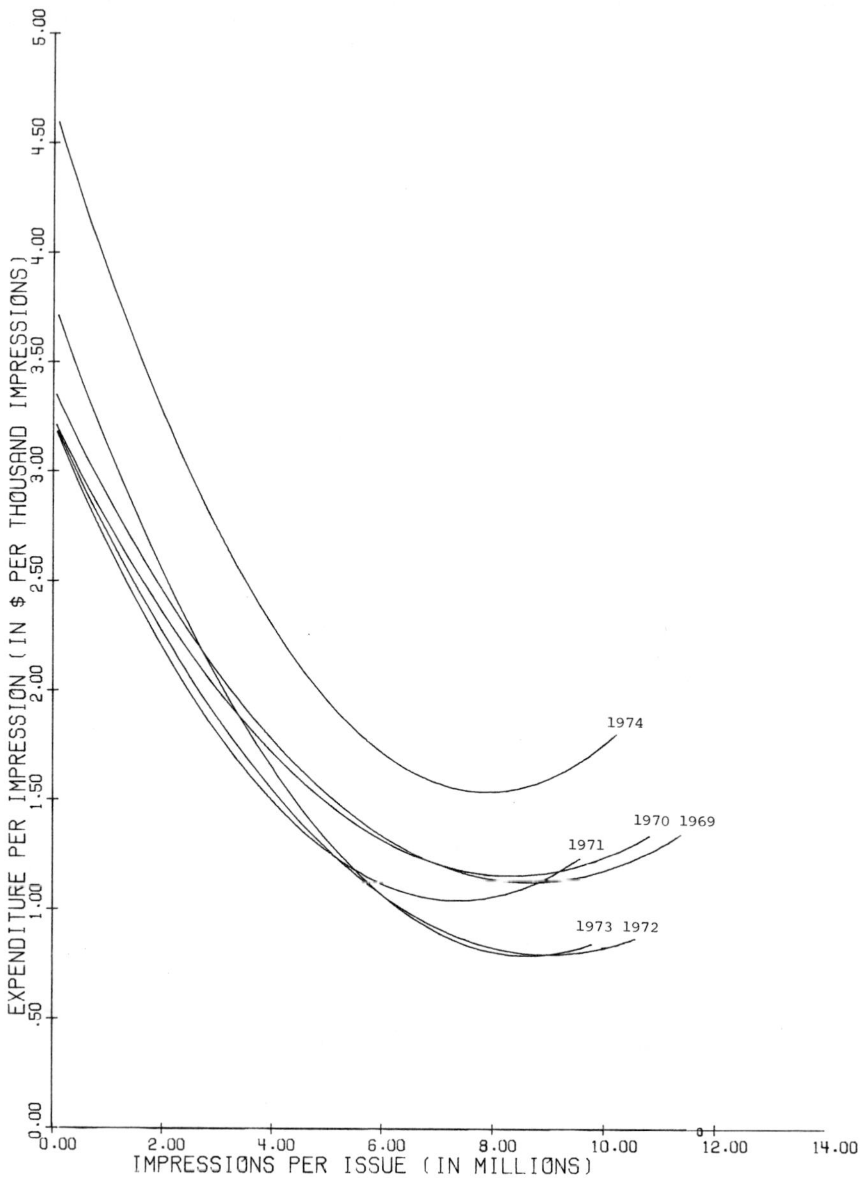

Source: Machlup, Leeson, and Associates (with Arthur Rosenzweig)

TABLE 8.3.2 Impressions per Issue in the Sample of 35 Journals and Properties of the Estimated Expense Functions

	Impressions per issue (in millions)						
Year	Number of observations (journals)	Minimum	Maximum	Mean	Standard deviation	Value of (PC/I) at which (EPB/PC) is at a minimum	Per cent change in (EPB/PC) per one per cent change in (PC/I), at sample mean
1969	35	0.05	11.50	1.70	2.45	8.67	-0.27
1970	35	0.05	10.91	1.54	2.21	8.33	-0.24
1971	35	0.06	9.66	1.35	1.95	7.38	-0.25
1972	35	0.08	10.66	1.37	2.15	9.00	-0.24
1973	35	0.08	9.87	1.31	2.03	8.63	-0.26
1974	35	0.08	10.32	1.28	2.08	7.90	-0.22

Source: Machlup, Leeson, and Associates (with Arthur Rosenzweig).

second shows the number of journals. The third through sixth columns give the minimum, maximum, mean, and standard deviation of the sample distribution of impressions per issue for each year. The seventh column gives the quantity of impressions per issue at which expenditure per impression attains its minimum value as calculated from the estimated expense function for that year. This quantity varies between 7.38 and 9.00 million. We note that the sample mean is considerably below this quantity and well into the range of decreasing expenditure per impression in all years.

Cost Savings for Larger Purchases

These results imply the presence of substantial economies in the purchasing of printing and binding services over most of the range of impressions per issue actually produced among journals in the industry. As a rule of thumb, we may state that for journals with less than seven million impressions per issue, printing and binding expenses per impression will fall as the number of impressions increases (or they will rise as the number of impressions decreases). Moreover, the decrease (increase) in expenditure per impression may be relatively large for many journals. To give an idea of the orders of magtude that may be involved, we compute, for each year, the percentage change in expenditure per impression that would be induced by a one per cent change in the number of impressions per issue at the sample mean. The value of this index, presented in the last column of Table 8.3.2, is computed according to the formula

$$[d(EPB/PC)/d(PC/I)]^* \cdot [(PC/I)^*/(EPB/PC)^*]$$

where $[d(EPB/PC)/d(PC/I)]^*$ is the derivative of the average expense function evaluated at the sample means of impressions per issue $(PC/I)^*$ and expenditure per impression $(EPB/PC)^*$. We see from the table that the value of this index ranged between -0.22 in 1974 to -0.27 in 1969. Hence, for example, for a journal with 1.28 million impressions per issue in 1974, expenditure per impression would have been 22 per cent smaller (greater) if the number of impressions had been 1 per cent greater (smaller).

These results suggest that, in terms of printing and binding costs, there is for many journals an inducement to increase circulation and publish more pages. On the other hand, falling circulation and fewer pages will generally mean rapidly increasing printing and binding expenses. We note that the mean values of impressions per issue presented in the fifth column of Table 8.3.2 actually decrease from year to year in four out of five cases. This might imply that many journals experienced declines in circulation and/or in pages published during the period, or that a few journals experienced very large declines. In such cases, the costs of printing and binding must have risen more rapidly than they otherwise would have.

We should emphasize at this point that increases in the number of impressions per issue from year to year does not mean that expenditure per impression will necessarily decrease, even when these changes occur well within the range of declining expenditure per impression along the expense function. This is because the position of the expense function does not remain the same from one year to the next. This is evident from Figure 8.3.1, where, in particular, the curve for 1974 is everywhere well above the others. The expense function may shift and bend from year to year for a number of reasons, primary among them is changes in the prices of resources used in printing and binding. In other words, part of the variation over time in prices paid for the printing and binding of a journal can be explained by the variation in the number of impressions; the rest must be attributed to such factors as cost inflation in the printing and binding industry.

To pursue this point further, we present a set of calculations based on statistics published by the United States Government which describe the pattern of changes in the prices of broad categories of resources used in printing and binding during the period 1969-1974. We are particularly interested to see if these figures suggest a clue as to why the graph of the estimated expense function for 1974 is substantially higher than the others.

The Role of Cost Inflation

The Bureau of Economic Analysis of the Department of Commerce publishes aggregate price indices for materials, and machinery and equipment used in the production of various producers' goods as well as average weekly earnings of production workers in various industries aggregated according to Standard Industrial Classification (SIC) code. From these we have chosen the three annual series that seem to be most relevant to the printing and binding activities: (1) the Producers Price Index for "book paper, #3 uncoated offset," (2) the series for average weekly earnings of production workers in printing and publishing (SIC code 27), and (3) the Producers Price Index for "machinery and equipment, printing trades." For each of these series, we calculate the year-to-year percentage changes for each year from 1969 through 1974. These percentage changes are presented in Table 8.3.3 under the abbreviated heading "Paper," "Labor," and "Machinery and Equipment."

As an example of how to interpret the figures in the table, consider the row for 1970. The figure in the column headed "Paper" represents the percentage change in the price of paper from 1969 to 1970. The figures in the next two columns repre-

TABLE 8.3.3 Percentage Changes from Year to Year in Selected Price Indices for Paper, Labor in the Printing Industries, and Machinery and Equipment used in Printing and Binding for the Period 1969-1974

Year	*Paper* (*Book paper, #3 uncoated offset*)	*Labor* (*Production workers in printing & publishing*)	*Machinery and equipment* (*Printing trades*)
1969	-	-	-
1970	*5.5*	*4.6*	*5.9*
1971	*3.8*	*6.7*	*3.0*
1972	*1.9*	*7.9*	*1.0*
1973	*2.0*	*5.3*	*5.4*
1974	*27.8*	*5.4*	*10.4*

Source: All three series are calculated from data published by the Bureau of Labor Statistics of the United States Department of Commerce. The figures for "Paper" and "Machinery and Equipment" are year-to-year percentage changes in Producers Price Indexes. The figures for "Labor" are percentage changes in annual average weekly earnings.

sent the percentage changes in the prices of labor and machinery and equipment, respectively, for the same period. These figures show that the prices of all three types of resources increased in 1970. They also imply that the price of machinery and equipment increased relative to the prices of the other two, and that the relative price of paper to labor also increased.

The most noticeable figure in the table is the 27.8 per cent increase in the price of paper in 1974. This is by far the largest percentage increase in the price of any of the resources in any of the years. By comparison, all the other figures in the table are of a uniform but much lower, order of magnitude, with the possible exception of the 10.4 per cent increase in the price of machinery and equipment which also occured in 1974. This suggests that the substantially higher price of paper in 1974 is a likely explanation of the relative position of the graph of the expense function for that year. The unusually large increase in the price of paper must have been passed on to the publishers of journals in the form of higher prices for printing and binding. Higher prices for machinery and equipment might also have contributed, although their effect is not likely to be as direct and widespread as that of the change in the price of paper.

EXPENSE FUNCTIONS: COMPOSITION

In recent years there has been considerable progress in developing new techniques of composition. Notable among them are methods of photocomposition, which have largely replaced older typesetting methods in the manufacturing of many types of publications. Some of the newest techniques of automatic composition, involving such recent innovations as computerized word processing, tend to integrate much of the editorial work with the composition stage and streamline the operation of large-volume publication programs.

The introduction of new composition techniques has induced some publishers to experiment with in-house composition. At the same time, many of the manufacturing firms that have traditionally done many kinds of typesetting and graphics work have been induced to specialize in a few, but to expand production to encompass more types of publications than previously. The general environment for this stage of the industry seems to be one of experimentation and continuing evolution.

Characterization of the Composition Process

In this context, it would be difficult to devise a characterization of the composition process which would provide a general explanation of how the costs of composition are determined. However, a few observations can be made to help us in formulating an empirical approach.

Many publishers of journals — perhaps most of them — have continued to farm out their composition work during this period of innovation. Given the large number of firms who do composition work on a contract basis, we can expect prices to be competitive. As in the case of printing and binding, publishers can choose a particular composition technique by contracting with a compositor who employs that technique. Various factors will determine the efficient technique for composing a given journal. However, it is not likely that the efficient technique will vary from journal to journal according to the quantity composed, which we shall here measure in terms of the number of pages in the issue, but rather from compositor to compositor according to the total quantity of jobs contracted for in a given period.

Given a number of jobs similar in all relevant respects except in the number of pages to be composed, these jobs can all be performed using the same composition equipment. Each job uses (or uses up) quantities of resources in proportion to its number of pages; set-up and clean-up costs are not significant. Hence all jobs can be performed in a continuous sequence, and costs do not vary from job to job either more than or less than proportionally with the number of pages.

The Hypothesis Tested

This does not rule out the possibility that different composition techniques are absolutely more efficient at different scales of production. But the scale here refers to the total volume per period of the compositor and not to the volumes of individual jobs. Thus compositors with more business might choose to use different techniques. In any case, with a given set of equipment, as total volume per period — i.e., total number of pages composed for all jobs — rises, the compositor's costs will eventually, if not always, rise more than proportionally. At least this will be so for all profit-conscious compositors in a competitive industry. Hence prices are likely to reflect costs at the margin of the compositor's total volume per period, and are unlikely to vary from job to job. This implies that journals with similar composition requirements in other respects will incur the same costs per page despite differences in the total number of pages composed.

It remains to consider how the costs of composition might vary among journals where composition requirements differ in other respects (other than the number of pages to be composed). They may differ, for example, in type face, use of mathematical and other special notation, color, and use of graphics (diagrams, graphs, charts). We shall not be able, in our statistical experiments, to investigate the influence of each of these on the costs of composition. However, we might obtain a measure of their collective influence by considering the fact that the composition requirements of journals in some scholarly fields of specialization (i.e., chemistry or physics) tend to be rather complex, while the requirements of journals in other fields (i.e., philosophy or literature) tend to be relatively simple.

We may classify all journals into two broadly defined groups: those that are scientific or technological and those that are non-scientific and non-technological. In the former group we include journals in the natural sciences, engineering, medicine, mathematics and some social sciences. These journals tend to make relatively heavy use of special notation, diagrams, graphs and charts. The second group includes journals in the humanities and most social sciences whose pages contain mainly prose (or poetry) and make little use of special notation and special graphics. We expect that the composition costs per page will, on average, be higher for the first group than for the second. We hope to offer some evidence on this hypothesis.

A Preliminary Test

Our statistical analysis of expenditures for composition utilizes the same sample of 35 journals for the same years, 1969 through 1974, as our previous analysis of printing and binding expenses. We have data on annual expenditures for composition, on number of pages per year, and on number of issues per year. As in the previous case, and for similar reasons, we shall not pool the data of different years but shall derive, instead, different estimates of the same expense function for each of the years separately.

In the previous section we argued that composition expenses should not vary with the number of pages in the issue in the same way as printing and binding expenses vary with the number of impressions. That is, we do not expect that composition costs rise, at first, less than proportionally, later, more than proportionally with the number of pages as the latter increases. Instead, we expect a proportional relation, other things being equal.

However, as a preliminary experiment we shall begin by positing an expense function for composition whose formulation follows those posited for printing and binding, i.e., one that is *not* proportional. We want to know whether the statistical results will allow us to doubt the appropriateness of this formulation. We take the cost of composition per issue to be a cubic function of the number of pages per issue; that is

$$EC/I = c_1(P/I) + c_2(P/I)^2 + c_3(P/I)^3 + e,$$

where

EC = annual expenditure for composition, in thousands of current dollars, and the other variables are defined as before. As before, if c_2 is negative and c_3 is positive, then expenditure per issue rises less than proportionally with the number of pages per issue until the latter variable attains a value of $-(c_2/2c_3)$, beyond which expenditure per issue rises more than proportionally.

Rather than report the detailed estimates for each of the six years, we shall confine ourselves to a summary of the overall results. We find that the estimated values of c_2 and c_3 are respectively negative and positive in all years. However, except for c_1, the coefficient values are generally not significantly different, in the statistical sense, from zero at any reasonably low levels of significance. This allows us to doubt the appropriateness of the above formulation.

The results of our initial experiment, then, do not constitute evidence sufficient to support the hypothesis that the expense function for composition is of the same form as those for printing and binding. This tends to confirm our expectation. We have argued that there is reason to expect the cost of composition per page to remain fairly constant across journals despite differences in the numbers of pages per issue, even though these differences may be great. This suggests a very simple formulation for the expense function for composition, in which expenses per issue vary directly with the number of pages per issue; that is,

$$EC/I = c(P/I) + e.$$

Results of the Regressions for Composition

We estimate six equations of this form for our sample of 35 journals, one for each year from 1969 through 1974. The results are presented in Table 8.3.4.

As expected, the coefficient c is highly significant in each year. In this case the estimated coefficient represents expenditure per page. It is interesting to note that while the estimated composition cost per page varies little over the period — from a low of $31.90 in 1969 to a high of $38.28 in 1972 — it falls from one year to the next in two out of five cases. The decrease from 1970 to 1971 is practically insignificant — only $.01 — but the decrease from 1972 to 1973 by $4.17 is much greater. The average for the six estimates is $35.28, suggesting that a ballpark figure of about $35.00 per page for composition expenses would be reasonable for any journal in any of these years.

Although the statistical results of this experiment are quite good, it ignores the question of the existence of a differential between the cost per page of composing a scientific or technological journal and the cost per page of composing a non-scientific, non-technological journal. Our final experiment is designed to investigate this question.

Hypothesizing that in any given year there might exist a constant differential between the composition costs per page of scientific and technological journals and non-scientific, non-technological journals, we estimate six equations of the form

$$EC/I = c(P/I) + d(D \cdot (P/I)) + e,$$

where

D = 1, if the observation is for a scientific or technological journal, and

TABLE 8.3.4 Results of the Regressions for the Expense of Composition, 1969-1974

Year	*Number of observations (journals)*	*Estimated coefficient (t-values in parentheses)* $(\frac{P}{I})$
1969	*35*	*+31.90*
		*(27.47)**
1970	*35*	*+35.67*
		*(23.01)**
1971	*35*	*+35.67*
		*(20.77)**
1972	*35*	*+38.28*
		*(19.70)**
1973	*35*	*+34.11*
		*(16.59)**
1974	*35*	*+36.04*
		*(16.35)**

*Note: * denotes significance at the .001 level.*
Source: Machlup, Leeson, and Associates (with Arthur Rosenzweig).

D = 0, if the observation is for a non-scientific, non-technological journal,

and the other variables are defined as before. In this formulation, the estimated composition cost per page of a scientific or technological journal is given by the sum of the two coefficients, c + d, while the estimated composition cost per page of a non-scientific, non-technological journal is given by the single coefficient c. The results of this experiment are presented in Table 8.3.5.

The table contains seven columns. As usual the first shows the years, the second the sample size. The next two show the estimated coefficients and their associated t-values.

TABLE 8.3.5 Results of the Regressions for the Expense of Composition, Using a Dummy Variable for Scientific and Technological Journals, 1969-1974

Year	Number of observations (journals)	Estimated coefficients (t-values in parentheses) $(\frac{P}{I})$	$(D \cdot \frac{P}{I})$	Cost of composition per page: Scientific, technological	Non-scientific, non-technological	Difference
1969	35	+18.31	+13.90	\$32.21	\$18.31	\$13.90
		(2.42)***	(1.82)***			
1970	35	+16.48	+19.74	\$36.22	\$16.48	\$19.74
		(1.87)***	(2.21)***			
1971	35	+14.61	+21.99	\$36.60	\$14.61	\$21.99
		(1.93)***	(2.84)**			
1972	35	+11.28	+28.08	\$39.36	\$11.28	\$28.08
		(1.28)	(3.12)**			
1973	35	+11.37	+23.67	\$35.04	\$11.37	\$23.67
		(1.16)	(2.38)***			
1974	35	+13.56	+23.49	\$37.05	\$13.56	\$23.49
		(1.35)	(2.29)***			

Note: ** Denotes significance at the .01 level; *** denotes significance at the .10 level.
Source: Machlup, Leeson, and Associates (with Arthur Rosenzweig).

We note that estimates for the coefficient of the second variable (D · P/I) are significant at at least the .10 level in all years. The estimates for the coefficient of the first variable (P/I) are significant at the .10 level in the first three years but not in the most recent three.

The last three columns present first the estimates of the composition costs per page for scientific and technological journals, then the estimates for non-scientific, non-technological journals, and finally, the differences between the two. The figures in the fifth column are the sums of the corresponding figures in the third and fourth columns. The sixth and seventh columns reproduce the numbers in the third and fourth columns, respectively.

Comparing these results with the estimates presented in Table 8.3.4, we note that in each year the estimated cost per page of composing a scientific or technological journal is slightly higher than the estimated cost for both types of journals combined given in Table 8.3.4. On the other hand, the estimated costs for non-scientific, non-technological journals is considerably lower in each year. It is interesting that the estimates for the two groups of journals change in opposite directions from one year to the next except from 1973 to 1974 when both increase. The estimated composition cost per page for scientific and technological journals increases steadily from 1969 to 1972, then decreases between 1972 and 1973, and finally increases again. The estimated costs for non-scientific, non-technological journals declines from 1969 to 1972, then increases from 1972 to 1974. The estimated cost per page of composing a non-scientific, non-technological journal is less than half that of composing a scientific or technological journal in all years except 1969.

The statistical results presented in Table 8.3.5 must be viewed with caution in at least one important sense. The sample values for the two variables (P/I) and (D · P/I) are highly correlated with each other in each year. The coefficient of correlation between the two variables ranges from a minimum value of .978 in 1974 to a maximum value of .989 in 1969. This indicates the presence of a very high degree of multicollinearity, which in turn suggests that the coefficient estimates may be inaccurate.

Conclusions

Overall, our results lend support to the hypothesis that composition costs per page remain fairly constant across journals, perhaps with a differential between scientific or technological journals and non-scientific, non-technological journals. This conforms to the characterization of the composition process previously outlined. Evidently there do not appear to be the same economies in composition as there are in the purchasing of printing and binding services.

However, given the rapidity of technological progress at this stage of publication, we feel that additional information about the techniques actually used to compose journals is required before any conclusion can be firmly established. Moreover, in this environment of innovation, knowledge of the production opportunities and costs of the present or recent past may not be helpful in predicting the conditions of even the near-term future.

PART 9

BIBLIOGRAPHIC SERVICES: ABSTRACTING AND INDEXING

CHAPTER 9.1

SCOPE, STRUCTURE, AND MARKET OF THE BIBLIOGRAPHIC-SERVICES INDUSTRY

When we set out to inquire into the book publishing industry, we began with an overview of the industry or, more specifically, with a chapter on its "Scope, Structure, and Markets," (Volume 1, Chapter 2). We did the same when we embarked on our inquiry into journals. There was in Volume 2 a chapter on "Scope, Structure, and Market of the Journal-Publishing Industry." If we find it appropriate to follow this pattern, it is not just for reasons of symmetry. As we are launching our inquiry into indexing, abstracting, and other bibliographic services, it is a natural beginning to survey the field with a chapter on the "Scope, Structure, and Market of the Bibliographic-Services Industry."

Indexing, abstracting, and other bibliographic services come nowadays in two forms: electronic and in print. The fact that electronic information services may use printed matter as an input and frequently furnish print-outs as one of their outputs is not a compelling reason for merging electronic and printed services into one category; we can still differentiate, and concentrate on bibliographic services in printed form. The title of our four-volume work is *Information Through the Printed Word* and we plan to stick with this delineation. Hence we shall confine ourselves to a discussion of those bibliographic services that are available in print.

BIBLIOGRAPHIC SERVICES

There is a trivial terminological problem: different designations have been used for the services we consider relevant for our purposes, chiefly (1) *indexing* of books, volumes of conference proceedings, journals, articles in journals, and papers in conference proceedings; (2) *abstracting* of journal articles and papers in conference proceedings; (3) *annotating* of books; and (4) *reviewing* of books. Perhaps we should also mention (5) *surveys* of the literature and (6) *specialized bibliographies* published as articles or books. The last two, however, are not regular or periodical services to which libraries, corporations, and individuals subscribe; they are more in the nature of *special* undertakings, not a continuing service offered for subscription.

There is also the question of the place to be accorded to secondary-research journals, those that are dedicated to reporting on findings of research first published in "primary-research journals." To identify all or most of the periodicals that serve chiefly or significantly as secondary-research journals would be too much of a task for our small research team and we shall therefore not include them in our survey of bibliographic services. Perhaps we should explicitly warn against confusing "secondary-research journal" — where secondary modifies the noun "research," not the noun "journal" — with secondary publications or secondary services — which are designed as bibliographic aids.

The widely used expression "secondary services" is rarely defined or circumscribed. Outsiders of the scholarly community would hardly know what is meant by secondary services. The expression covers, by and large, what we understand by bibliographic services and we shall therefore give preference to the latter term. Bibliographic services covers more than abstracting and indexing (A and I) services; it includes, for example, annotated book lists, book reviews, review digests, etc.

Serials, Periodicals, Journals

In Volume 2, *Journals*, we made an attempt at a classification of types of serials. This was a bold undertaking since librarians had never agreed on a classification of serials, and their officially agreed definitions were found to be ambiguous and inconsistent. We discussed this problem in Volume 2 on pp. 3-7.

Our tentative "Classification of Serials, Periodicals, and Journals" (Table 3.1.1, Volume 2, p. 10) recognized a hierarchy of categories. Serials, of which we distinguished nine types, included periodicals. Periodicals in turn were divided into magazines (five types) and journals (four types). One type of journal was the "learned journal," which we subdivided into primary-research journal and secondary-research journal.

This brave effort at classifying should have been empirically tested. We have tried to interest some librarians in this task, but unfortunately have not succeeded. We can well understand why the librarians refused our request: it would be a difficult and time-consuming task without any promising pay-off. One of the librarians showed us that he had not even a list of the journals, periodicals and other serials received by his library. All he had was a card file containing the titles of 30,000 serials regularly received. The cards were in alphabetical order and there was no separation of the type or form in which these serials came, no separation by the field which they served, no breakdown of any sort. To have these 30,000 cards reproduced, listed, sorted, and classified in any way could not be done without major expense. As a matter of fact, some librarians did not see any purpose to such an undertaking, satisfying nothing but "idle curiosity."

We sympathized with the librarians' point of view, particularly when we tried to answer the question where within our classification we would place the indexing and abstracting services. At least three of the "boxes" that we had designed could accommodate, however awkwardly, bibliographic services. First, the category "secondary-research journals" had a parenthetic explanation: "Reviews, Abstracts, Literature Surveys, etc." Second, among the serials, a category "Annuals, Biennials, etc." seemed to invite bibliographic services that appeared only once a year or even less frequently. Third, there was a category called "Nonsuperseding Serial Services, bound, sewn, stapled, or loose-leaf, including bibliographic and statistical data." We must admit that it would be difficult to justify the selection of any one of these three boxes as the appropriate home of all bibliographic services. The first of them, secondary-research journals, would not be the right place for any index that included magazines or articles in magazines which cannot be considered to report on scholarly research. Moreover, journals are a sub-class of periodicals, which were defined as being published "more than once per year." This definition, therefore, would exclude all those bibliographic services that are published annually, or still less frequently. The most suitable box would then be "Nonsuperseding Serial Services," but we shall probably have to reconsider the separation of annuals from serials published more often per year.

We have engaged in this self-criticism because we are anxious that our taxonomy be critically examined and improved before it is accepted for practical application. In any case we regard all bibliographic services in printed form as serial publications and we recommend against separating services that are published only once a year (or with even greater intervals) from services that are published more often than once a year.

The fact that indexing and abstracting services may take the form of printed publications about printed publications should not bother us — this, of course, is the very reason they are often called "secondary publications." Since some of the publications listed in serial indexing services are journals (or articles in journals) and therefore serial publications, we should not mind that we deal with serials covering serials. Indeed, we even know of a third layer: published indexes of published indexes of books, journals, articles, reviews, etc.

Just What Is An Index? A Proposed Taxonomy

Leaving aside the meanings of index not pertinent to our inquiry — for example, a numerical index, such as an arithmetic ratio (index number) relating a quantity to a chosen base; or a symptom of a phenomenon chosen as an indicator of some related quality or property — we still have to deal with a family of meanings that *are* pertinent to a study of printed matter. What all of these meanings have in common is that they are lists prepared as aids in locating something printed somewhere. We have to make a few essential distinctions.

A. *Non-serial Indexes* (Published only once)

1. *Contained in the publication being indexed* — Lists of the subjects treated or authors cited within the same book, journal, or other publication, usually alphabetically arranged, giving the page number where references to or discussions of particular subjects or names can be found.

2. *Separate from the publication being indexed* — Lists of the subjects treated or authors cited in a particular book, volume, or set of volumes, but published separately, perhaps because the original publication lacked an index or in order to provide an integrated index of subjects and authors for a set of volumes, as an encyclopaedia or any other multi-volume work.

B. *Serial Indexes* (Published at regular intervals)

1. *Classified lists of periodicals* — Lists of titles of periodicals, such as journals, in particular disciplines or subject groups. These are not lists of subjects or authors, but lists of journals, magazines, and perhaps also other serials (newsletters, etc.), with information regarding publishers or places of publication.

2. *Classified lists of the contents of periodicals, with or without annotations or abstracts* — Lists of the contents of (articles in) preselected periodical publications in particular disciplines or subject groups, arranged in various ways, for example, (a) by issue or volume of the periodical (reproducing the table of contents); (b) by subject matter (key words or formal subject classes); (c) by title of the article in alphabetic order; and/or (d) by name

of the author in alphabetic order. Included in this category are cumulative indexes for several consecutive volumes of a single journal.

3. *Classified lists of books, with or without annotations* — Lists of titles of books in particular disciplines or subject groups (bibliographies), arranged (a) by subject matter (keywords or formal subject classes); (b) by title of the books in alphabetic order, and/or (c) by name of the author in alphabetic order. (This definition seems broad enough to include publishers' catalogues, either of their books in print or of their new publications during the season or year. Such catalogues, however, would serve as indexes or bibliographies only if the publisher had a monopoly in books in particular subjects or subject areas. Otherwise, if several publishers were cultivating the same field, the searcher would have to consult several, perhaps many, such catalogues and the purpose of an index or bibliography would be defeated.)

4. *Classified lists of book reviews* — Lists of reviews or notices of books (sometimes with digests of the reviews) in particular disciplines or subject groups, arranged (a) by subject matter (keywords or formal subject classes), (b) by title of the books reviewed in alphabetic order, and/or (c) by name of the author of the book in alphabetic order, and (d) by name of the reviewer of the book in alphabetic order. (Indexes of book reviews, even with digests of all or selected reviews, should be distinguished from yearbooks surveying the literature on a subject published during the year. The difference is that these surveys are not guides to the reviews published elsewhere but are themselves reviews, by one author or a small team of authors, of the entire literature or of selected major publications — books, pamphlets, journal articles, and conference papers — in a particular year (or longer period). In recent practice the designation "yearbook" is being replaced by "annual review of [this or that field]." We may recognize it as a bibliography, since it usually includes a list of the items covered in the survey, but it is not a serial index.)

5. *Classified lists of publications of all kinds, with or without abstracts or annotations* — Lists of books, articles in journals, papers in conference proceedings, etc., in particular disciplines or subject groups (bibliographies), arranged (a) by subject matter (key-words or formal subject classes); (b) by titles of books, articles, papers, etc., in alphabetic or chronological order; and/or (c) by name of the author in alphabetic or chronological order. (This type of index differs from that described under No. 3 by its inclusion of journal articles and conference papers, whereas the Index described under No. 3 was confined to books. Perhaps we should have provided a separate category for indexes specialized in conference proceedings.)

6. *Classified lists of citations* — Lists of citations of books, articles in journals, papers in conference proceedings, etc., in broadly defined subject groups, arranged (a) by authors of the cited publications, (b) by authors of the citing publications, (c) by affiliations (universities, corporations) of the citing authors, and/or (d) by subject matter (key-words) treated in the cited publications; all in alphabetic order.

7. *Classified lists of bibliographies* — Lists of bibliographies (on different subjects or subject groups) which have been published as separate books, reports, or pamphlets intended as bibliographic aides or appended to monographic books or to journal articles that contain some selected minimum — say, 50 — of items published or forthcoming. (Coverage of the periodical literature from which the lists of references — the bibliographies — are recorded, is arbitrary.)

Given the large variety of indexes, we cannot claim this list to be exhaustive or our descriptions to be appropriate. Any dictionary will inform the reader that our list omitted, for example, the index of publications proscribed or prohibited by church authorities; but there are probably other omissions too. Our list, on the other hand, is unduly comprehensive in that it includes indexes that are not furnished by indexing services: Types A1 and A2, the indexes of references to subjects or names in a particular volume or set of volumes, are one-time affairs, not serial services. Indexing *services* should be defined as continuing undertakings, offered to subscribers and available through serial publication. All seven types listed under B satisfy this condition.

Index versus Bibliography

Some of the types of indexes listed above have been characterized as "bibliographies." Indexes of books, of periodical literature, or of all publications (including conference papers) are usually called bibliographies if they provide a good overview of the writings on a more narrowly circumscribed *subject* or by a particular *author*. The bibliography of a particular author, however, is not the product of a continuing indexing service; it is prepared for particular occasions, such as anniversaries, memorials, or other appraisals. Bibliographies on particular subjects, however, are often continuing undertakings of regular bibliographic services.

The difference between abstracting and indexing seems to be clear enough to make definitions unnecessary. On closer inspection, however, we have found that there is more to that difference than we first thought. This can be best shown by describing one of the publications of this type: the *Current Physics Index*. This publication consists of three parts, one appearing four times a year, the other two annually. The quarterly is in actual fact an abstracting service. Every item — carefully classified according to the classification scheme of the American Institute of Physics (with ample cross-references to multiple entries under different classes or subclasses) — is abstracted. (These abstracts are taken over from the source journals). In the back part of each issue is an alphabetic author index with page references to the publications abstracted in the issue. Of the two annual publications one is a subject index, the other an author index. The latter, usually in two volumes, includes the affiliations and addresses of the authors. From this description it is clear that the title of the publication is an understatement. The quarterly is an abstracting service and the two annuals are indexing services, although all are confined to the journals published by the American Institute of Physics.

Not every publisher is so systematic as the American Institute of Physics, although some are more comprehensive in the coverage of journals. There are some services that *combine* abstracting and indexing without, however, furnishing abstracts of every item in the index. In the classified list of items some may be with and others without abstracts. Again in other serial services there may be a virtually complete indexing service *separate* from a less complete, merely selective abstracting service.

Indexes to Indexes

It goes without saying that most serial indexes need their own built-in indexes to each issue or volume, and are more serviceable if they have also periodic cumulative indexes to guide the searcher to the pages, issues, and volumes where particular entries have appeared. Where different indexing services cover the same fields or subject groups and compete with one another by providing virtually the same kind of information, overlapping in coverage, there may be a supplementary indexing service to tell the searcher in which of the competing abstracting or indexing services information on particular authors, books, or reviews of books can be found.

This kind of tertiary service designed as guides to secondary services is more frequent for biographical than for bibliographical information. There are indexes to biographies, presenting lists of authors with codes signifying the biographical publications in which the particular authors can be looked up. If there exist, say, 20 biographical services, a tertiary service may save the searcher a little time by directing him to the ones that contain the biographical sketch of the author in question.

Purposes, Frequencies, Cumulations

Secondary services, or bibliographic information services, may serve different purposes: (1) to provide researchers with current awareness of materials relevant to their fields of interest, (2) to provide them with guides for retrospective search in their fields of interest, (3) to provide them with easy access to the literature outside their own field, either to satisfy their general interest or for interdisciplinary research, and (4) to help students, novices to the field, to get their initial orientation.

Serial indexes that are intended to serve current-awareness purposes — for example, to tell the searcher what papers, articles, or books in his area of interest have appeared in the last few months — are most useful if they are published with great frequency: weekly, bi-weekly, monthly, or at least quarterly. On the other hand, indexes intended for retrospective searches or for purposes (3) and (4) listed above are more serviceable if they appear less frequently or if they are from time to time supplemented by a cumulative index. For retrospective searches a monthly or quarterly index is actually a nuisance; an annual index may be a sensible compromise; but a cumulative five-year index is probably the ideal as a guide for researchers either new to the field or returning to it after a temporary absence, and for those engaged in "checking," in looking up something they vaguely remember having read or seen "some time ago." Without a cumulative index, the searcher may have to go back to several volumes to look for the wanted entry, which could easily be found in a single cumulative volume.

As an example of such cumulative indexes we may mention a recent publication by ISI, the Institute for Scientific Information, the *Social Sciences Citation Index, 5-Year Cumulations* (1966-1970 and 1971-1975). The blurb says: "For retrospective searches or verifications. . .The easiest, most efficient way to search the literature of the social sciences. . ." The two volumes together contain over 3 million citations to 1,340,000 items cited in 385,000 source items (the citing publications) in 2,676 journals.

A Widespread Shortcoming

Many special bibliographies and several serial abstracting and indexing services suffer from a shortcoming that could be corrected only with the cooperation of the primary-research journals, the editors of conference proceedings, and the publishers of books. We refer to insufficient identification of authors by suppression of their first names; if only initials are offered, authors with common last names remain virtually unidentified. Bibliographers and indexers are helpless if the sources suppress the authors' first names, perhaps at the request of authors who lack the imagination to know what inconvenience or actual cost they impose on other researchers. (The Library of Congress used to spend large sums of money to dig up missing first names of authors of books for the entries on catalogue cards.)

The chief inconvenience from the omission of first names is to readers of books, or rather to all who search for books in the library. Any searcher looking for books by authors whose names are listed or cited merely by initials, instead of first names, may have to thumb through hundreds of cards in the catalogue of the library. Assume that a searcher has to find the call numbers of the books he needs: a simple task if he knows the first names of the authors, but a time-consuming drudgery if he has only the initials. This is especially true in the case of authors with rather common last names, like Brown, Miller, Smith, etc.

The point is that there may be only a few authors named Ronald M. Hartwell, but if a searcher knows only R.M. Hartwell, he may have to search all the cards for Ralph, Randall, Randolph, Rebecca, Reginald, Rendigs, Rexford, Richard, Robert, and Robin Hartwell before he arrives at Ronald, the author whose book he seeks.

In a test in the card catalogue of a large university library, it was established that there were only eleven cards for Hugh Jones, but 373 cards for Joneses whose first names begin with H. Hence, if your bibliographical reference gives you only H. Jones, you have to thumb through 372 cards before you reach the one you are looking for. (Middle initials would be of no help in this task.) Similar findings in the experiment of looking for the catalogue cards of authors whose first names had been spelled out in the searcher's list or of finding them if the searcher had only the authors' initials, showed the following ratios:

Number of Cards in Catalogue to be Inspected

	If the First Name is Furnished	*If Only the Initial is Furnished*
Gordon Brown	4	167
Julius Cohen	18	105
Azriel Green	1	149
Josephine Johnson	11	277
Eva Meyer	2	174
Joseph Miller	35	336
Arthur Pollard	9	118
Judith Robinson	5	313
Winthrop Smith	1	680
Jonathan Williams	10	429

These figures may somewhat exaggerate the differences in the required searching effort, because among the cards that precede the ones that are sought there may be packs referring to the same very prolific writer which the searcher may be able to skip. Still, if the catalogue does not have special markers to show the end of such packs, the effort of thumbing will not be substantially reduced.

The translation of the number of cards examined into seconds or minutes of time wasted in the process depends on the thumbing-and-reading skill of the searcher. In many instances it is the time of a busy research scientist or scholar that is wasted; considering the alternative uses of the researcher's time, the waste is a serious matter, especially since it could so easily be avoided if authors, editors, and publishers were willing to cooperate.

A similar waste of time is imposed on the researcher who has come upon an article that interests him but now wants to know whether the same author has published a book on the general subject. Alas, if he knows only the author's initial, he will have a hard time searching the catalogue for a book of which he does not know the title and has only the last name of the author.

A third group of victims of the mischievous omission of first names in primary and secondary publications are the persons interested in citation-search or citation-count. If the citation index throws all G. Brown's, all J. Johnson's, and all W. Smith's together, the user of the index who is interested in the publications of a Gordon Brown, Josephine Johnson, or Winthrop Smith, has to try to separate the cited publications that look more likely to be by the particular authors than by some namesake with the same initial. The searcher will have a difficult time, and his assistant or secretary may find it impossible to do this job for him.

In order to stop these wasteful practices, one should put pressures on authors, editors, and publishers urging them to include the fully spelled-out first name with every last name of an author or editor. The publishers of abstracts and indexes ought to start immediately to include first names whenever furnished by the sources, and they should exert all their influence, inducements or pressures, upon editors and publishers of books, journals, and proceedings to insist on printing first names in the publications for which they are responsible. (There is no excuse for the suppression of first names where the primary journal and the bibliographical service are published by the same organization.)

SURVEYS OF THE INDUSTRY

Several attempts have been made to survey the sector of the publishing industry that produces bibliographic services. Back in 1925 the *Index Bibliographicus* was published in its first edition. Volume I, *Science and Technology*, of the 4th edition, appeared in 1959. It was published in The Hague by the Fédération Internationale de Documentation (FID). In 1960 the National Federation of Abstracting and Indexing Services (NFAIS) published *A Guide to U.S. Indexing and Abstracting Services in Science and Technology* (Washington, D.C.), a compilation containing approximately 500 entries, all published in the United States. *A Guide to the World Abstracting and Indexing Services in Science and Technology* was published in 1963 by NFAIS, containing 1,855 titles from 40 countries, 365 of them from the United States. (Thus, not all of the 500 U.S. entries of the 1960 guide were included in the 1963 guide.) The Fédération Internationale de Documentation published, in 1965 and 1969, lists of abstracting services for practically all disciplines, including social sciences and humanities. The 1969 edition indicates an increase of 30 per cent in the number of bibliographical services over the ones listed in the NFAIS *World Guide* of 1963. If these two lists, the NFAIS guide of 1963 and the FID list of 1969, were combined, 2,671 bibliographic services would be counted for all subject fields.[1]

[1]Much of this information is drawn from *Statistical Indicators of Scientific and Technological Communication (1960-1980), Volume 2: A Research Report*, prepared by Donald W. King *et al.* for the National Science Foundation under Contract #NSF-C878 (Rockville, Maryland: King Research, May 1976), pp. 285-288.

Several years ago NFAIS and FID announced a joint project to prepare an inventory of abstracting and indexing services for all fields and for the entire world, with a full description of each of approximately 2,100 abstracting and indexing services. Originally they were hoping for completion early in 1976, but as of now (1979) no publication date seems to be in sight.

At the request of the Committee on Scientific and Technical Information (COSATI) a survey of the Abstracting and Indexing industry was commissioned in the 1960s. The report, with findings for 1966, was released under the title *A Systems Study of Abstracting and Indexing in the United States*.[2] We are not aware of any more up-to-date study, and we could not possibly undertake, with our limited funds, to attempt an update of the findings.

The Size of the Industry

An attempt to estimate the size of the bibliographical-services sector of the publishing industry in the United States would normally begin with a look into the census data. According to the Standard Industrial Classification, publishing falls into Major Group 27, Printing, Publishing, and Allied Industries. Code Number 2721 covers periodicals, 2731 covers book publishing, and 2741, miscellaneous publishing. Since there are no further subdivisions of these sectors relevant for our purpose, we get no help from census data. We assume that most abstracting or indexing services would be listed under periodicals, but cannot rule out the possibility that some, published annually or even less frequently, would be under book publishing, and some under miscellaneous publishing (which includes publishing of catalogues and directories).

In the absence of any guidance from the census, the *Systems Study* of 1966 went out to obtain primary data, through mail questionnaires and site interviews with the A and I publishers. According to the report, 100 different organizations produced, in 1966, 200 different Abstracting and Indexing publications, covering 1,856,000 individual items from source publications. Of these, 1,040,000 were covered in the form of abstracts. (This was less than the 2,000,000 items estimated by another, less systematic study for 1962.[3] This larger estimate had included some double-counting through overlap of coverage.) The *Systems Study* estimated — by "blowing up" the sample of 100 to

[2]Systems Development Corporation, *A Systems Study of Abstracting and Indexing in the United States* (Falls Church, Virginia, 16 December 1966), produced under contract NSF-C-464, distributed by the United States Department of Commerce, TM-WD-394, PB 174-249.

[3]Charles P. Bourne, *et al.* "The World's Technical Journal Literature: An Estimate of Volume, Origin, Language, Field, Indexing, and Abstracting," *American Documentation*, Volume 13 (April 1962), pp. 159-168.

what might be the entire A and I population — that in 1966 a total of 2,573,000 items had been produced by domestic abstracting and indexing services. If the ratio of abstracts was the same for the whole as for the sample, the estimated total divides into 1,440,000 abstracts and 1,133,000 items indexed but not abstracted.

The *Systems Study* went on to translate this "physical" measure of output into a dollar value. For a very small sample of respondents cost data had been obtained, which were, somewhat daringly, assumed to be representative for all producers of abstracting and indexing services. An amount of $30.00 was taken to be the average cost for an abstract (including the bibliographic citation), and $7.50 for an item indexed but not abstracted (p. 8). On this basis the total cost of producing the 2,573,000 items in the abstracting and indexing publications of 1966 relating to literature on natural sciences and technology was estimated to have amounted to over $50 million.

Possibility of Updating the Estimate

We considered the possibility of an update of that estimate. One, rather primitive way would have been to work with a constant annual rate of growth, perhaps the 8.5 per cent per year which had been suggested by a comparison of abstracting and indexing data for 1962 and 1966. This we rejected as completely illegitimate. Another way would have been to estimate the growth in the number of publications regarded as serial abstracting and indexing services. Unable to do a count of our own, we hoped to find some help from *Ulrich's International Periodicals Directory* (New York: R.R. Bowker). This directory has separate headings for "Abstracts and Indexes" and for "Bibliographies." Each entry is given the Dewey decimal code number, which would even allow us to assign it to the discipline or subject group to which it belongs. We excerpted no less than 946 entries for abstracts, indexes, and bibliographies in the 32 subject groups designed for our study; we intended to include the list in this volume.

We have changed our collective mind when we found that *Ulrich's* included many titles that clearly should not be classed as bibliographic services at all. We have a wide choice of examples of entries in *Ulrich's* that should not be included among abstracts, indexes, and bibliographies. A large number of publishers' catalogues is included, though, strangely enough, not consistently: the catalogues of the largest publishers are left out, while those of some small publishers are included. The accession lists of some libraries are included, though only in a rather spotty selection. The catalogues of copyright entries of the U.S. Copyright Office are included. In the field of Business Administration, we find *Standard Rate and Data Services*, giving the price lists of advertising in various print media, and in radio and television, included among bibliographies.

In these circumstances we gave up the idea of producing a more up-to-date estimate of the size of the A and I industry.

THE STRUCTURE OF THE INDUSTRY

We may be forgiven if we quote from our Volume 2 what we said about the meaning of structure:

> Structure ordinarily stands for "composition" and for "relationships among the parts;" sometimes it stands for anything at all for which no better word is found; but if one speaks of the structure of an industry, what is usually meant is the number of firms or enterprises that produce the output, their size distribution, preferably in terms of physical units sold or dollar volumes of sales, and their market positions and degrees of cooperation or rivalry in capturing or maintaining their shares of the market. Of course, findings will differ according to the chosen definition of the market. For example, the markets for serials, for periodicals, for journals, for scholarly journals, for scholarly journals in the life sciences, for scholarly journals in molecular biology, and so forth, are different, and hence the structures of the "industries" serving these markets will surely be different.

Noncompeting Sectors of the Industry

This statement, written with regard to the journal-publishing industry, is equally applicable to the abstracting and indexing industry. An abstracting service for music literature is no substitute for an abstracting service for articles on the health effects of environmental pollutants, although the two may compete for dollars allocated to research libraries in their budgets for serial services. Not all problems of industrial structure, however, relate to the competitive situation in the markets. One may have other reasons for being curious to see how different disciplines or subject groups are served by the abstracting and indexing industry, or what types of publisher produce these services.

The Publishers and the Fields

We find six categories of publishing organizations in the abstracting and indexing industry: 1. Governmental (Federal and State); 2. Societal (Professional associations, learned societies); 3. Commercial (business firms operated for profit); 4. Industrial (firms and trade associations, producing bibliographical services for internal use, for distributions among their members, and only in exceptional instances for outside distribution, sometimes gratis and on a controlled basis); 5. Institutional (Not-for-profit organizations, serving research, teaching, or other public purposes, including university presses); 6. Others.

Although we decided against using *Ulrich's* for estimates of the total size of the industry, we thought that we might use this directory for a compilation of the relative composition of producers of A and I services in different fields, provided we make cautious reservations and warn against taking the "structure" revealed by the compilation too seriously. The incidence of mistaken inclusions may be much larger in some fields than in others and larger also with regard to some publishers than to others. For example, if *Ulrich's* classifies publishers' catalogues as bibliographies, we should expect disproportionally large figures of "Interdisciplinary bibliographies" published by commercial publishers. If *Ulrich's* classifies governmental releases of statistical series about prices and rates as indexes or bibliographies, we should expect disproportionately large figures of "business" indexes or bibliographies published by governmental agencies. These expectations are actually confirmed by our computation in Table 9.1.1 — which reinforces our warnings against relying on the proportions of abstracting and indexing services by different categories of publishers catering to the various fields of inquiry.

Nonetheless we take a look at Table 9.1.1 to see how 946 serial bibliographic services in a sample compiled from *Ulrich's* are distributed over the six categories of publishers and over the 32 fields or subject areas distinguished. The columns of the table show us the distribution among categories of publishers. Of all the services in this sample, 17.7 per cent are published by governmental agencies; 13.5 per cent by societal organizations; 36.3 per cent by commercial publishers; 3.1 per cent by industry organizations; 22.3 per cent by institutional publishers or non-profit organizations; 0.7 per cent by university presses; and 6.4 per cent by others.

On the right side of the table we see the percentage distribution among fields or subject areas. Singling out only those with relatively large representations, we find that the group "interdisciplinary" services has the largest share with 13.8 per cent of the whole sample. It is followed by "other applied sciences" with 13.2 per cent, "medical sciences" with

TABLE 9.1.1 *Number of Abstracting, Indexing, and Other Bibliographic Services Published Serially and Listed in Ulrich's International Periodicals Directory, Broken Down by Type of Publisher and by Field or Subject Area*

		Govern-ment	Soci-etal	Commer-cial	Indus-trial	Institu-tional	Univer-sity press	Other	Total	Per cent distribution by field
01	Life sciences	1	5	21	1	6	0	2	36	3.8%
02	Physical sciences	11	17	19	4	8	0	2	61	6.4%
03	Environmental sciences	9	4	7	1	4	0	0	25	2.6%
04	Mathematics	0	3	1	0	0	0	0	4	0.4%
05	Statistics	0	1	0	0	0	0	0	1	0.1%
06	Engineering	25	23	15	2	14	0	4	83	8.8%
07	Medical sciences	30	12	36	0	22	0	8	108	11.5%
08	Other applied sciences	39	11	35	1	29	1	8	124	13.2%
09	Psychology	0	4	2	0	0	0	0	6	0.6%
10	Economics	2	2	13	0	5	0	0	22	2.3%
11	Business administration	6	3	14	17	17	0	3	60	6.3%
12	Political science	8	2	11	0	4	0	3	28	3.0%
13	Law	0	1	10	0	6	0	3	20	2.1%
14	Philosophy and religion	0	7	3	0	6	0	1	17	1.8%
15	History and archaeology	0	2	17	0	12	1	1	33	3.5%
16	Geography	0	1	0	0	0	0	0	1	0.1%
17	Anthropology, sociology, and urban studies	6	5	6	0	8	2	6	33	3.5%

(continued)

TABLE 9.1.1, continued

		Govern-ment	Soci-etal	Commer-cial	Indus-trial	Institu-tional	Univer-sity press	Other	Total	Per cent distribution by field
18	Physical education	0	0	1	0	0	0	0	1	0.1%
19	Occupational education	0	0	0	0	1	0	0	1	0.1%
20	Education	5	5	6	0	15	0	2	33	3.5%
21	Home economics	1	1	4	0	1	0	1	8	0.8%
22	Language and linguistics	0	3	2	0	1	0	0	6	0.6%
23	English composition, communication, and speech	0	2	8	1	3	0	3	17	1.8%
24	Literature	1	1	11	0	6	2	0	21	2.2%
25	Music	2	1	3	0	1	0	0	7	0.7%
26	Art and art history	2	0	6	0	5	0	1	14	1.5%
27	Fiction	0	1	0	0	0	0	1	2	0.2%
28	General, adult	0	0	1	0	0	0	0	1	0.1%
29	General, juvenile	1	2	3	0	0	1	2	9	1.0%
30	Games and sports	1	0	1	0	0	0	1	3	0.3%
31	Other	7	1	12	1	6	0	4	31	3.3%
32	Interdisciplinary	10	8	75	1	31	0	5	130	13.8%
	Total	167	128	343	29	211	7	61	946	
	Per cent distribution by type of publisher	17.7%	13.5%	36.3%	3.1%	22.3%	0.7%	6.4%		100.0%

Source: Machlup, Leeson, and Associates. Compiled from Ulrich's International Periodicals Directory, Seventeenth Edition, 1977-78 (New York: R.R. Bowker, 1977).

11.5 per cent, and "engineering" with 8.8 per cent. The next two largest subject groups are "physical sciences" and "business administration," with 6.4 per cent and 6.3 per cent, rerespectively. This rank order seems quite plausible, so that we need not feel too embarrassed about presenting a set of numbers in the accuracy of which we have little confidence.

Natural Monopolies

Inquiries into the market structure of an industry are usually intended to throw some light on the competitive positions of firms who control a relatively large share of the market. If something like 75 per cent of a market in A and I services were controlled by only one or two firms, one might have to suspect that their dominating market position would imply a high degree of monopolistic power. But what should be regarded as a market in an industry that is catering to a large variety of fields? As we suggested above, no buyer interested in an abstracting service on environmental science will substitute for it an abstracting service on Old-English literature, no matter what the price difference between the two might be. On the other hand, we can hardly expect that there will be a large number of firms producing abstracting or indexing services for the literature in a single field. The market in any specialized field is not large enough to make it commercially attractive for several publishers to undertake producing competing bibliographies. We conclude from these theoretical considerations that we cannot expect much competition in the A and I industry as far as special fields are concerned. In a sense, the situation in this industry is similar to what economists have called natural monopolies. The point is that the total demand for the product is so small that it would not be profitable to have this small total divided among many producers, each supplying a minuscule number of units.

These considerations apply chiefly to bibliographic services for special fields. There may be indexes, readers' guides, and similar services for the total book trade, services for which the total demand may be sufficiently large to allow competing publishers to serve it. Even this would hardly allow situations in which *many* publishers compete with one another. It would at best be competition among very few or, to use the technical jargon, oligopolistic competition. Our remarks about monopolistic and oligopolistic markets should not be mistaken as raising suspicions of illegal activities. If a firm produces a service in which only a small number of buyers are interested, there is nothing the firm or anyone else can do to create competition from other publishers. No other publisher would seriously consider entering the market, except perhaps in the unusual case where he can provide so superior a product that he would drive out the existing publisher and take his place after a costly period of rivalry.

The arguments presented here may have an air of unreality, largely because the producers in the A and I industry are to such a large extent governmental agencies and non-profit organizations. With commercial publishers serving not much more than one third of the total market for A and I services, the question of "monopoly profits" is not very likely to arise or to excite the observer. This does not mean that the librarians will not complain about the high cost of subscribing to A and I services. Some of them may have the impression that they are being gouged — and perhaps, in some instances, they are.

THE MARKET

The preceding discussion included considerations about the market for bibliographic services, because the structure of the industry is commonly analyzed in terms of market shares, concentration, and dominance. What still remains to be done is to answer the question of who are the buyers in the market for bibliographic services.

Who Subscribes to A and I Services?

Unfortunately we cannot offer any substantial amount of statistical data to answer this question. We did try to get such data for six publications selected for closer analysis, but we cannot pretend that this small sample is at all representative for the entire industry. Four of the six selected publications supplying abstracts and indexes of the journal literature in different fields of specialization did provide breakdowns of their subscription lists between individuals and institutions. (See Table 9.2.2.)

It happened that one of these services was embodied in a regular journal distributed to the members of the learned society that produced it, so that a great many individuals were receiving the abstracts or indexes in question. This seems to be a rather unusual situation. It is our impression that most of the bibliographic services are catering largely to institutions, that is, chiefly to research libraries, special libraries, specialized research institutes, and specialized research departments of industrial corporations. Needless to say, this observation — or rather, speculation — is pertinent mainly to bibliographic services in the life sciences, the physical sciences, environmental sciences, and engineering. It is probably no coincidence that the prices of A and I services in these areas of study are very much higher than the prices in other special fields.

The correlation between subscription prices for bibliographic services and the ratio of institutional to individual subscribers should not suggest that cause and effect run only in one direction. The price may be higher for services catering to larger institutions for two reasons. (1) Publishers know that institutions are less sensitive to high prices than individuals, that is, (expressed in technical language) the price-elasticity of demand will be small on the part of institutions with large budgets; they will not cancel their subscriptions so readily when subscription rates are raised. (2) The flow of primary publications is far greater in natural sciences and engineering than in other fields; this implies that the number of items to be abstracted and indexed is much greater and the cost of the service much higher. At the subscription prices that cover the high costs, we must expect that institutions will constitute an overwhelming ratio of the subscribers.

These remarks have addressed chiefly the question of the market for bibliographic services in special fields. If we now consider the market for interdisciplinary bibliographic services, we must immediately realize that we are dealing with even more ambitious undertakings: many more source journals have to be covered, many more articles, papers, etc. have to be abstracted and indexed, and consequently, much higher costs have to be incurred in producing the services. Thus, more comprehensive bibliographic services may run into really big money and, where this is the case, the market will be almost necessarily confined to larger libraries serving readers with a variety of interests. We can hardly expect that many individuals will subscribe to, say, the *Science Citation Index* at a subscription rate of $3,500 per year; on the other hand, some libraries may consider this an indispensable item in their reference department. (With this remark we have again been indulging in pure speculation, but where information is lacking we cannot help but resort to speculating.)

The Cost of Bibliographic Services to a Hypothetical Library

Our hypothesis that the market for bibliographic services consists chiefly of research libraries and other research institutions suggested a modest experiment. Assume that a new research library is established at a new or expanding university; that the librarian is asked to prepare a budget for serial subscriptions which provide what he considers indispensable bibliographic aids; that he, after consultation with members of various departments, prepares a sort of shopping list and, after obtaining prices, calculates the amount of the required allocation. How may his shopping list look, what are the prices for the selected serial services, and what is the sum total required?

The reader may ask why such a hypothetical experiment is needed when the country has a hundred research libraries that could be asked for information. This is a reasonable question, and the answer is rather distressing. We have tried our question on a few librarians and have learned that the available records do not furnish the answers. Neither the accounting records nor the budgets of most libraries are sufficiently broken down to enable them to tell us how much they spend on serial bibliographic services. Thus we had to resort to the primitive technique of preparing a hypothetical budget for an imaginary library.

In selecting the serial services for this budget, we did not impose on our overburdened librarians or our friends in various departments. We merely tried to make selections that seemed reasonable to us and satisfied the requirement that there be some pertinent publications in each of our disciplines; we chose only the smallest possible number from the long lists contained in *Ulrich's*.

In Table 9.1.2 we present the list prepared by us pretending that we are an acquisitions librarian. We cannot possibly vouch for the quality of our selection, since we must modestly disavow competence in most of the 32 subject groups. If experts take exception to some of our choices, they can easily disqualify some items and replace them with better ones. We doubt that the order of magnitude of the total bill would be very different as a result of such substitutions. Only the elimination of particularly expensive items would make a substantial difference. A thrifty librarian may be prepared to sacrifice, for example, the expensive citation indexes.

Some of the abstracts or indexes in special fields are also quite costly, but we suppose that our imaginary librarian would not be willing to do without them. If our list is in serious error, this error is on the side of excessive modesty. We are bold enough to advance the hypothesis that the majority of research libraries in the United States spend a multiple of the total at which we arrived. The total subscription cost for the 72 serial publications in our list amounts to $21,566.85 in prices prevailing in 1979.

In order to test whether this figure is reasonable, we may compare it with the annual expenditures of small academic libraries for serial subscriptions. From Table 6.5.5 in Volume 3, *Libraries*, we learned that in a sample of 75 academic libraries, the smallest twenty (namely, libraries which had total annual expenditures of less than $1 million each) spent as a group in 1976 $1,280,000 for serials. This would mean that the average library in this size-class spent $64,000 for serials in 1976. The amount we figured in the list of desirable bibliographic services was therefore approximately one-third of the budget for serials. Though it may seem not unreasonable, we wish we could check this array of figures against recorded facts. We can only repeat our hope that it

TABLE 9.1.2 List of Bibliographic
Serials for the Reference Department of an Emerging Research Library

	Annual subscription price in 1979	Number of issues in an annual subscription
Life sciences		
Biological Abstracts	$1,102.50	24 issues
Bioresearch Index	$ 549.00	12 issues
Annual Cumulative Index to Bioresearch Index	$ 220.50	1 issue
Current Contents/Life Sciences	$ 135.00	52 issues
Physical sciences		
Chemical Abstracts	$3,700.00	52 issues
Current Contents/Physical & Chemical Sciences	$ 135.00	52 issues
Current Physics Index	$ 95.00	4 issues
Environmental sciences		
Environment Abstracts	$ 325.00	12 issues
Current Contents/Agriculture, Biology, and Environmental Sciences	$ 150.00	52 issues
Environment Index	$ 95.00	1 issue
Mathematics		
Index of Mathematical Papers	$ 40.00	2 issues
Mathematical Review	$1,050.00	12 issues
Statistics		
Current Index to Statistics	$ 18.00	1 issue
Engineering		
Engineering Index (with Annual)	$ 985.00	12 issues & annual
Current Contents/Engineering, Technical and Applied Sciences	$ 135.00	52 issues
Medical sciences		
Index Medicus	$ 170.00	12 issues
Current Contents/Clinical Practices	$ 135.00	52 issues
Other applied sciences		
Computer & Information Systems Abstracts	$ 440.00	20 issues
Information Science Abstracts	$ 95.00	6 issues
Library Literature	$ 45.00-50.00	6 issues
Psychology		
Psychological Abstracts	$ 315.00	12 issues
Economics		
Journal of Economic Literature (with American Economic Review)	$ 39.35	4 issues
Business administration		
Business Periodical Index	$ 45.00-50.00	11 issues

(continued)

TABLE 9.1.2, continued

	Annual subscription price in 1979	Number of issues in an annual subscription
Political science		
ABC Pol Sci. (Advance Bibliography of Contents: Political Science and Government)	$ 82.00	6 issues
CIS Index (Congressional Information Service)	$ 310.00	12 issues
Law		
Criminal Justice Abstracts	$ 40.00	4 issues
Contents of Current Legal Periodicals	$ 62.00	12 issues
Index to Legal Periodicals	$ 70.00-80.00	12 issues
Philosophy & religion		
Religious and Theological Abstracts	$ 26.00	4 issues
Index to Religious Periodical Literature	$ 58.50	2 issues
Philosopher's Index	$ 40.00	4 issues
History & archaeology		
Historical Abstracts. Part A: Modern History Abstracts, 1450-1914	$ 325.00 (Parts A and B)	4 issues
Historical Abstracts. Part B: Twentieth Century, 1914 to Present		4 issues
America: History & Life. Part A: Article Abstracts and Citations	$ 196.00 (Parts A, B, C and Annual Index)	7 issues
America: History & Life. Part B: Index to Book Reviews		7 issues
America: History & Life. Part C: American History Bibliography		7 issues
America: History & Life. Annual Index		1 issue
Geography		
Current Geographical Publications	$ 25.00	12 issues
Anthropology, Sociology, and Urban Studies		
Abstracts in Anthropology	$ 48.00	4 issues
Sociological Abstracts	$ 150.00	6 issues
Contemporary Sociology	$ 20.00	6 issues
Physical Education		
Current Index to Physical Education and Recreation	$ 50.00	12 issues
Occupational education		
Resources in Vocational Education	$ 34.00	6 issues
Education		
Education Abstracts	$ 8.50	12 issues
Education Index	$ 45.00-50.00	12 issues
Resources in Education	$ 42.70	12 issues
Home Economics		
Home Economics Research Abstracts	$ 37.50	1 issue

(continued)

TABLE 9.1.2, continued

	Annual subscription price in 1979	Number of issues in an annual subscription
Language & linguistics		
MLA International Bibliography of Books and Articles on the Modern Languages and Literature	$ 75.00	1 issue
English composition, communication, speech		
Abstracts of English Studies	$ 40.00	10 issues
Literature, English, Foreign, Comparative, Drama		
Essay & General Literature Index	$ 45.00	2 issues
Biography Index	$ 44.00	4 issues
Short Story Index	$ 25.00	1 issue
Music		
RILM Abstracts of Music Literature	$ 45.00	4 issues
Music Index (with Annual)	$ 420.00	12 issues & annual
Art & art history		
Art & Archaeology Technical Abstracts	$ 20.00	2 issues
Art Index	$ 45.00-50.00	4 issues
Art & Architecture Bibliography	$ 96.80	irregular
General, juvenile		
Subject Index to Children's Magazines	$ 12.00	12 issues
Children's Books in Print	$ 28.50	1 issue
Interdisciplinary publications		
Book Review Index	$ 68.00	6 issues
Readers' Guide to Periodical Literature	$ 58.00	24 issues
Bibliographic Guide to Government Publications	$ 150.00	irregular
Books in Print	$ 92.50	1 issue
Subject Guide to Books in Print	$ 65.00	1 issue
Dissertation Abstracts International Section C: European Abstracts	$ 295.00	4 issues
National Union Catalog: A Cumulative Author List	$1,100.00	12 issues
Dissertation Abstracts International Section B: Physical Sciences and Technology	$ 125.00	12 issues
Applied Science & Technology Index	$ 45.00-50.00	11 issues
Science Citation Index	$3,500.00	4 issues
Dissertation Abstracts International Section A: Humanities and Social Sciences	$ 125.00	12 issues
Social Science Citation Index	$1,500.00	3 issues
Social Science Index	$ 30.00-40.00	4 issues
Current Contents/Social and Behavioral Sciences	$ 135.00	52 issues
Arts & Humanities Citation Index	$1,500.00	3 issues
Humanities Index	$ 30.00-40.00	4 issues
Current Contents/Humanities	$ 135.00	3 issues
TOTAL	$21,566.84	for 72 publications

Source: Ulrich's International Periodicals Directory, Seventeenth Edition, 1977-78 (New York: R.R. Bowker, 1977) and Faxon 1979 Librarians' Guide, (Westwood, Massachusetts: F.W. Faxon Company, Inc., 1979).

will not take too many years until librarians will be able to furnish corroborating or disconfirming information.

GATHERING DATA ON BIBLIOGRAPHIC SERVICES

In each of the first three volumes of this study, "Book Publishing," "Journals," and "Libraries," we devoted a separate chapter to discussions of the procedures followed in gathering our data. We showed, for example, the kinds and amounts of data *sought* from each respondent and compared this with what we were actually able to *obtain*. We also showed the sizes and compositions of our samples as they had "evolved" over the course of our piece-meal method of data collection, a method that involved contacting only a few respondents at a time and, in most cases, having our own staff collect the data first-hand from the files and internal reports of the cooperating organizations.

In our research on abstracting and abstracting services, we attempted to follow the same procedures. We prepared statistical questionnaires fashioned after the ones used in our study of primary-research journals; we contacted publishers of A and I services to ask for their cooperation; and we tried to arrange for members of our staff to visit the organizations and to participate in the actual collection of data, both to increase the willingness of the respondents to cooperate with us by reducing the burden imposed on them by nosy outsiders and to improve the comparability of data obtained from different organizations.

Regrettably, we were far less successful in our attempts to persuade publishers of A and I services to participate in our study, and those that did agree to cooperate were, with a few notable exceptions, unable to provide much of the data we were after.

The disappointing show of cooperation, the scarcity of data suited to our needs, and the large variations among A and I publications in subscription prices, circulation, contents, format, and coverage, eventually forced us to abandon any attempt to present "aggregative statistics" on this sector of the information industry, as we had done, for instance, on journals — average number of subscribers, average subscription price, average manufacturing costs, gross margins, and so on.

As an alternative approach, we decided to select from our original sample of over fifty organizations selected for coverage (we were successful in obtaining sparce data from only 24 of these) a small group of the most cooperative, those who were able to provide a great deal of information and who would allow us to present in a considerable amount of detail, several characteristics about their operations and their abstract or index publications. These cooperating publishers are:

Biosciences Information Services
American Institute of Physics
Engineering Index, Inc.
American Psychological Association
American Economic Association
Modern Language Association

The results of this second and comparatively successful attempt at covering secondary services are presented in the next chapter.

CHAPTER 9.2

PROFILES OF SIX ABSTRACTING AND INDEXING PUBLICATIONS

We have already noted the large variety of information that may be contained in bibliographic publications. For example, some contain only enumerations of articles in the *journal* literature in a particular subject area, while others, in addition, list *monographs*, *reports*, *conference papers*, and other types of publications; some contain abstracts of *all* of the scholarly works listed in their indexes, others contain abstracts of only *some* of the listed works; some contain, in addition to abstracts and lists of publications, book *reviews* and *annotations* of books; some make an attempt to cover all of the literature published in a given field, others cover only a portion of the relevant literature; some are large, containing tens of thousands of abstract or index items in the issues published over a one-year period, while others are comparatively small with perhaps just a few hundred abstracts or a few thousand index items; some are available in both computerized form and in the conventional printed form, others are available only in printed form; some are too expensive for individual subscribers to afford, with prices of an annual subscription in some instances of more than a thousand dollars.

As we mentioned in the previous chapter, with publications of such wide variety falling under the rubric "abstracting and indexing services," we found it virtually impossible to provide meaningful descriptions of this sector of the information industry with aggregative statistics such as average number of subscribers, average subscription price, average manufacturing cost, gross margins, etc., as we had done for the publications analyzed in Volumes 1 and 2, that is, books and primary-research journals. Furthermore, our initial attempts to study abstracting and indexing in this "aggregative" vein were frustrated by the scarcity of the kinds of data we would need for such an analysis, a scarcity owing as much to the unwillingness of many publishers to provide what we needed as to their inability to do so.

We were compelled by these considerations to seek an alternative method of analysis. We decided on a method similar to the one used in a portion of the analyses of book publishing in Volume 2 (Chapter 2.9 "Life Profiles and Cohort Analysis"). There we selected a small sample of individual book titles and presented a detailed "profile analysis" for each, showing in considerable detail the life histories of costs, prices, and sales involved in their production and distribution. In this chapter we shall present profile analyses of six abstracting and indexing publications. The approach, however, will be somewhat different from that used for books, because unlike books, secondary services are serial publications issued at regular intervals and hence the notion of a "lifetime" profile of any particular issue is not pertinent. The profiles presented below will consist of descriptions of several characteristics of the publications and their publishers, as well as the steps involved in producing the finished products. Before turning to this collection of "case studies," however, it might be helpful to provide a more general description of the steps involved in producing A and I services, without making direct reference to particular publishers or publications.

STEPS IN THE PRODUCTION OF BIBLIOGRAPHIC PUBLICATIONS

In this general account of the production of A and I publications, we shall refer to the flow chart in Table 9.2.1 which depicts the sequence of major activities.[1]

The first step involves acquiring the source material — primary-research journals, books, conference proceedings, festschriften, dissertations — whose contents are to abstracted or indexed. The source material may be obtained from libraries, from paid subscriptions, or from complimentary copies supplied by publishers.

The second step involves examining the source publications to determine which items treat subject matter that actually fall within the scope of coverage of the bibliographic publication. While some primary journals are considered "core" journals in particular fields and are thus indexed (or abstracted) from cover to cover, others are "interdisciplinary" or "peripheral" and contain articles that deal with subjects of little or no relevance to the interests of those who are likely to use the bibliographic publication. Articles in such journals are usually covered only selectively.

---

[1]This flow chart was constructed from information obtained from our respondents. It is similar to the flow chart appearing in a study of A and I services done under an NSF contract by the Systems Development Corporation, entitled *A System Study of Abstracting and Indexing in the United States*, TM-WD-394, PB 174 249, (Falls Church, Virginia: 1966).

TABLE 9.2.1 Steps in the Production of Abstract and Index Publications

	Source Material — consisting of primary-research journals, books, conference proceedings, etc.
Step 1 — Acquisition of source material	*Acquire from libraries, from paid subscriptions, or from complimentary copies supplied by publishers of the primary publications the material to be abstracted and/or indexed.*
Step 2 — Selection of Material to be Abstracted or indexed	*Select the articles, books, proceedings, etc. from among the source material that fall within the scope of coverage of the bibliographic publication.*
Step 3 — Editorial and "bibliographic" activities	*Write the abstracts or edit those prepared by authors of the source material; prepare the index items and annotations, book reviews, or other relevant references; classify and arrange these according to subject area, author's name, or by other lexicographic schemes that may be used.*
Step 4 — Production activities	*Composition (typesetting) done in most cases by computer. The abstracts and index items are entered on computer tapes by key-board operators. The tapes are then used to produce preliminary proofsheets for proofreading. After proofreading, corrections are made by adjusting the computer tapes and the "clean" tapes are sent to the printer who produces the final camera-ready copy. From these the hardcopy versions of the publication are printed and then bound. The tapes are also reproduced, sometimes by the firm that does the printing or by an outside computer service.*
Step 5 — Distribution	*Copies of issues are sent to subscribers; copies of tapes are sent to outside vendors.*

Source: Machlup, Leeson, and Associates.

The third step involves the editorial functions, that is, preparing (writing and/or editing) and classifying the abstracts and/or index entries of each of the publications (or individual articles) selected for coverage.

Preparation of abstracts may require writing the abstract from scratch, or it may only require editorial adjustments to be made on abstracts that have already been written by the authors of the original articles.

Once the abstracts and index items have been written and edited to conform with the publisher's specifications, particularly with regard to vocabulary, length (in words), punctuation, and syntactic or grammatical structure, the items are classified by one or more lexicographic schemes to provide the means by which users can locate entries relevant to their interests. The abstracts, for instance, may be arranged according to subject area, the index entries according to authors' surnames. Entries are often numbered to facilitate cross referencing. For many bibliographic publications, the editors scan the abstracts during preparation and select key-words or phrases. These are listed in the index to the publication as a means of directing users to items that deal with topics not mentioned explicitly in the titles of the articles.

The fourth major step in the sequence involves the production activities. The classified bibliographic entries are "key-boarded," that is, entered on the computer tapes usually by CRT (Cathode-Ray Tube) operators. The tapes are eventually used to produce camera-ready copy or photographic plates from which the conventional printed copies are produced. First, however, preliminary proof sheets are prepared from the tapes and proofread by the production staff or, in some instances, by the editorial staff. After proofreading, corrections are made directly on the computer tapes. The resulting "clean" tapes are sent to the printer, who prepares the final camera-ready copy. From these, the conventional hard-copy versions of the publication are printed and then bound. For publishers who offer computerized search services in addition to hard-copy issues of their publications, the tapes themselves are reproduced, either by the same firm that does the printing or by an outside computer service.

The fifth and final step depicted in Table 9.2.1 is distribution. This involves sending issues of the finished publication to subscribers, a function commonly performed by the printer, rather than the publisher. The reproducer of the tapes sends copies to vendors.

THE CASE STUDIES

We chose for the profile or case-study analysis, six of the most cooperative organizations, those that had, in addition, the most comprehensive records and statistical data on their publications and publishing operations.

Participating Publishers

The following are the organizations that provided, through personal interviews, the information required for the analysis:

Publisher	*Abstract/Index Publication Covered in this Profile Analysis*
Biosciences Information Service	*Biological Abstracts*
American Institute of Physics	*Current Physics Index*
Engineering Index, Inc.	*Engineering Index*
American Psychological Association	*Psychological Abstracts*
American Economic Association	*Journal of Economic Literature*
Modern Language Association	*MLA International Bibliography of Books and Articles on the Modern Languages and Literature*

Thus, in the order of their position in the list, our sample contains one abstract publication in the life sciences; one in the physical sciences; one in engineering (these last two are publications containing abstracts even though they are called *Index* by their titles); one in psychology; one in economics, containing besides indexes, selected abstracts, book reviews, and book annotations; and lastly, an index (no abstracts) of the literature in languages and literature.

Table 9.2.2 lists for each of these publications twenty-three characteristics that will serve as the basis for our discussion.

PROFILES OF THREE PRODUCTION PROCESSES

Before turning our attention to these twenty-three characteristics, however, we will extend our general discussions of the production process presented above by describing in some detail how a few of the organizations in our sample produce their publications. For this purpose we have selected three: *Current Physics Index*, *Psychological Abstracts*, and the *MLA International Bibliography of Books and Articles on the Modern Languages and Literature*. Descriptions of these are primarily intended to convey an idea of some of the similarities and differences among the production processes of publishers of A and I services.

Current Physics Index

Current Physics Index (CPI) published by the American Institute of Physics (AIP) presents an interesting case study. Unlike most other A and I publications, its "source materials," that is, the articles of which abstracts are published in the conventional hard-copy form, include articles contained only in the 44 primary-research journals published by AIP. (Approximately 20 primary-research journals of other publishers are abstracted selectively, but are available only on computer tapes, not in the hard-copy version of interest in this analysis.) Still, the extent of coverage of significant research in physics is substantial. The American Institute of Physics, an organization composed of several member societies in various specialized fields of the physical science, publishers, according to their own estimates, some 90 per cent of all physics articles published in the United States and about 25 per cent of of the total published throughout the world. That all abstracts appearing in CPI are of articles of primary research published by the American Institute of Physics means that the publisher incurs virtually no acquisitions costs for source material, at least not in the same sense that other publishers of secondary services incur such costs. Furthermore, since abstracts of all articles appearing in the primary-research journals are automatically published in CPI, the actual selection of source material is done, in effect, not by the staff of CPI, but by the editors and editorial boards of the primary-research journals who select the original articles for publication.

Thus, in both the acquisition of source material and in the selection of the items to be abstracted — Steps 1 and 2 in the flow chart of Table 9.2.1 — procedures followed by the publisher of *Current Physics Index* depart somewhat from those outlined in our general model.

After an article has been accepted for publication in one of the primary-research journals, the manuscript of the article and of its abstract are copy-edited; these two functions — editing the article and the abstract — are not performed by separate staffs. The work done at this stage of the process contributes jointly to the production of the primary-research journals and to the production of CPI. (As a matter of fact, the same abstracts published in CPI are published along with the full-length version of the articles in the primary-research journals.) Approximately 85 per cent of the abstracts are prepared by the author of the original article; 8 per cent are prepared by the in-house staff and 7 per cent by free-lance abstracters.

After copy-editing, the articles and the abstracts are classified according to subject area. The abstracts are then entered on computer tape by keyboard operators. The computer produces proof sheets by a process of photocomposition. These are proofread. When all corrections have been made, the "clean" tapes are used by AIP to produce camera-ready copy. This is sent to an outside printer who produces the hard-copy versions of *Current Physics Index.*

A serious shortcoming of this index is the suppression of most first names of authors, thus making their full identification difficult, if not impossible. Since the source material is also published under the auspices of the American Institute of Physics, it would be easy for the publisher to insist on fully-spelled-out first names. Any additional cost to the AIP would be negligible, while the cost imposed on searchers of particular authors' work is substantial.

Psychological Abstracts

Steps in the production of *Psychological Abstracts* (PA), a publication of the American Psychological Association (APA), are similar to those outlined in the general model depicted in Table 9.2.1. APA publishes 17 primary-research journals in addition to *Psychological Abstracts*. Unlike the previous example, however, the two publishing programs are not joint operations. The subdivision of the American Psychological Association that publishes *Psychological Abstracts*, along with other information services in psychology, is called PsycINFO which employs its own staff and has separate facilities. *Psychological Abstracts* covers over 1,000 journals in psychology and related fields. Most of the source journals are supplied to PsycINFO free of charge by their publishers; a few are obtained through paid subscriptions. Three members of the staff of *PA* scan the journals and select the articles to be abstracted. (In addition to full-size articles, pertinent notes, comments, and even obituaries may be selected; editorials are exluded.)

After acquiring the source material and selecting the items to be abstracted, the editorial and bibliographic activities begin. Eight staff members are responsible for preparing the abstracts. This involves either "lifting" from the source material the abstract written by the author of the original article and making whatever editorial adjustments are required to bring it into conformance with *PA*'s terminology and format, or, when an author-prepared abstract is not available, writing the abstract from scratch. The eight staff members prepare approximately 80 per cent of the abstracts, including both "lifts" and those prepared from scratch. Some 19 per cent are prepared by volunteer abstracters, psychologists throughout the country who contribute their services free of charge; one per cent of the abstracts are prepared by free-lance abstracters.

After the abstracts have been prepared they are classified under one of 16 major subject headings and 65 subheadings by a staff of nine "indexers." The abstracts are arranged by subject and, within subject classifications, alphabetically by author. In addition, the indexers select from each abstract up to ten key words. These are listed alphabetically in the "Brief Subject Index" to each issue of *PA* and direct the reader by means of a reference number to the pertinent abstracts. An author index is also published in each issue. A number of *phrases* are also selected from the abstracts for listing, not in the hard-copy version, but only on the machine-readable version of the service to assist users with computer searches.

In addition to the three "scanners" of source material, eight "abstracters," and nine "indexers," there are nine CRT (Cathode-Ray Tube) operators, who enter the abstracts and accompanying data onto the computer system, the next step in the production process.

The procedures described above are followed on a routine basis from day to day. Once each month, a day is designated as a cut-off date; all abstracts that have been prepared and entered into the computer system by that time are selected to appear in the next monthly issue. (The goal is to produce 2,500 abstracts per month.) The abstracts on the tapes are then put into final form (e.g., special characters are inserted in place of temporary "tags" used earlier in the editing process; abstracts are sorted by field and within field alphabetically by author; sequence numbers are assigned). The tape is then sent to the photocompositor, an outside service. Proof sheets are made and sent back to PsycINFO for proofreading. This is done by the nine CRT operators. After corrections have been made, the final camera-ready copy is prepared and sent to the printer. Approximately 6,000 copies of *Psychological Abstracts* are printed per issue.

MLA International Bibliography of Books and Articles on the Modern Languages and Literatures

The *MLA Bibliography* is published annually in three separate volumes. Volume I is entitled "General, English, American, Medieval and Neo-Latin, Celtic Literatures; and Folklore;" Volume II, "European, Asian, African and Latin American Literature;" and Volume III, "Linguistics." A special library edition that combines all three volumes is also available. Unlike the previous two publications discussed in this section, the *MLA Bibliography* is an *index* to publications in the modern languages and literature and contains no abstracts.

A staff of five editors, or research assistants as they are referred to at MLA, in cooperation with 215 off-site volunteers, scan altogether nearly 3,000 titles, including books, journals, festschriften, collected works, and series. From these they select the publications that fall within the scope of coverage of the *MLA Bibliography* — some 40,000 index items per year. The in-house staff of five are themselves responsible for indexing between 500 and 600 journals and generate 50 per cent of the total index items. In addition, they verify the authenticity of all items sent in by the off-site indexers.

Source material is obtained in any one of the following four ways: through libraries; through special arrangements with publishers (university presses often send complimentary copies of their monographs, commercial publishers usually notify MLA of new titles); through personal correspondence with authors; and from the *American Book Publishing Record*, a publication of the R.R. Bowker Company that provides a comprehensive listing of all new book titles published each year in the United States. (Catalogues of individual publishers are not used.) The 500 to 600 journals indexed by the in-house staff are supplied free of charge by their publishers.

When a publication is found to fall within the scope of coverage of Volumes I or II, the index entry is prepared and classified by the five in-house staff according to national literature — English, American, French, and so on — and within national literature by period — medieval, sixteenth century, etc. Within these categories, items are classified alphabetically according to the name of the literary figure to whom the original publication refers. The entries prepared for Volume III, "Linguistics," are classified according to a somewhat different scheme. They are assigned to one of three broad subject headings — general linguistics; theoretical and descriptive linguistics; or comparative and historical linguistics — and within these categories, according to language group or regional interest — Indo-European, African, etc.

The selected index items are entered first on paper "index" cards by the research assistants. From these a keyboard operator enters the items onto computer tape, specifying in coded form the subject classification, diacritical markings, punctuation, italics, and so on. A preliminary "proofreading" is performed electronically by a specially prepared validation program to assure, for example, that standard acronyms or initializations are used for the titles of journals, that titles of books and journals are italicized, and that individual journal articles are within quotation marks. Next, printouts of the index items are obtained and proofread visually by the research assistants. Corrections are entered on the computer files and the final "clean" tapes are sent to an outside service that prepares the camera-ready copy for the printer. A separate tape is prepared for outside venders who offer computer-search services.

Each annual issue (three volumes) of the *MLA Bibliography* takes a full twelve months to produce. Approximately eight months are devoted to gathering the source material, writing the index items and entering them on computer tapes, and four months to proofreading and editing the items in preparation for the production of camera-ready copy and to printing and distributing final copies of the publication.

TWENTY-THREE CHARACTERISTICS OF SELECTED ABSTRACT AND INDEX PUBLICATIONS

Table 9.2.2 lists 23 characteristics of each of the six bibliographic publications chosen for our profile analysis. Since numerous references will be made to these publications and their publishers, it will conserve a good deal of space if we adopt a logogram to represent each. The full names of the six publications, with their abbreviations in parentheses, are shown as column headings in the table. The full names of the publishers, along with their abbreviations, are listed as the first characteristic in the table.

Publisher

The next two characteristics shown in Table 9.2.2 are type of publisher and any other information services provided by the same publisher.

All six publishers are not-for-profit organizations. BIOSIS and EI, Inc. are independent. The remaining four are associated with the major learned society in their respective fields.

Without exception, the six publishers, or the learned societies with which they are affiliated, provide a number of information services in addition to the abstract or index publications chosen here for detailed description. The independent organizations, BIOSIS and EI, Inc., do not publish any primary-research journals but specialize in secondary services. BIOSIS publishes five additional bibliographic publications in conventionally printed form. Four of these contain abstracts in specialized fields of biology, selected from the same computer file used to produce the more comprehensive *Biological Abstracts*. The fifth is an index publication containing tables of contents of publications generally not covered by *BA*. EI, Inc. publishes, in addition to *Engineering Index*, two abstract journals in specialized fields of engineering, each containing abstracts selected from the master file used to produce *EI*.

Among the learned societies, AIP has by far the largest publication program, including 44 primary-research journals in the physical sciences. *Current Physics Index*, first published in 1975, is one of their most recent additions. We noted earlier that the 44 journals constitute the entire universe of source material covered by *CPI* and that these journals and the abstract publication are, in large measure, jointly produced.

TABLE 9.2.2 Twenty-Three Characteristics of Selected Abstract and Index Publications: *Biological Abstracts*, *Current Physics Index*, *Engineering Index*, *Psychological Abstracts*, *Journal of Economic Literature*, *MLA International Bibliography of Books and Articles on the Modern Languages and Literatures*

	Publications					
	Biological Abstracts (BA)	*Current Physics Index (CPI)*	*Engineering Index (EI)*	*Psychological Abstracts (PA)*	*Journal of Economic Literature (JEL)*	*MLA International Bibliography of Books and Articles on the Modern Languages and Literatures (MLA Bibliography)*
1. Name of publisher	Biosciences Information Service (BIOSIS)	American Institute of Physics (AIP)	Engineering Index, Inc. (EI, Inc.)	American Psychological Association (APA)	American Economic Association (AEA)	Modern Language Association (MLA)
2. Type of publisher	Independent; not for profit	Professional society; not for profit	Independent; not for profit	Professional society; not for profit	Professional society; not for profit	Professional society; not for profit
3 Other information services provided by this publisher	Five abstract or index journals in specialized fields of the biological sciences; various computer search services, standardized or customized to meet individual needs; available also through outside vendors	44 primary-research journals in the physical sciences; three indexes to physics journals; photocopy service for reprints of articles; computer searches of abstracts in data base available through outside vendors	Two abstract or index journals in specialized fields of engineering; computer searches of records in data base available through outside vendors	17 primary-research journals in psychology; an index to *Psychological Abstracts*; a thesaurus of index terms; computer searches of abstracts in data base available through both APA and outside vendors	One primary-research journal; papers and proceedings of annual meeting	One primary-research journal; about 5 books and pamphlets per year; computer search services available through outside vendors
4. Principal contents	Abstracts of journal articles, conference papers, monographs, etc.	Abstracts of journal articles	Abstracts of journal articles, conference papers, etc.	Abstracts of journal articles; dissertations	Journal articles, abstracts of journal articles, index to the journal literature, book reviews, annotated listing of new books	Index of journal articles, books, and analyzed collections
5. Type of abstracts/index items published (see text for definitions)	Informative — 100 per cent	Informative — 100 per cent	Informative — 75 per cent Indicative — 25 per cent	Informative — 80 per cent Indicative — 20 per cent	Informative — 100 per cent	Not applicable

(continued)

TABLE 9.2.2, continued

6. Attempted scope of coverage of all relevant publications in the field	Complete coverage of relevant subject areas	Coverage of publications of the American Institute of Physics (estimated to be 90 per cent of the number of articles in physics published in the United States; 25 per cent of the number published in the world)	Complete coverage of relevant subject areas	Complete coverage of relevant subject areas	Complete coverage of relevant subject areas	Approximately 80 per cent of relevant subject areas
7. Number of publications covered, totally or in part	8,000 journals and conference papers, monographs, etc. — abstracts are prepared for most but not all of the source material covered	44 journals of the American Institute of Physics and member societies — 100 per cent are abstracted	2,000 journals and conference papers; 90 to 100 per cent of articles in "core" journals are abstracted; only selected articles in peripheral journals are abstracted	1,000 journals; 90 to 100 per cent of articles in "core" journals are abstracted; only relevant articles in peripheral journals are abstracted	250 journals; all articles are indexed, selected articles are abstracted; reviews or annotations appear on some 1,200-1,300 books each year	3,000 books, journals and series, all publications that fall within MLA's subject scope are indexed
8. Estimated percentage of total abstracts/index items prepared from source material published abroad	75 to 80 per cent	25 per cent (these are all journals from the U.S.S.R. with English translations published in the United States by AIP)	50 per cent	18 per cent	Unknown	50 per cent
9. Who translates the material written in foreign languages?	In-house staff plus a few free-lance translators for less common languages	Free-lance translators	Translation of material written in Romance Languages done in-house; other languages translated by free-lance translators	Translations done largely by volunteers from the profession; also by free-lance translators	No translating required. Only articles written in English or with English summaries are classified. (Journal articles with foreign-language titles are listed without translation but not classified by subject area.)	Index items appear in the original languages as long as they are written in the Roman alphabet. Items written in non-Roman alphabets are transliterated, but not usually translated

(continued)

TABLE 9.2.2, continued

	Biological Abstracts (BA)	Current Physics Index (CPI)	Engineering Index (EI)	Psychological Abstracts (PA)	Journal of Economic Literature (JEL)	MLA International Bibliography of Books and Articles on the Modern Languages and Literatures (MLA Bibliography)
10. Size of staff 1979:						
Administrative	15 employees	Not possible to separate accurately the staff that produces *Current Physics Index* from staff that produces other publications of AIP	6 employees	4 employees	5 full-time employees, 3 part-time employees	3 employees
Editorial	122 employees		29 employees	20 employees		5 employees
Production	46 employees		18 employees	9 employees		1 employee
Marketing	3 employees		4 employees	2 employees		-
Other	84 employees		5 employees	1 employee		1 employee
Total	270 employees		62 employees	36 employees	8 employees	10 employees
11. Proportion of total abstracts prepared by:						
Author of original article	0 per cent	0 per cent	0 per cent	0 per cent	100 per cent	Not applicable
Author, with editorial adjustments by this publisher	65 per cent	85 per cent	85 per cent	75 per cent	0 per cent	Not applicable
In-house staff	30 per cent	8 per cent	15 per cent (in-house staff, free-lance abstracters/indexers, and volunteers combined)	5 per cent	0 per cent	50 per cent
Free-lance abstracters/indexers	5 per cent	7 per cent		1 per cent	0 per cent	Not applicable
Volunteers from the profession	0 per cent	0 per cent		19 per cent (by 300 volunteers)	0 per cent	50 per cent (by 215 volunteers)
Total	100 per cent	100 per cent	100 per cent	100 per cent	100 per cent	100 per cent
12. Estimated average number of abstracts/index items prepared (written and/or edited) in one week by a member of the in-house staff	180 abstracts per week or 450 index items per week	130 abstracts per week; mostly editorial work on abstracts written by authors	100 abstracts per week (This total contains a combination of abstracts written by the authors and free-lance abstracters, and edited by the in-house staff, as well as those created from scratch by the in-house staff.)	90 abstracts per week (This total contains a combination of abstracts written by the authors, free-lance abstracters and volunteers, as well as those created from scratch by the in-house staff.)	Abstracts are not prepared by the staff; annotations of books take, on average, 24 minutes to prepare; book reviews (editorial functions only) take about 48 minutes to prepare	Not known

(continued)

TABLE 9.2.2, continued

13. The estimated direct cost of labor to the publisher of preparing (writing and editing) a typical abstract/index item*						
For those prepared by the:						
Author of original article	Not available	Not available	$4.05 in 1977	Not applicable	$.07 in 1977 (all abstracts are published as written by the original author). Costs of other contents: book reviews, $18.30 in 1977 (the reviews themselves are written free of charge by members of the profession); annotations of books, $8.05 in 1977; index item, $1.30 in 1977	Not available
Author, with editorial adjustments by this publisher	Not available	Not available	$4.05 in 1977	$4.45 in 1978		Not available
In-house staff	Not available	Not available	$4.05 in 1977	$9.85 in 1978		Not available
Free-lance abstracters/indexers	Not available	Not available	$4.05 in 1977	$6.50 in 1978; $11.20 including in-house editorial work		Not available
Volunteers from the profession	Not applicable	Not available	Not applicable	$6.60 in 1978, including in-house editorial work	Not applicable	Not available
14. First year of publication	1927	1975	1884	1927	1969 (preceded by the <u>Journal of Economic Abstracts</u>)	1922
15. Frequency of publication at present	24 issues per year (plus a separate semi-annual index to the abstracts contained in these issues)	4 issues per year (plus a separate annual index to the abstracts contained in these issues)	12 issues per year (plus an annual cumulation of the 12 issues)	12 issues per year (plus a triennial index to the abstracts contained in these issues)	4 issues per year (plus an annual index to economic articles)	Issued once per year in three volumes
16. Cumulative number of abstracts/index items published from first year of publication through 1977	3,133,780 abstracts since 1927; of these some 500,000 are on computer tapes, all produced since 1976	45,700 abstracts since 1975; all on computer tapes	2,400,000 abstracts since 1884; of these, 940,000 are on computer tapes, all of these produced since 1970	528,800 abstracts since 1927; of these, 251,100 are on computer tapes, all of these produced since 1967	13,440 abstracts of articles; 40,128 index items (since 1972); 1,580 book reviews; 10,880 book annotations, all of these since 1969	Not known

*Exclusive of the cost of acquiring the source material and of entering the finished abstract onto computerized data base.

(continued)

TABLE 9.2.2, continued

	Biological Abstracts (BA)	Current Physics Index (CPI)	Engineering Index (EI)	Psychological Abstracts (PA)	Journal of Economic Literature (JEL)	MLA International Bibliography of Books and Articles on the Modern Languages and Literatures (MLA Bibliography)
17. Number of pages published in 1977 (excluding periodic cumulations and separate indexes)	27,940 pages	2,050 pages	8,033 pages	3,428 pages	1,713 pages	879 pages
18. Number of abstracts/ index items published in 1977	145,000 abstracts	17,340 abstracts	95,000 abstracts	27,000 abstracts	1,589 abstracts of articles; 7,164 index items; 172 book reviews; 1,212 book annotations	39,950 index items
19. Annual subscription price in 1977:						
Individuals (or society members)	No subscriptions held by individuals	$30.00	No subscriptions held by individuals	$70.00	From $26.25 to $36.75, depending on income of the subscriber. Prices cover subscription to the American Economic Review and membership in the American Economic Association	$20.00
Institutions	$1,200.00	$95.00	$695.00	$240.00	$39.35	$75.00
20. Subscription price per 1,000 abstracts in 1977:						
Individuals	-	$1.70	-	$2.60	Because of the diversity of contents, price per abstract is not a meaningful measurement	$0.50 per 1,000 index items

(continued)

TABLE 9.2.2, continued

Institutions	*$8.30*	*$5.50*	*$7.30*	*$8.90*		*$1.90 per 1,000 index items*
21. Number of subscribers in 1977:						
Individuals	*Not available*	*Held in confidence*	*None*	*1,883*	*17,300*	*30,000*
Institutions			*2,900*	*4,307*	*6,700*	*2,500*
22. Average elapsed time from publication of the original (source) material to publication of abstracts/index items	*Varies widely among journals*	*2 months*	*5 to 14 months*	*Varies widely among journals*	*4 to 7 months*	*9 to 16 months*
23. Average elapsed time from receipt of the original (source) material to publication of abstracts/index items	*3 to 6 months*	*2 months*	*3 months*	*2 to 3 months*	*3 to 6 months*	*Less than 9 months*

Source: Machlup, Leeson, and Associates.

APA publishes, in addition to *Psychological Abstracts*, 17 primary journals in psychology, but the two publishing operations are, for the most part, separate undertakings. AEA and MLA each publish one primary-research journal besides their secondary publication. The language association produces about five books and pamphlets per year.

Of the six publications profiled in Table 9.2.2, five offer their information services also in computerized form, with computer search services available directly from the publisher and from an outside vendor who leases or purchases the publisher's computer tapes. The one exception is the American Economic Association, though plans to provide such services in the future have been given some consideration.

Cumulative indexes to the publications of abstracts are not counted among the "Other information services" but, instead, are mentioned under a later heading, "Frequency of publication at present." There we see that such indexes are produced by five of the six publishers.

The remaining nineteen characteristics listed in Table 9.2.2 refer to the publications themselves, rather than to their publishers.

Contents and Coverage

From Characteristic No. 4, "Principal Contents," we see that *JEL* offers the largest variety of material. Each issue contains three or four full-length articles — most often survey articles of selected topics in economics — , abstracts of journal articles, an index to the journal literature, book reviews, and an annotated listing of new books in the field. The first four publications in the table, *BA*, *CPI*, *EI*, and *PA*, contain abstracts of journal articles; *PA* also covers dissertations. The *MLA Bibliography* is an index to journal articles, books, and analyzed collections, but contains no abstracts.

Some publishers, librarians, and industry analysts find it useful to categorize abstracts according to the type of information they are intended to convey about the source articles. So-called "informative" abstracts, for example, provide a comprehensive summary of the information contained in the source article, often in sufficient detail to be used in lieu of the original article, while "indicative" abstracts are intended primarily to advise the reader of the existence of an article and provide only enough information about its contents to enable the user to decide if the source article is pertinent to his interests. There are also "critical" abstracts, sometimes called "evaluative" abstracts, that provide a brief critical review of the source article. (In fact, one reference publication, *The Librarians' Glossary*, published by Seminar Press, lists no fewer than ten types of abstracts. Besides informative, indicative, and evaluative, abstracts may be characterized as general, selective, traditional, telegraphic, locative, and illative.)

We asked the publishers in our sample to indicate which of these definitions would best describe the type of abstracts they publish. The results, which require no additional discussion here, are given as Characteristic No. 5 in Table 9.2.2.

Characteristics Nos. 6 and 7 convey an idea of the coverage by each of the six publications of the primary literature in their respective fields. Four of the publications, *BA*, *EI*, *PA*, and *JEL* attempt to cover all of the relevant publications in their fields. The staff of *Biological Abstracts* scans some 8,000 journals in addition to conference papers and monographs and prepares abstracts of most of this source material. Approximately 2,000 journals and conference papers are covered by *Engineering Index* and 1,000 by *Psychological Abstracts*. Each of these publishers abstract 90 to 100 per cent of the articles in "core" journals in their fields and abstract selectively the articles in "peripheral" journals. In economics, fewer primary journals are published than in biology and engineering, and *JEL* accomplishes nearly complete coverage of the relevant subject areas by covering 250 journals; abstracts, however, are published only for selected articles. As mentioned earlier, the coverage of *CPI* is confined to the 44 primary-research journals of *AIP*. All articles appearing in these journals have their abstracts published in *CPI*; it is estimated by the publisher that articles in these 44 journals account for 90 per cent of all physics articles published in the United States. Finally, the index publication, *MLA Bibliography*, counts among its source material some 3,000 books, journals, and series, accounting for an estimated 80 per cent of the relevant subject area.

Foreign Source Material

Characteristics Nos. 8 and 9 in Table 9.2.2 show, respectively, the estimated percentage of abstract or index items prepared from source material published abroad and who does the translating of foreign materials. Of the six publications, *Biological Abstracts* contains the highest estimated percentage of abstracts of material published abroad — 75 to 80 per cent. Most of the translation of the foreign source material is done by the in-house staff of BIOSIS, though free-lance translators are relied on for less common languages.

Approximately half of the abstracts in *EI* and half of the index items in *MLA Bibliography* pertain to source material published abroad. In the case of *EI*, most translation is done by the in-house staff, particularly of Romance Languages, with some other languages done by free-lance translators. In the *MLA Bibliography*, the titles of the indexed items are given in their original languages, or are transliterated by volunteer indexers if a non-Roman alphabet is used in the original. They are not translated into English.

Although *CPI* contains abstracts only of articles published in the primary journals of the American Institute of Physics, there is still some coverage of foreign source material; because among AIP's 44 primary journals are several "translation" journals: AIP translates, publishes, and distributes in the United States some journals published in the Soviet Union. These account for approximately 25 per cent of the abstracts in *CPI*; translation is done by free-lance translators.

Psychological Abstracts contains the smallest percentage of abstracts of foreign source material — 18 per cent. Translation is done, for the most part, by volunteers from the psychology profession; to a lesser extent by free-lance translators.

An estimate of the coverage of foreign material by *JEL* was made by our own staff. They checked the 865 abstracts published in the March and September issues of *JEL* for 1978 and found that 216, or 25 per cent were of articles published in foreign journals. As a rule, only articles from English-Language journals published abroad are abstracted, hence no translation is required. (In a section of the *JEL* entitled "Contents of Current Periodicals," the names of articles in foreign tongues are listed, but without translation, unless an English summary is published along with the article in the source journal.)

Production and Costs

The next four characteristics listed in the table, Nos. 10 through 13, answer for the publications that could provide the information, the following questions: How large is their staff? What percentages of the abstracts or index items are prepared by the authors, editors, staff, and others? How many abstracts per week are produced on the average by one member of the in-house staff? What is the average direct labor-cost incurred in preparing a typical abstract?

BIOSIS, with 270 employees has, by far, the largest staff. As we shall note later on, they also produce the thickest publication and the largest number of abstracts per year among the six publishers. For *CPI* it was not possible to list the number of staff members solely responsible for its preparation and publication, because many of their functions performed contribute jointly to the production of AIP's primary-research journals. Of comparatively small size are the staffs of *JEL* and *MLA Bibliography*, with only eight and ten employees, respectively.

Most of the publishers were uneasy about trying to divide their total staff among the five functional categories shown in the table — administrative, editorial, production, marketing, and other. They warned that such a breakdown might be misleading, because many of the same employees perform duties that fall under two or more of the categories shown. Hence, the reported distributions should be taken as rough approximations. Still, for the four publications that provided the breakdowns, *BA*, *EI*, *PA*, and *MLA Bibliography*, there is a rough similarity in the proportion of employees slotted in a few of the categories. Editorial personnel, for example, account for 45 per cent, 47 per cent, 56 per cent, and 50 per cent, respectively, of the total for these four publications. In relation to the others, *BA* has a disproportionately large number of employees listed under "other," 84 out of 270, or 31 per cent. This may reflect the fact that BIOSIS does a lot of in-house translation and offers rather extensive "in-house" computer search services for their customers. For example, they provide a search service customized to individual needs called "Current Literature Alerting Search Service" (CLASS), in which they search their computer files three times per month for references that match the research interests of a particular customer. The "hits"[2] are printed on index cards and sent to the customer from four to six weeks before the printed version of *BA* is published.

Characteristic No. 11 shows who prepares the abstracts for each publication, or the index items in the case of *MLA Bibliography*. There are five possibilities listed: (1) the author of the original article, (2) the author of the original article with substantial editorial adjustments by the publisher's in-house staff, (3) the in-house staff, (4) free-lance abstracters, and (5) volunteers from the profession.

All of the abstracts published by *JEL* are prepared by the authors of the source material. Work performed by the staff of *JEL* on abstracts is confined to "marking-up" the abstracts received with instructions for the compositor. The remaining four publications that contain abstracts, *BA*, *CPI*, *EI*, and *PA*, also publish a high percentage of author-prepared abstracts, but often after substantial editorial adjustments — rewording of sentences, replacement of some terms with terms from a standardized vocabulary, lengthening, shortening.

Abstracts prepared from scratch by the in-house staffs, using the full text of the original articles, account for 30 per cent of *BA*'s output. This is the largest percentage among the five reporting publications. *CPI* prepares 8 per cent of their abstracts from scratch (presumably, some source articles

---

[2]A "hit," for those who may be unfamiliar with the language of the trade, occurs each time a bibliographic reference is found on the computer tape that matches the interests of the customer.

are not accompanied by author-prepared abstracts as required by the primary journals published by AIP). We need not repeat here the percentage breakdowns shown in the table. Free-lancers are, to a large extent, relied on to prepare abstracts of articles written in foreign languages. Among the abstract publications, *PA* is the only publication that obtains a significant part of their total abstracts from volunteers from the profession — approximately 19 per cent, contributed by 300 volunteers. For the single publication devoted solely to indexing the literature, the *MLA Bibliography*, half of the index items are prepared by the in-house staff and half by a group of some 215 volunteers from the profession.

Characteristic No. 12, estimated average number of abstracts or index items prepared in one week by a member of the in-house staff, ought to be viewed with a good deal of caution, largely because the actual functions performed by members of the staffs of the various publication vary widely. Thus, it would make no sense to use the figures shown as a basis for judging the relative productivity of the different staffs. The figures will vary, for instance, according to the proportion of abstracts in the total that are prepared from scratch versus these proportions prepared initially by authors or by free-lance abstracters; according to the technical complexity or sophistication of the articles in the various fields; according to the amount of editorial adjustment required, and so on. Beyond these qualifications and the explanatory notes provided along with the figures displayed in the table, there is little additional discussion to offer, particularly if we intend to play down the significance of the values presented.

Turning now to the final topic pertinent to this discussion on "Production and Costs," we present as Characteristic No. 13 in Table 9.2.2, "the estimated direct cost of labor to the publisher of preparing (writing and editing) a typical abstract/ index item." (We should emphasize that the figures shown, as noted in a footnote to the table, exclude the cost of acquiring the souce material and of entering the finished abstract onto a computerized data base.)

It is obvious from the gaps in the table that data on costs were hard to come by in our survey. Three of the publishers, of *BA*, *CPI*, and *MLA Bibliography*, were not prepared to provide any estimates. The publishers of *EI* were able to provide a single figure, $4.05 in 1977, representing a weighted average of the costs of preparing a mixture of abstracts, those written by authors and edited by the in-house staff, those prepared from scratch by the in-house staff, and those prepared by free-lance abstracters.

It stands to reason that abstracts prepared by authors, whether or not editorial adjustments are required, are less costly to the publishers than abstracts prepared either from scratch by the in-house staff or by free-lance abstracters. The cost figures on *PA* and *JEL* tend to support this assertion.

All of the author-prepared abstracts published in *PA* are edited by the in-house staff. The publisher calculated that the direct cost of labor involved in preparing these abstracts was $4.45 in 1978. On the other hand, abstracts prepared from scratch by the in-house staff cost almost twice as much, $9.85. Those prepared by free-lance abstracters were the most expensive of the three types shown, costing, on average, $6.50 in fees to the free-lancer and $4.70 in in-house editorial processing, a total of $11.20.

Although we cannot offer the labor cost to the *JEL* of processing an author-prepared abstract (taken as is, with no editorial adjustments) as a basis for generalization, we may note that the comparatively minute expense of $.07 stands in stark contrast to the costs incurred by *EI* and *PA*. The difference, of course, can be attributed to the fact that author-prepared abstracts are published in *JEL* without extensive editorial processing. The cost of $.07, as estimated by the publisher of *JEL*, includes half a minute of secretarial time to "check in" the author-prepared abstract upon its receipt, and one-and-a-half minutes of an assistant editor's time to "mark up" the abstract for the compositor.

We were able to obtain estimates of the cost of preparing some of the other items contained in the *JEL*. A single book review, on the average, cost $18.30 in 1977, a figure that includes selecting a reviewer, preparing and sending requests for review to the individual chosen, sending the book to be reviewed along with general instructions, sending reminders, and finally, assessing and editing the submitted review and marking it up for the compositor. The cost excludes the time spent by the reviewers; they contribute their time free of charge. Annotations of books cost, in 1977, $8.05 each, a figure that includes the writing (24 minutes, by a graduate student), typing and "logging-in" the annotation (12 minutes of secretarial time), review of the annotation first by an assistant editor, then by the chief editor (13 minutes), and finally, marking-up for the compositor by an assistant editor (4 minutes). The estimated cost of preparing an index item was $1.30 in 1977, including checking-in the source journal (half a minute of secretarial time) classifying the individual articles by subject (four minutes for each entry, by a graduate student), having the classification checked by an outside consultant (approximately $.30), review of the item by an assistant editor (on a sample basis), and finally, typing the item in preparation for composition (one-and-a-half minutes of secretarial time).

Age and Output

Characteristics Nos. 14 through 18 show the first year of publication, frequency of publication at present, cumulative number of abstracts or index items published from the first year of publication through 1977, number of pages published in 1977, and number of abstracts or index items published in 1977.

The oldest publication is *EI*, first published in 1884; the youngest is *CPI*, first published in 1975. *JEL* is relatively young, first appearing in its present form in 1969, though prior to that year the AEA published on a quarterly basis a secondary journal containing abstracts, but with none of the other features of the *JEL*, under the title *Journal of Economic Abstracts*. The remaining three publications *BA*, *PA*, and *MLA Bibliography* have been published for just over 50 years, the first two since 1927 and the third since 1922.

Of the six publications, *BA* is published most frequently with 24 issues per year, and *MLA Bibliography* least frequently with one issue per year issued in three volumes. We also note from the table that the five abstract journals have triennial, semi-annual, or annual indexes to their issues. *EI* publishes an annual cumulation of 12 monthly issues, including all abstracts.

An idea of the volume of output of each of the six publications, in terms of number of pages and number of abstracts or index items, can be obtained from Characteristics Nos. 16, 17, and 18. No. 16 shows the cumulative number of abstracts or index items published from the first year of publication through 1977. Note that four of the abstract journals, *BA*, *CPI*, *EI*, and *PA*, have the abstracts published in the more recent past available also on computer tapes.

With regard to number of pages published in 1977, *BA* is by far the largest with 27,940 pages, more than three times the number of pages published that year in the second-voluminous publication, *EI*, with 8,033 pages. The large number of pages in *BA* can be attributed, in part, to the fact that it publishes more issues per year and more abstracts per year than the others, and in part, to the fact that each issue contains five separate indexes: (1) an author index; (2) a "biosystematic" index arranged according to taxonomic categories; (3) a "generic" index arranged according to genus and species; (4) a "concept" index arranged according to broad subject areas; and (5) a subject or "key-word" index arranged according to words found in the titles of articles.

The five abstract publications have the same rank-ordering in terms of number of abstracts as they have in terms of number of pages.

Prices and Number of Subscribers

Characteristics No. 19, 20, and 21 provide information on annual subscription price in 1977, subscription price per 1,000 abstracts or index items, and number of subscribers in 1977, respectively.

Four of the six publications charged different prices for subscriptions by individuals (including, in the cases of *CPI*, *PA*, and *JEL*, the members of the respective professional societies) and for subscriptions by institutions, mostly libraries. *BA* and *EI* each charged a single price, $1,200 and $695, respectively. It is not surprising that no individuals hold subscriptions at these prices. In the case of *JEL*, the subscription price to individuals is actually the membership dues charged by the AEA on a sliding scale according to annual salary; it covers, in addition to the subscription to *JEL*, a subscription to the *American Economic Review*, the society's primary journal. The differential between even the lowest member rate of $26.25 and the institutional rate of $39.35 is smaller than for any of the other publications on the table that charge two rates. *CPI* charged $95.00 to institutions, 3.2 times the rate of $30.00 to individuals; *PA* charged $240.00 to institutions, 3.4 times the rate of $70.00 to individuals; and *MLA Bibliography* charged $75.00 to institutions, 3.8 times the rate of $20.00 to individuals.

We have calculated subscription prices per 1,000 abstracts or, in the case of *MLA Bibliography*, per 1,000 index items, by using the number of abstracts or index items published per year and annual subscription prices. The results are given as Characteristic No. 20.

This averaging technique does not apply to *JEL* because this publication includes other services such as book reviews, book annotations, and indexes to nonabstracted journals. For the remaining abstract publications, institutions pay from $5.50 per 1,000 abstracts in *CPI* to $8.90 per 1,000 abstracts in *PA*. The index items published in *MLA Bibliography* are, not surprisingly, the least expensive, with a cost to individuals of $.50 per 1,000 items and a cost to institutions of $1.90 per 1,000 items.

Publication Lags

The final two characteristics presented in the table, Nos. 22 and 23, show the publishers' estimates of, first, average elapsed time from *publication* of the original source material to publication of the abstract or index item in the final form and, second, average elapsed time from *receipt* of the original source material to publication of the abstract or index item in final form. These are, of course, overlapping time periods, with the length of the former exceeding the length of the latter by the time that lapses between publication of the source material and receipt of the material by the publisher of the abstract or index publication. As a short-hand device we shall refer to the longer period as the "publication lag" and to the shorter period as the "production lag." (Note that because of the unique circumstances surrounding *CPI*, these two lags coincide in this instance.)

Publishers found it difficult to come up with what they would consider useful estimates of publication and production lags, principally because of the wide variations in the lags among journals and other source publications. We nevertheless pressed them to provide us with some idea of the lengths of time involved. As we see from Table 9.2.2, two of the publishers, of *BA* and *PA*, preferred not to venture a guess, choosing instead to say "varies widely among journals." The estimates of publication lags provided for the remaining four publications range from two months in the case of *CPI* to from 9 to 16 months in the case of the *MLA Bibliography*. The organization of these two publication programs and the frequency of publication of their issues can account for the wide differences reported. Since all abstracts in *CPI* are of journal articles published in AIP's primary-research journals and since *CPI* is published every four months, any given issue of *CPI* will contain some abstracts of articles that are at most four months old and some of articles just published; hence, the average publication lag will be two months.

The situation is quite different for the *MLA Bibliography*, which is issued only once a year. In our description of the steps involved in producing this publication, we noted that approximately eight months are devoted to gathering the source material and entering the index items on computer tapes, and four months to proofreading, editing, preparation of camera-ready copy, and, finally printing and distributing the issue. Thus, the shortest possible publication lag for any index item would be four months, and this assumes that the staff of *MLA* receives the source material for such an item as soon as it has been published. Alternatively, it would not be unusual to find some index items published only after sixteen or more months from the time the original material appears in the source literature. If, for example, a source journal arrives at *MLA* just after the four-month production process for the next issue has begun, index items on its articles might have to wait to be included in the issue subsequent to the next, published a full year and four months later.

All six publishers ventured an estimate of their production lags. Compared with their estimates of publication lags, the publishers, in general, felt more confident about their estimates of production lags — how long it takes them to process the average abstract or index item once the source material is received and enters their flow of work.

The publishers of *CPI* estimate the *production* lag to be of the same duration as the *publication* lag. We can attribute the equivalence to the nature of AIP's publication program, in which both the original articles and the abstracts are prepared simultaneously as described in some detail above.

About the Authors

Fritz Machlup, born in 1902, received his doctorate in 1923 from the University of Vienna. After spending ten years in industrial management, he came to the United States in 1933 on a research fellowship of the Rockefeller Foundation. He was visiting professor at Harvard University in 1935, 1936, and 1939; Goodyear Professor of Economics at the University of Buffalo, 1935-1947; Hutzler Professor of Political Economy at the Johns Hopkins University, 1947-1960; Walker Professor of Economics and International Finance at Princeton University, 1960-1971; and he is now Professor of Economics at New York University.

Dr. Machlup holds six honorary degrees from American and European universities. He served as president of the Southern Economic Association, the American Economic Association, the International Economic Association, and also the American Association of University Professors. The list of his writings enumerates over 800 titles, of which 112 were articles in major economic journals, 28 were books of sole authorship, and 13 books of joint authorship, not counting the 3 volumes now being published.

Kenneth Leeson recently received his doctorate in economics from New York University and is currently research associate at the Center for Applied Economics at N.Y.U. Chief among his interests are the economics of knowledge and information, technology and technological change, industrial organization, and international trade and finance. As Senior Research Associate on the project culminating in these three volumes on *Information through the Printed Word* he has spent the last three years directing the research activities of the staff that gathered and compiled the reported data. He has authored or co-authored publications on, "The Economic Viability of Scientific and Scholarly Journals," "Major Journals in Economics: A User Study," "Sources and Uses of Funds of Academic Libraries," and "The Effects of Innovations on the Demand for and Earnings of Factors of Production."